SELECT LAB SE

PROJECTS FOR
MICROSOFT® EXCEL 97

MICROSOFT® CERTIFIED BLUE RIBBON EDITION

Philip A. Koneman
Colorado Christian University

Yvonne Johnson

Pamela R. Toliver

▲▲ ADDISON-WESLEY

An imprint of Addison Wesley Longman, Inc.

Reading, Massachusetts • Menlo Park, California • New York • Harlow, England
Don Mills, Ontario • Sydney • Mexico City • Madrid • Amsterdam

Acquisitions Editor: Anita Devine
Editorial Assistant: Holly Rioux
Senior Marketing Manager: Tom Ziolkowski
Senior Marketing Coordinator: Deanna Storey
Production Supervision: Elm Street Publishing Services, Inc.
Composition and Art: Gillian Hall, The Aardvark Group
Cover Illustration: © Frederic Joos/SIS
Cover Designer: Anthony Saizon
Design Supervisor: Regina Hagen
Manufacturing: Sheila Spinney

0-201-43863-1

Ordering from the SELECT System
For more information on ordering and pricing policies for the SELECT Lab Series and supplements, please contact your Addison Wesley Longman sales representative or fax 1-800-284-8292 or email: exam@awl.com. Questions? Email: is@awl.com

Addison-Wesley Publishing Company
One Jacob Way
Reading, MA 01867
http://hepg@awl.com/select

1 2 3 4 5 6 7 8 9 10-DOW-01009998

Preface

Microsoft Certified

Welcome to the *Microsoft® Certified Blue Ribbon Edition of Select PLUS: Projects for Microsoft Excel 97*. This project-based visual text is approved courseware for the Microsoft® Office User Specialist program. After completing the projects in this book, students will be prepared to take the Expert level exam for Excel 97. Successful completion of this exam proves students marketable skills. *Microsoft® Certified Blue Ribbon Edition of Select PLUS: Projects for Microsoft Excel 97* allows students to explore the essentials of the software application and learn the basic skills that are the foundation for business and academic success. Step-by-step exercises and full-color illustrations show students what to do, how to do it, and the exact result of their action.

In addition, your school may qualify for full Office 97 upgrades or licenses. Your Addison Wesley Longman representative will be happy to work with you and your bookstore manager to provide the most current menu of application software in addition to *Select Lab Series* offerings. Your representative will also outline the ordering process, and provide pricing, ISBNs, and delivery information. Call 1-800-447-2226 or visit our Web site at http://hepg.awl.com and click on ordering information.

Organization

The *Microsoft® Certified Blue Ribbon Edition of Select PLUS: Projects for Microsoft Excel 97* familiarizes students with the operating system before launching into the features of Excel 97. Students learn the basics of starting Windows 95, using a mouse, using the basic features of Windows 95, and organizing files. Your computers may also be set up with Windows 95 Active Desktop or Windows 98—we have included a new section that shows what the different desktops may look like, what makes them similar, and what differentiates them.

Microsoft® Certified Blue Ribbon Edition of Select PLUS: Projects for Microsoft Excel 97 can be used for either a survey course that extensively covers Microsoft Excel 97, a one credit or full semester course. Each section begins with an overview that introduces the basic concepts of the application and provides hands-on instructions to put students to work using the applications immediately. Students learn problem-solving techniques as they work through the projects that provide practical, real life business scenarios that students relate to.

Approach

The *Microsoft® Certified Blue Ribbon Edition of Select PLUS: Projects for Microsoft Excel 97* uses a document-centered approach to learning that focuses on running case studies that help students understand how the applications are used in a business setting. Each project begins with a list of measurable **Objectives**, a realistic case scenario called **The Challenge**, a well-defined plan called **The Solution**, and an illustration of the final product. **The Setup** enables students to verify that the settings on the computer match those needed for the project.

The project is arranged in carefully divided, highly visual objective-based tasks that foster confidence and self-reliance. Each project closes with a wrap-up of the project called **The Conclusion**, followed by summary questions, exercises, and assignments geared to reinforcing the information taught throughout the project.

Other Features

In addition to the document-centered, visual approach of each project, this book contains the following features:

- An **Overview** of Windows 95 and Active Desktop with Windows 98 Preview.
- A **Function Reference Guide** for each application. Functions are arranged alphabetically rather than by menu.
- **Keycaps** and **toolbar button icons** within each step so students can quickly perform the required action.
- A comprehensive, well-organized end-of-the-project **Summary** and **Exercises** section for reviewing, integrating, and applying new skills.
- **Results of each step** are illustrated or described so students know they're on the right track throughout the project.

Student Supplements

QWIZ Assessment Software is a network-based skills assessment-testing program that measures student proficiency with Windows 95, Word 97, Excel 97, Access 97, and PowerPoint 97. Professors select the tasks to be tested and get student results immediately. The test is taken in a simulated software environment. On-screen instructions require students to perform tasks just as though they were using the actual application. The program automatically records responses, assesses student accuracy and reports the resulting score both in a printout or disk file as well as to the instructor's gradebook. The students receive immediate feedback from the program, including learning why a particular task was scored as incorrect and what part of the lab manual to review.

Student data files can be easily downloaded from the Internet at http://hepg.awl.com/select

1

PROJECT
Creating a Workbook

In order to use Excel 97 effectively, you must know how to create, save, and print workbooks. In this project, you will enter text and numbers and calculate the numbers with formulas and functions to create a simple worksheet. (This might sound like a lot, but I promise you won't have to use all 16,777,216 cells!)

Objectives

After completing this project, you will be able to:

➤ Create a new workbook
➤ Move around in a worksheet and a workbook
➤ Name worksheets
➤ Enter data
➤ Enter simple formulas and functions
➤ Save a workbook
➤ Preview and print a worksheet
➤ Close a worksheet

The Challenge

Mr. Gilmore, manager of The Grande Hotel, wants a down-and-dirty worksheet to compare the January receipts to the February receipts for both restaurants in the hotel (the Atrium Café and the Willow Top Restaurant). Since the worksheet is just for him, you won't have to worry about formatting right now.

EX-16

The Introduction sets up the real-world scenario that serves as the environment for learning.

Clearly defined and measurable **Objectives** give students direction and focus they need to learn new material.

The **Challenge** introduces the case and outlines the goal of the project, the document, spreadsheet, database, or presentation to be created.

EX-100

You need to delete some information, add some information, make some adjustments in the columns and rows, and add a header and footer.

The Solution

You will begin your edits by deleting one of the worksheets, inserting a new worksheet, and rearranging worksheets. Then you will adjust the width of columns and the height of rows as needed. Next, you will insert and delete columns, rows, and cells, and, finally, you will add the headers and footers. Figure 4.1 shows the first worksheet in the workbook.

To obtain the files you need for this project, download them from the Addison Wesley Longman web site (http://hepg.awl.com/select or obtain them from your instructor.

Figure 4.1

The Setup

So that your screen will match the illustrations and the tasks in this project will function as described, make sure that the Excel settings listed in Table 4.1 are selected on your computer. Because these are the default settings for the toolbars and view, you may not need to make any changes to your setup.

Table 4.1: Excel Settings

Location	Make these settings:
View, Toolbars	Deselect all toolbars except Standard and Formatting.
View	Use the Normal view and display the Formula Bar and Status Bar.

The **Solution** describes the plan for completing the project, tasks leading to the final product.

An illustration shows the outcome of the project.

The Setup tells the students exactly which settings should be chosen to match those in the illustrations.

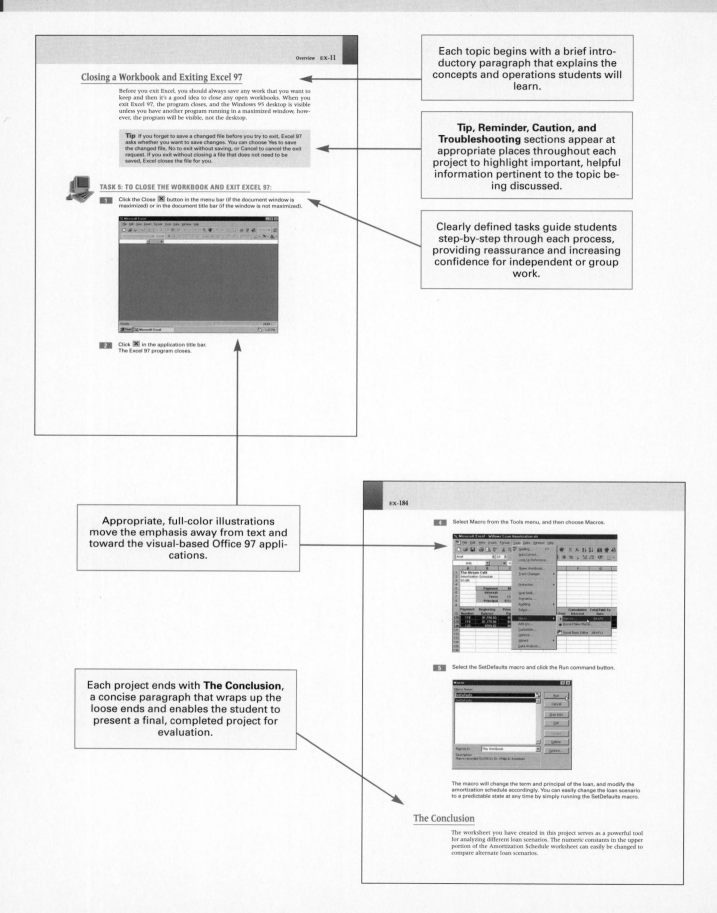

Each topic begins with a brief intro-ductory paragraph that explains the concepts and operations students will learn.

Tip, Reminder, Caution, and Troubleshooting sections appear at appropriate places throughout each project to highlight important, helpful information pertinent to the topic be-ing discussed.

Clearly defined tasks guide students step-by-step through each process, providing reassurance and increasing confidence for independent or group work.

Appropriate, full-color illustrations move the emphasis away from text and toward the visual-based Office 97 appli-cations.

Each project ends with **The Conclusion**, a concise paragraph that wraps up the loose ends and enables the student to present a final, completed project for evaluation.

Overview EX-11

Closing a Workbook and Exiting Excel 97

Before you exit Excel, you should always save any work that you want to keep and then it's a good idea to close any open workbooks. When you exit Excel 97, the program closes, and the Windows 95 desktop is visible unless you have another program running in a maximized window, how-ever, the program will be visible, not the desktop.

Tip If you forget to save a changed file before you try to exit, Excel 97 asks whether you want to save changes. You can choose Yes to save the changed file, No to exit without saving, or Cancel to cancel the exit request. If you exit without closing a file that does not need to be saved, Excel closes the file for you.

TASK 5: TO CLOSE THE WORKBOOK AND EXIT EXCEL 97:

1 Click the Close ✕ button in the menu bar (if the document window is maximized) or in the document title bar (if the window is not maximized).

2 Click ✕ in the application title bar. The Excel 97 program closes.

EX-184

4 Select Macro from the Tools menu, and then choose Macros.

5 Select the SetDefaults macro and click the Run command button.

The macro will change the term and principal of the loan, and modify the amortization schedule accordingly. You can easily change the loan scenario to a predictable state at any time by simply running the SetDefaults macro.

The Conclusion

The worksheet you have created in this project serves as a powerful tool for analyzing different loan scenarios. The numeric constants in the upper portion of the Amortization Schedule worksheet can easily be changed to compare alternate loan scenarios.

Summary and Exercises

Summary

- You can format text with bold, italic, underline, different fonts and font sizes, and so on.
- Data in a cell can be left, right, or center aligned.
- Excel provides many formats for displaying numbers.
- You can apply a border to any side of a cell.
- You can apply a background color to a cell.
- You can apply a color to text.
- The Page Break view shows where page breaks are located.
- You can rearrange page breaks in the Page Break view.
- An AutoFormat can be applied to a worksheet or a range.

Key Terms and Operations

Key Terms	Operations
border	add a border
fill	add fill
page break	align cells
Page Break view	AutoFormat
pattern	change a page break
shading	format dates
	format numbers
	format text
	view a page break

Study Questions

Multiple Choice

1. If you type text in cell A1 and you want to center the text across cells A1 through A5,
   a. merge the cells and click the Center button.
   b. select A1:A5 and click the Center button.
   c. select A1:A5 and choose Format, Cells, Alignment, Center, and click OK.
   d. merge the cells, and choose Format, Align, Center.

2. You can apply an AutoFormat
   a. to a cell.
   b. only to a complete worksheet.
   c. to a single range.
   d. to noncontiguous ranges.

3. To make text bold,
   a. click in the cell, type the text, click the Bold button, and press Enter.
   b. select the cell and click the Bold button.
   c. select the cell and choose Format, Bold.
   d. All of the above.

EX-94

A **Summary** in bulleted-list format further reinforces the Objectives and the material presented in the project.

Key terms are boldface and italicized throughout each project, and then listed for handy review in the summary section at the end of the project.

Study questions (Multiple Choice, Short Answer, and For Discussion) bring the content of the project into focus again and allow for independent or group review of the material learned.

EX-188

For Discussion

1. What is the FV function? How does the data it returns differ from the PV function?

2. What is a macro? How is a macro recorded and applied?

3. How can worksheets, such as the amortization schedule you created in this project, be protected from changes?

4. What arguments are required by the PMT function? Is the order in which these appear in a formula significant?

Review Exercises

1. Protecting cells in a workbook
In many settings, portions of a worksheet should be protected to prohibit users from inadvertently making destructive changes to the workbook. By unlocking the cells to which users need access and protecting the worksheet, this objective can easily be achieved. Open the *Willows Loan Amortization* workbook and do the following:

1. Select the following nonadjacent ranges: C6:C8 and A13:H370.
2. Select Cells from the Format menu.
3. Click the Protection tab.
4. Deselect the Locked check box in the Format Cells dialog box.
5. Click the OK button.
6. Select Protection from the Tools menu.
7. Select Protect Sheet from the cascading menu.
8. Do not enter a protection password in the Protect Sheet dialog box.
9. Click OK.
10. Save the updated workbook as *Protected Loan Analysis.xls*.

2. Creating a worksheet to predict the future value of an investment
The FV function is similar to the PV function, except that it returns the future value of an investment, assuming a constant interest rate. Create the workbook shown below as follows:

Project 6: Using Financial Functions **EX-189**

1. Launch Excel if isn't already running.
2. Create a new workbook.
3. Save the workbook as *Future value.xls*.
4. Enter the text and numeric constants shown in the figure on the previous page into the worksheet.
5. Type **=FV(B3/12,B4*12,−B5,−B6,1)** as the formula in cell B7. Look up FV in the Excel Help System for information about the arguments.

Assignments

1. Creating macros to enable and disable protection for a worksheet
Open the *Protected loan analysis.xls* workbook. Create two macros: one that sets the protection for the worksheet, and one that removes the worksheet protection. Save the workbook as *Protected Loan Y-N.xls*.

2. Repaying a loan early
Visit Microsoft's New Spreadsheet Solutions site, which contains spreadsheet solutions created by Village Software. (http://www.microsoft.com/excel/freestuff/templates/villagesoftware/). Download the Loan Manager file self-extracting file(*Loan.exe*), and install the *Loan.xlt* template to your floppy diskette. Open the *Loan.xlt* file, and enter the loan data from this project. Make three additional payments of $100.00 each. Save the workbook as *Prepaid.xls*.

Review Exercises present hands-on tasks for building on the skills acquired in the project.

Assignments invoke critical thinking and integration of project skills.

Instructor Supplements

Instructors get extra support for this text from supplemental materials that can be downloaded from our password-protected Web site at http://hepg.awl.com/selectteacher/. These materials include:

- Screen shots, diagrams, and tables from the text, as well as files that correspond to key figures in the book that can be used for classroom presentation. Screen by screen steps in a project can be displayed in class or reviewed by students in the computer lab.
- The entire Instructor's Manual in Microsoft Word format.
- Computerized Test Bank to create printed tests, network tests, and self-assessment quizzes for the Internet. Computerized Test Bank files allow you to view and edit test bank questions, create multiple versions of tests, easily search and arrange questions in the order you prefer, add or modify test bank questions, administer tests on a network, and convert your tests to HTML and post to the Web for students to use for practice.
- Project Outlines and solution files
- Text updates
- Helper applications

Student data files are located at http://hepg.awl.com/select

Contact your Addison Wesley Longman Sales Representative for your ID and password for the Instructor's site.

The printed Instructor's Manual includes a Test Bank and Transparency Masters for each project in the student text, as well as Expanded Student Objectives, Answers to Study Questions, and Additional Assessment Techniques. The Test Bank contains two separate tests with answers, and consists of multiple choice, true/false, and fill-in questions referenced to pages in the student text and Transparency Masters.

The Select Lab Series

Greater access to ideas and information is changing the way people work and learn. The *Select Lab Series* software application manuals help you take advantage of these valuable resources, with special assignments devoted to the Internet.

Dozens of proven and class-tested lab manuals are available within the *Select Lab Series*, from the latest operating systems and browsers to the most popular applications software for word processing, spreadsheets, databases, presentation graphics, desktop publishing, and integrated packages to HTML and programming. The *Select Lab Series* also offers individually bound texts for each *Office 97* application. Knowing that you have specific needs for your lab course, we offer the quick and affordable *TechSuite* program. For your lab course, you can choose the combination of software lab manuals in *Brief*, *Standard*, or *PLUS* Editions that best suits your classroom needs. Your choice of lab manuals will be sent to the bookstore in a *TechSuite* box, allowing students to purchase all books in one convenient package at a significant discount.

Acknowledgments

When a *team* combines their knowledge and skills to produce a work designed to meet the needs of students and professors across the country, they take on an unenviable challenge.

To **Anita Devine** for the steady editorial focus needed to make the *Microsoft Certified Blue Ribbon Editions* happen. **Holly Rioux** was instrumental in keeping the project organized and on schedule.

Thanks to **Emily Kim** and **Pauline Johnson** who were more than just technical editors, but who also made sure things worked the way we said they would. To those in production, especially to **Gillian Hall**, **Diane Freed**, and **Pat Mahtani**, your efforts have paid off in a highly user-friendly book!

To **Tom Ziolkowski** and **Deanna Storey**, thanks for your strong marketing insights for this book.

Many people helped form the cornerstone of the original work, and we would like to thank **Barb Terry**, **Robin Drake**, **Chuck Hutchinson**, **Martha Johnson**, **Robin Edwards**, and **Deborah Minyard**.

And, finally, thanks to everyone at Addison Wesley Longman who has followed this project from start to finish.

P. K.
Y. J.
P. T.

Acknowledgments

Addison-Wesley Publishing Company would like to thank the following reviewers for their valuable contributions to the *SELECT Lab Series*.

James Agnew
Northern Virginia
Community College

Joseph Aieta
Babson College

Dr. Muzaffar Ali
Bellarmine College

Tom Ashby
Oklahoma CC

Bob Barber
Lane CC

Robert Caruso
Santa Rosa Junior
College

Robert Chi
California State
Long Beach

Jill Davis
State University of New
York at Stony Brook

Fredia Dillard
Samford University

Peter Drexel
Plymouth State College

David Egle
University of Texas, Pan
American

Linda Ericksen
Lane Community College

Jonathan Frank
Suffolk University

Patrick Gilbert
University of Hawaii

Maureen Greenbaum
Union County College

Sally Ann Hanson
Mercer County CC

Sunil Hazari
East Carolina University

Gloria Henderson
Victor Valley College

Bruce Herniter
University of Hartford

Rick Homkes
Purdue University

Lisa Jackson
Henderson CC

Martha Johnson
(technical reviewer)
Delta State University

Cynthia Kachik
Santa Fe CC

Bennett Kramer
Massasoit CC

Charles Lake
Faulkner State Junior
College

Ron Leake
Johnson County CC

Randy Marak
Hill College

Charles Mattox, Jr.
St. Mary's University

Jim McCullough
Porter and Chester
Institute

Gail Miles
Lenoir-Rhyne College

Steve Moore
University of South
Florida

Anthony Nowakowski
Buffalo State College

Gloria Oman
Portland State University

John Passafiume
Clemson University

Leonard Presby
William Paterson
College

Louis Pryor
Garland County CC

Michael Reilly
University of Denver

Dick Ricketts
Lane CC

Dennis Santomauro
Kean College of
New Jersey

Pamela Schmidt
Oakton CC

Gary Schubert
Alderson-Broaddus
College

T. Michael Smith
Austin CC

Cynthia Thompson
Carl Sandburg College

Marion Tucker
Northern Oklahoma
College

JoAnn Weatherwax
Saddleback College

David Whitney
San Francisco State
University

James Wood
Tri-County Technical
College

Minnie Yen
University of Alaska
Anchorage

Allen Zilbert
Long Island University

Contents

Overview of Windows 95

Microsoft Windows 95 is an *operating system,* a special kind of computer program that performs three major functions. First, an operating system controls the actual *hardware* of the computer (the screen, the keyboard, the disk drives, and so on). Second, an operating system enables other software programs such as word processing or spreadsheet *applications* to run. Finally, an operating system determines how the user operates the computer and its programs or applications.

As an operating system, Windows 95 and all other programs written to run under it provide *graphics* (or pictures) called *icons* to carry out commands and run programs. For this reason, Windows 95 is referred to as a *Graphical User Interface* or GUI (pronounced *gooey*). You can use the keyboard or a device called a *mouse* to activate the icons.

This overview explains the basics of Windows 95 so that you can begin using your computer quickly and easily.

Objectives

After completing this project, you will be able to:

➤ **Launch Windows 95**

➤ **Identify the desktop elements**

➤ **Use a mouse**

➤ **Use the basic features of Windows 95**

➤ **Organize your computer**

➤ **Work with multiple programs**

➤ **Get help**

➤ **Exit Windows 95**

Launching Windows 95

Because Windows 95 is an operating system, it launches immediately when you turn on the computer. Depending on the way your computer is set up, you may have to type your user name and password to log on — to get permission to begin using the program. After Windows 95 launches, the working environment, called the *desktop,* displays on the screen.

Identifying the Desktop Elements

Figure W.1 shows the Windows 95 desktop with several icons that represent the hardware and the software installed on the computer. *My Computer* enables you to organize your work. The *Recycle Bin* is a temporary storage area for files deleted from the hard disk. At the bottom of the desktop is the *Taskbar* for starting programs, accessing various areas of Windows 95, and switching among programs.

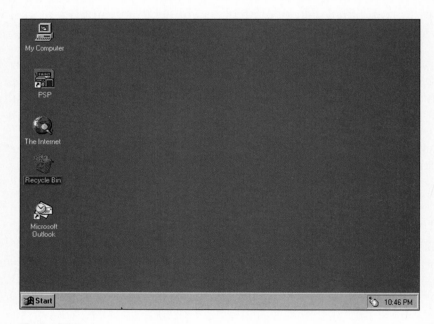

Figure W.1

> **Note** The desktop can be customized, so the desktop on the computer you're using will not look exactly like the one shown in the illustrations in this overview.

Using a Mouse

A pointing device is almost an indispensable tool for using Windows 95. Although you can use the keyboard to navigate and make selections, using a mouse is often more convenient and efficient.

When you move the mouse on your desk, a pointer moves on the screen. When the pointer is on the object you want to use, you can take one of the actions described in Table W.1 to give Windows 95 an instruction.

Table W.1 Mouse Actions

Action	Description
Point	Slide the mouse across a smooth surface (preferably a mouse pad) until the pointer on the screen is on the object.
Click	Press and release the left mouse button once.
Drag	Press and hold down the left mouse button while you move the mouse, and then release the mouse button to complete the action.
Right-click	Press and release the right mouse button once. Right-clicking usually displays a shortcut menu.
Double-click	Press and release the left mouse button twice in rapid succession.

TASK 1: TO PRACTICE USING THE MOUSE:

1 Point to the My Computer 🖳 icon, press and hold down the left mouse button, and then drag the mouse across the desk.
The icon moves.

2 Drag the My Computer icon back to its original location.

3 Right-click the icon.

Your shortcut menu may not match this menu

Open
Explore
Find...

Map Network Drive...
Disconnect Network Drive...

Create Shortcut
Rename

Properties

My Com

The Int

Recycle Bin

Microsoft Outlook

Start   10:46 AM

4 Click a blank space on the screen.
The shortcut menu closes.

5 Double-click the My Computer icon.

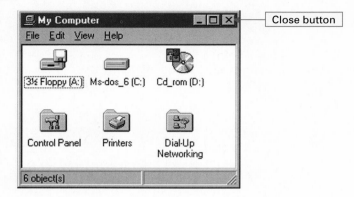

6 Click the Close ☒ button to close the My Computer window.

Using the Basic Features of Windows 95

The basic features of Windows 95 are menus, windows, menu bars, dialog boxes, and toolbars. These features are used in all programs that are written to run under Windows 95.

Using the Start Menu

Menus contain the commands you use to perform tasks. In Windows 95, you can use the Start menu shown in Figure W.2 to start programs and to access other Windows options.

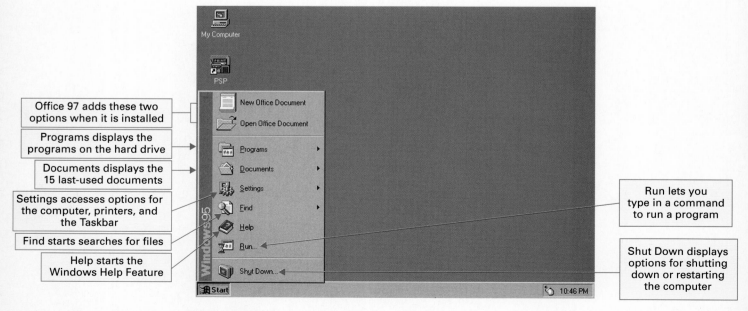

Figure W.2

TASK 2: TO USE THE START MENU TO LAUNCH A PROGRAM:

1 Click the Start button.
The triangles beside several of the menu options indicate that the options will display another menu.

2 Point to Programs and click the Windows Explorer icon on the cascading menu.
The Exploring window opens (see Figure W.3). You can use this feature of Windows 95 to manage files.

Using Windows

Clicking on the Windows Explorer icon opened a **window**, a Windows 95 feature that you saw earlier when you opened the My Computer window. Figure W.3 shows the common elements that most windows contain.

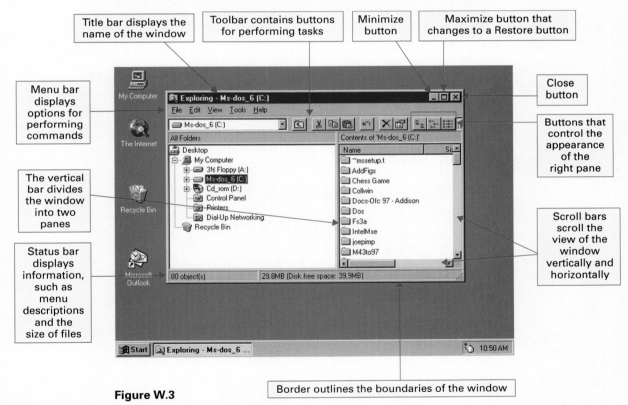

| Title bar displays the name of the window | Toolbar contains buttons for performing tasks | Minimize button | Maximize button that changes to a Restore button |

Menu bar displays options for performing commands

Close button

Buttons that control the appearance of the right pane

The vertical bar divides the window into two panes

Scroll bars scroll the view of the window vertically and horizontally

Status bar displays information, such as menu descriptions and the size of files

Border outlines the boundaries of the window

Figure W.3

TASK 3: TO WORK WITH A WINDOW:

1 Click the Maximize ⬜ button if it is displayed. If it is not displayed, click the Restore 🗗 button, and then click the Maximize button.
The Maximize button changes to a Restore 🗗 button.

2 Click the Minimize ➖ button.

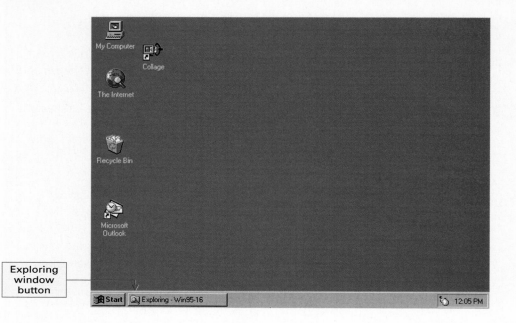

Exploring
window
button

Warning When you minimize a window, the program in the window is still running and therefore using computer memory. To exit a program that is running in a window, you must click the Close button, not the Minimize button.

3 Click the Exploring button on the Taskbar and then click [icon].

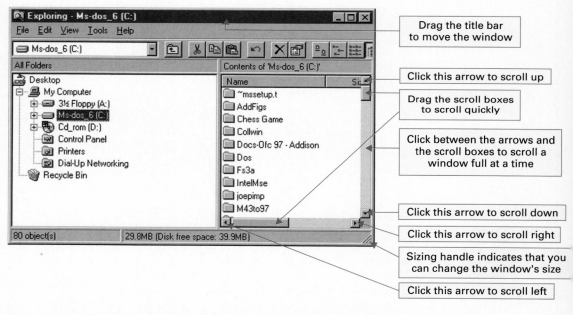

Drag the title bar to move the window

Click this arrow to scroll up

Drag the scroll boxes to scroll quickly

Click between the arrows and the scroll boxes to scroll a window full at a time

Click this arrow to scroll down

Click this arrow to scroll right

Sizing handle indicates that you can change the window's size

Click this arrow to scroll left

4 Point to the border of the Exploring window until the pointer changes to a double-headed black arrow, and then drag the border to make the window wider. (Be sure that all the buttons in the toolbar are visible.)

5 Practice scrolling.

6 When you are comfortable with your scrolling expertise, click [icon].

Using Menu Bars and Toolbars

Menu bars and toolbars are generally located at the top of a window. You can select a menu option in a menu bar by clicking the option or by pressing (ALT) and then typing the underlined letter for the option. When you select an option, a drop-down menu appears. Figure W.4 shows a menu with many of the elements common to menus.

Note Because you can select menu commands in two ways, the steps with instructions to select a menu command will use the word choose instead of dictating the method of selection.

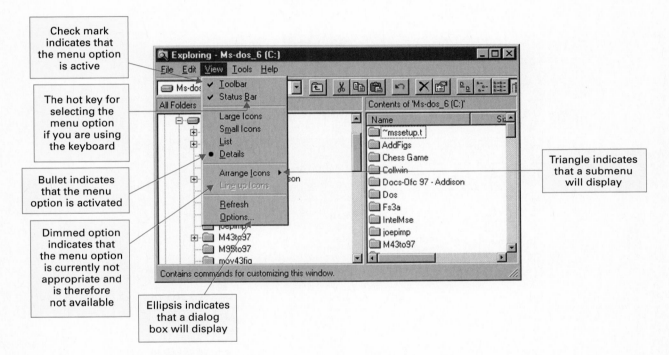

Check mark indicates that the menu option is active

The hot key for selecting the menu option if you are using the keyboard

Bullet indicates that the menu option is activated

Dimmed option indicates that the menu option is currently not appropriate and is therefore not available

Triangle indicates that a submenu will display

Ellipsis indicates that a dialog box will display

Figure W.4

Toolbars contain buttons that perform many of the same commands found on menus. To use a toolbar button, click the button; Windows 95 takes an immediate action, depending on the button's function.

Tip If you don't know what a button on the toolbar does, point to the button; a ToolTip, a brief description of the button, appears near the button.

TASK 4: TO USE MENUS AND TOOLBARS:

1 Choose View in the Exploring window.
The View menu shown in Figure W.4 displays.

2 Choose Large Icons.

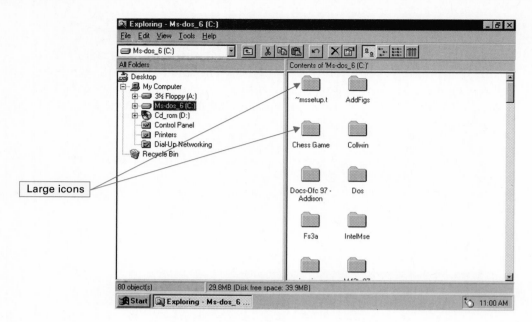

Large icons

3 Click the Details 🏛 button on the toolbar.

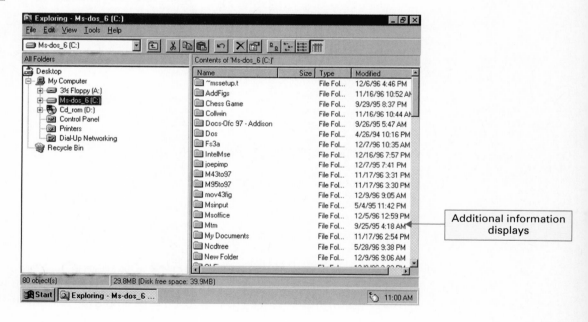

Additional information displays

Using Dialog Boxes

When many options are available for a single task, Windows 95 conveniently groups the options in one place, called a ***dialog box.*** Some functions have so many options that Windows 95 divides them further into groups and places them on separate pages in the dialog box. Figures W.5 and W.6 show dialog boxes with different types of options. Throughout the remainder of this project, you practice using dialog boxes.

Click its tab to display a page

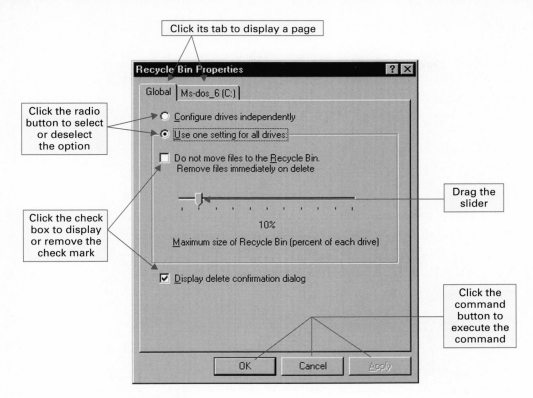

Click the radio button to select or deselect the option

Click the check box to display or remove the check mark

Drag the slider

Click the command button to execute the command

Figure W.5

Usually you can click in any text box and then type a value

Click the up or down arrow in the spin box to increment or decrement the value

Click the down arrow and then click an option in the drop-down list that appears

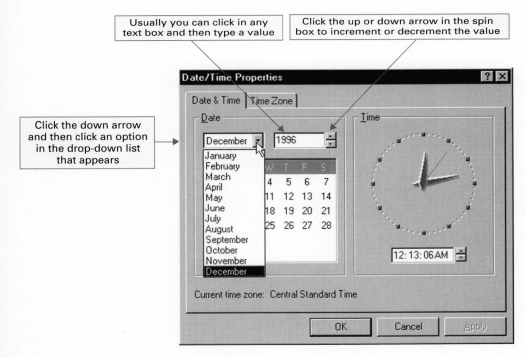

Figure W.6

Getting Help

Windows 95 provides you with three methods of accessing help information: You can look up information in a table of contents; you can search for information in an index; or you can find a specific word or phrase in a database maintained by the Find feature.

Additionally, Windows 95 provides *context-sensitive help,* called *What's This?* for the topic you are working on. This type of help is generally found in dialog boxes.

After you learn to use Help in Windows 95, you can use help in any Windows program because all programs use the same help format.

TASK 12: TO USE HELP CONTENTS, INDEX, AND FIND:

1 Click the Start button on the Taskbar and click Help.

2 Click the Contents tab if a different page is displayed. The Contents page displays.

3   Double-click Tips and Tricks.

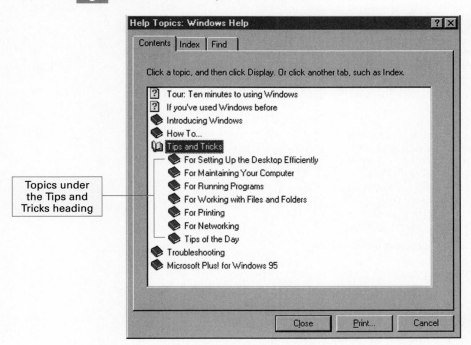

Topics under the Tips and Tricks heading

4   Double-click Tips of the Day.

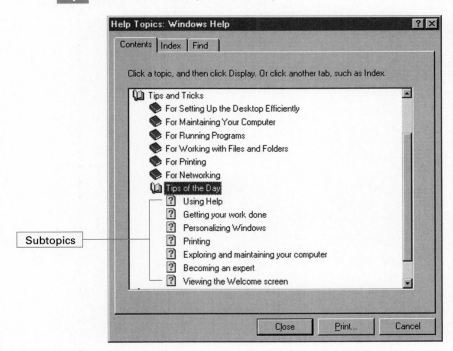

Subtopics

5 Double-click Using Help.

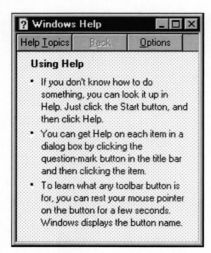

6 Read the information, click the Help Topics button, and then click the Index tab.

Text box

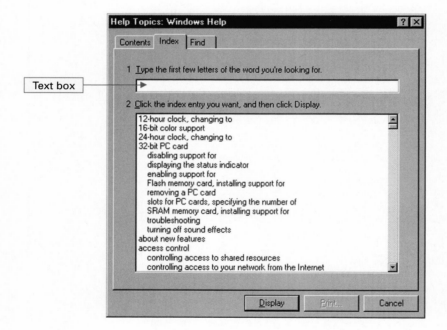

7 Type **shortcut** in the textbox.

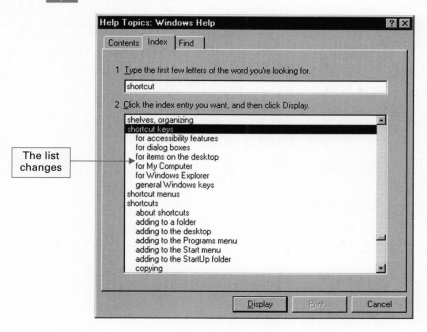

The list changes

8 Double-click "shortcut menus" in the list.

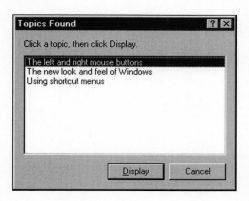

9 Double-click "Using shortcut menus."

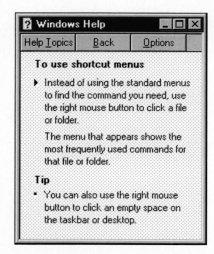

10 Read the information, click the Help Topics button, and then click the Find tab.

11 Click the What's This [?] button in the Help Topics title bar.
A question mark is attached to the mouse pointer.

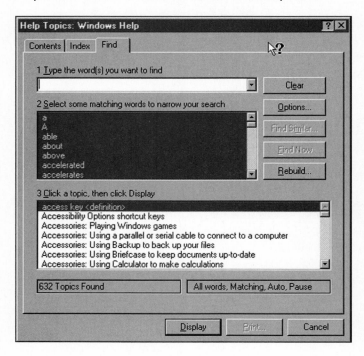

12   Click the Options button.

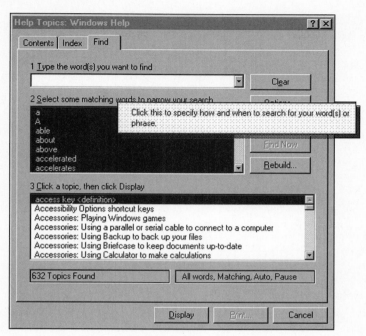

13   Read the pop-up message and then click it.
The message closes.

14   Type **printing help.** (If the list at the bottom of the screen doesn't change, click the Find Now button.)

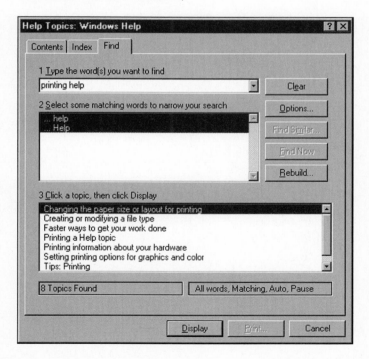

15   If necessary, scroll to "Printing a Help topic" in the list that displays and then double-click it.

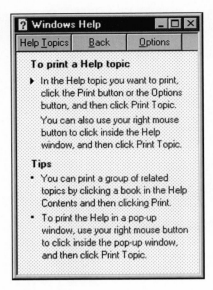

16 Click ✖.
The Help dialog box closes.

Tip You can print any help article by right-clicking anywhere in the article and choosing Print Topic.

Exiting Windows 95

When you are ready to turn off the computer, you must exit Windows 95 first. You should never turn off the computer without following the proper exit procedure because Windows 95 has to do some utility tasks before it shuts down. Unlike most of us, Windows 95 likes to put everything away when it's finished. When you shut down improperly, you can cause serious problems in Windows 95.

TASK 13: TO EXIT WINDOWS 95:

1 Click the Start button and then click Shut Down.

2 Click Shut down the computer? and then click Yes.

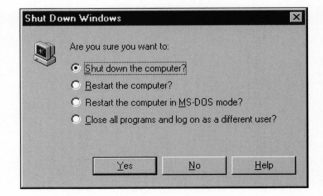

3 When the message "It's now safe to turn off your computer" appears, turn off the computer.

Windows 95 Active Desktop and Windows 98 Preview

Active Desktop and Windows 98 Preview

If you are running Windows 95 and your desktop looks significantly different from the desktop pictures found in the Overview of Windows 95, you may have Internet Explorer 4.0 installed with the Active Desktop. The Active Desktop contains features such as Taskbar toolbars, Internet Explorer Channel bar, and a Web-designed desktop background—features also available in Windows 98.

Other Windows 98 features—such as memory managers and file allocation tables—operate behind the scenes to improve the efficiency of your computer. Like Windows 95, Windows 98 is an operating system. Windows 98, however, operates with increased memory management capabilities. As a result, unless your computer is an older computer running less than 166 MHz, you should notice smoother transition when you move between programs, increased speed when performing basic tasks, and fewer program errors.

Many of the basic Windows 95 features, such as toolbars, are updated with a new look in Windows 98 because of the Active Desktop enhancement and the integration of Internet Explorer 4.0. Other features—such as the title bar and the minimize, maximize, and close buttons—remain unchanged. You will find that both Windows 98 and the Windows 95 Active Desktop are intimately integrated with the Internet and the World Wide Web. With the Active Desktop features, these "worlds" are literally just a click away.

This Active Desktop overview provides a preview of what to expect with Windows 98. You'll find that, in most cases, the procedures for using Windows 95 Active Desktop/Windows 98 features are identical to the procedures for using Windows 95 features.

Objectives

After completing this project, you will be able to:

➤ **Identify elements of the Windows 95 Active Desktop**

➤ **Use desktop ToolTips**

➤ **Launch programs**

➤ **Customize the Windows 95 Active Desktop**

➤ **Edit the Start menu**

➤ **Restore the desktop to its original format**

Identifying Elements of the Windows 95 Active Desktop

Both Windows 95 and Windows 98 start automatically each time you power up your computer. The appearance of the Active Desktop is controlled by options you choose when you install Internet Explorer 4.0. When you install Windows 98 the Active Desktop is installed, and the Web Channels bar displays automatically on your computer. You can choose to view your desktop as a Web page and to view the Internet Explorer Channel bar to provide easy access to pre-defined Web sites. These features are identified in the Active Desktop displayed in Figure A.1. If these features were not selected when you installed Internet Explorer 4.0 or Windows 98 on your computer, you can display the features from the Active Desktop.

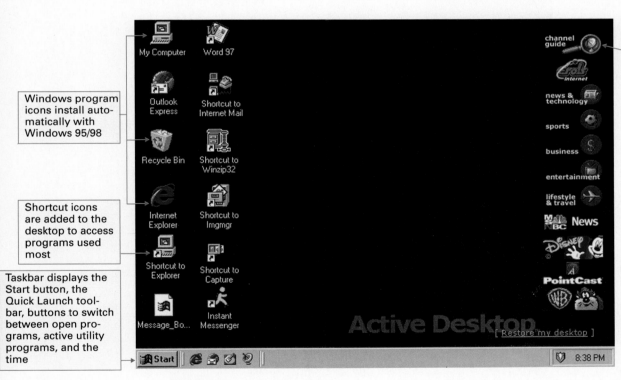

Figure A.1

Note Because the desktop can be customized, your desktop may not appear exactly as the one shown in the illustrations in this preview — even if you choose to display the Internet Explorer Channel bar and the desktop as a Web page.

Displaying the Internet Explorer Channel Bar

The Internet Explorer Channel bar appears in its own window when it is active. As a result, you can close the window by clicking the Close button that appears when you position the mouse pointer near the top edge of the Channel Guide button at the top of the Channel bar. Then use these procedures to restore the Internet Explorer Channel bar.

TASK 1: TO DISPLAY THE INTERNET EXPLORER CHANNEL BAR AFTER INSTALLATION:

1 Right-click a blank area of the Active Desktop and choose Active Desktop, as shown in the following figure.

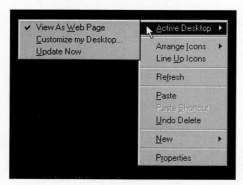

2 Choose Customize my Desktop.
The Display Properties dialog box opens.

3 Click the Web page tab, if necessary, as illustrated in the following figure.

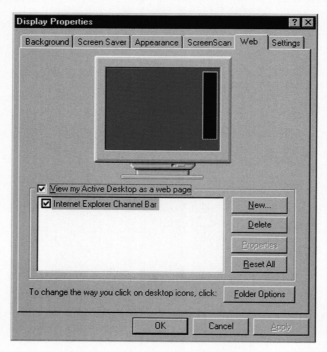

4 Check the View my Active Desktop as a web page check box, if necessary.

5 Check the Internet Explorer Channel Bar check box.
The Internet Explorer Channel bar shape appears in the preview monitor.

6 Choose Apply and then choose OK.

Displaying the Active Desktop Wallpaper

The default Active Desktop Web wallpaper displays a pre-formatted background. If your desktop is formatted with a different background, you can change the wallpaper to the Active Desktop Web wallpaper.

TASK 2: TO DISPLAY THE ACTIVE DESKTOP WALLPAPER AFTER INSTALLATION:

1 Right-click on a blank area on the Active Desktop and choose Properties.
The Display Properties dialog box opens.

2 Click the Background page tab, if necessary, to display the options shown in the following figure.

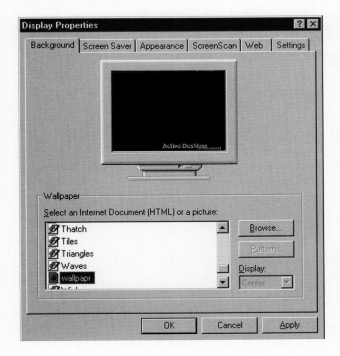

3 Select wallpapr from the Wallpaper list.
The preview monitor displays the Active Desktop Web wallpaper.

> **Note** The list of background designs varies depending on programs previously installed on your computer. If wallpapr is unavailable, select the background identified by your instructor.

4 Choose Apply and then choose OK.
The desktop is reformatted.

Using Desktop ToolTips

Other features that have been enhanced by the Active Desktop and Windows 98 include desktop ToolTips and shortcut menus. With the Active Desktop, simply pointing to an icon or desktop feature identifies the feature and, in some instances, displays explanatory information about the feature.

TASK 3: TO DISPLAY DESKTOP TOOLTIPS:

1   Click on a blank area of the Desktop to make it active.
The Desktop must be active before ToolTips appear.

2   Position the mouse pointer on the selected icon, as shown in the following figure.

The ToolTip explains how to use the My Computer program.

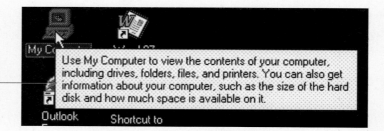

Note   The ToolTip appears different, depending on how the Active Desktop is installed on your computer. If it is installed using Internet Explorer 4.0 with Windows 95, it displays as shown in the figure. If the Active Desktop is installed with Windows 98, the information provided by the ToolTip will be different.

3   Point to the Start button.

4   Point to a button on the Internet Explorer Channel bar, as shown here.

5   Point to the Time at the right end of the Taskbar, as shown in this figure.

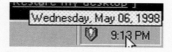

6   Point to an icon on the Quick Launch toolbar, as shown here.

Launching Programs

The same basic techniques used to launch programs in Windows 95 can be used to launch programs from the Active Desktop and Windows 98 Start menu and desktop shortcuts. The Active Desktop, however, enables you to use the Quick Launch toolbar located on the Taskbar to launch programs. In addition, you can change the setup of your desktop so that all program icons, shortcuts, and filenames act as hyperlinks. Clicking a filename, program icon, shortcut, or folder that is formatted as a hyperlink automatically opens the item. You'll also find that when Start menus contain more items than will fit on a cascading menu, the cascading menu displays an arrow at the top and/or bottom to indicate the presence of additional items.

TASK 4: TO LAUNCH PROGRAMS FROM THE ACTIVE DESKTOP:

1   Click the Outlook Express button on the Quick Launch toolbar, to launch the program shown here.

Title bars and title bar buttons are unchanged

Toolbars have a new look

The Internet Explorer icon has a new design

2 Choose Start, Programs, to display the Programs list shown here.

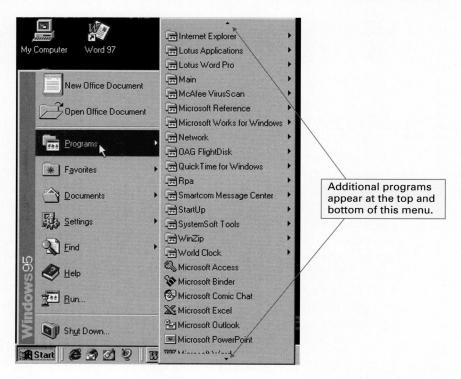

Additional programs appear at the top and bottom of this menu.

3 Click the arrow at the top or bottom of the cascading menu. Additional menu items scroll onscreen.

4 Double-click My Computer. The My Computer window opens.

5 Maximize the window and click once on the hard disk drive for your computer, as shown in the next figure.

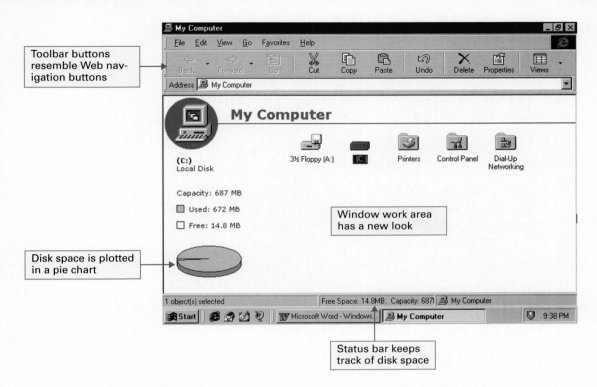

Toolbar buttons resemble Web navigation buttons

Window work area has a new look

Disk space is plotted in a pie chart

Status bar keeps track of disk space

6   Choose View, Folder Options to display the dialog box shown here.

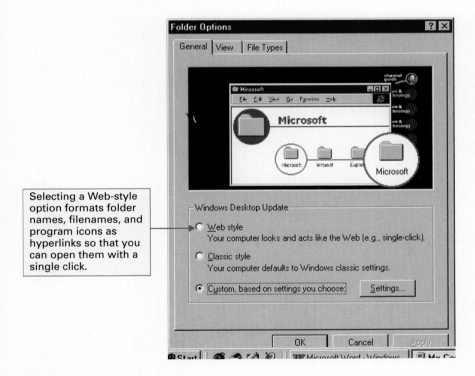

Selecting a Web-style option formats folder names, filenames, and program icons as hyperlinks so that you can open them with a single click.

7   Choose Cancel and close the My Computer window.

Customizing the Windows 95 Active Desktop

Windows 95 Active Desktop enables you to customize the Windows 95 environment for the way you work. You've already explored changing the Desktop background to the Web-style wallpaper. Now you'll move and size the Taskbar.

Sizing and Repositioning the Taskbar

The default position for the Taskbar is at the bottom of the desktop. The Taskbar can be expanded to provide more space for the features displayed and moved to a new location on the desktop.

TASK 5: TO MOVE AND SIZE THE TASKBAR:

1 Position the mouse pointer on the border between the desktop and the Taskbar.
The mouse pointer appears as a two-headed vertical arrow.

2 Drag the border toward the top of the desktop, as shown in this figure.

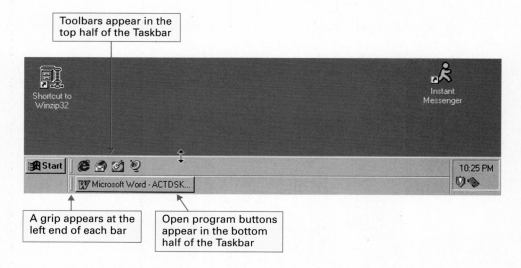

Toolbars appear in the top half of the Taskbar

A grip appears at the left end of each bar

Open program buttons appear in the bottom half of the Taskbar

3 Drag the border of the Taskbar to its original size.

4 Position the mouse pointer on a blank area of the Taskbar.
The mouse pointer should be a white arrow.

5 Click and drag the Taskbar to the top of the desktop, and drop it.
The Taskbar appears at the top of the desktop.

6 Drag the Taskbar to the right or left side of the desktop, and drop it.
The Taskbar appears as a vertical bar down the side of the desktop.

7 Return the Taskbar to its original position.

Displaying Additional Toolbars on the Taskbar

The Active Desktop provides four toolbars that you can display on the Taskbar. The Quick Launch toolbar is displayed by default. You can also display the Address, Links, and Web toolbars.

TASK 6: TO DISPLAY ADDITIONAL TOOLBARS:

1   Point to a blank area of the Taskbar, and right-click.
The Taskbar shortcut menu opens.

2   Choose Toolbars, as shown in this figure.

3   Choose Desktop, illustrated in this figure.

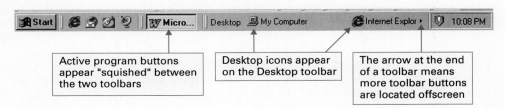

4   Right-click a blank area of the Taskbar, choose Toolbars, and choose Desktop to remove the toolbar.
The Desktop toolbar is removed from the Taskbar, and the Taskbar program buttons are restored.

Customizing Taskbar Toolbars

Each of the toolbars displayed on the Taskbar can be customized to contain the tools you use most. To remove tools from the toolbars, drag the button from the toolbar. To add a tool, drag a program item or feature onto the toolbar.

TASK 7: TO CUSTOMIZE THE QUICK LAUNCH TOOLBAR:

1   Click the Show Desktop 🗗 button on the Quick Launch Toolbar.
All open programs minimize and the Active Desktop is visible.

2 Click and drag the Launch Internet Explorer Browser 🅔 button from the Quick Launch Toolbar onto the desktop, and drop it.
The program button appears as a shortcut on the desktop, and the button no longer appears on the toolbar.

3 Select the Launch Internet Explorer Browser shortcut icon on the desktop, and drag and drop it in its original position on the Quick Launch toolbar.
The toolbar button appears on the toolbar, and the shortcut remains on the desktop.

4 Click the shortcut icon on the desktop, and press ⸤DEL⸥.
The Confirm File Deletion dialog box opens.

5 Choose Yes to confirm the deletion.

Floating and Restoring Toolbars

Toolbars take up valuable space on the Taskbar. When you have more programs active than will comfortably fit on the Taskbar, you can drag a toolbar to the desktop so that program buttons have more space.

TASK 8: TO MOVE AND RESTORE A TASKBAR TOOLBAR:

1 Position the mouse pointer on the Quick Launch toolbar grip.

> **Note** The mouse pointer appears as a horizontal mouse shape when you point to the grip.

2 Click and drag the toolbar from the Taskbar onto the desktop.
Your screen should look like the one in the following figure.

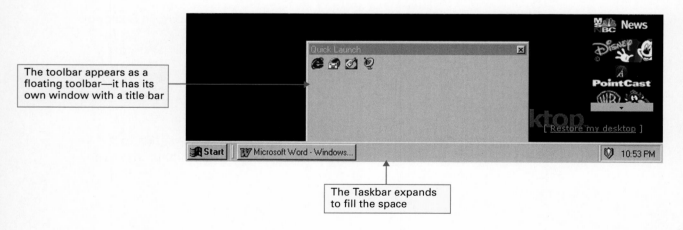

The toolbar appears as a floating toolbar—it has its own window with a title bar

The Taskbar expands to fill the space

3   Click and drag the Quick Launch title bar until the mouse pointer crosses the border of the Taskbar, as shown in this figure.

The toolbar stretches across the desktop just above the Taskbar after the mouse pointer crosses the Taskbar border—the toolbar will hop onto the Taskbar when you release the mouse button.

4   Release the mouse button.
The Quick Launch toolbar appears at the right side of the Taskbar.

5   Drag the grip beside the Start button to the right end of the Taskbar.
When the Taskbar grip is dragged past the Quick Launch toolbar, the toolbar assumes its original position.

6   Drag the toolbar and Taskbar grips until the Taskbar returns to normal.

Editing the Start Menu

The Active Desktop makes customizing the Start menu quick and easy. You can remove items from the Start menu to the desktop, or you can drag items from dialog boxes, the desktop, and folders and then place them on the Start menu.

Creating Shortcuts from the Start Menu

Dragging an item from the Start menu removes the item from the menu. To leave items on the Start menu and create shortcuts for the item on the desktop, you generally want to copy the Start menu item as you drag it to the desktop. You can drag Start menu items to the desktop or to an open dialog box or folder.

TASK 9: TO CREATE SHORTCUTS FROM THE START MENU:

1   Choose Start, Programs.
The Programs cascading menu opens.

2   Press and hold (CTRL), then click and drag the Windows Explorer icon and title to the desktop.

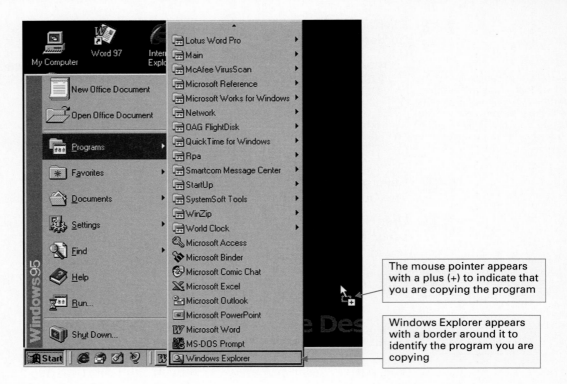

The mouse pointer appears with a plus (+) to indicate that you are copying the program

Windows Explorer appears with a border around it to identify the program you are copying

3 Drop the program on the desktop.
A Windows Explorer shortcut appears on the desktop.

4 Choose Start, Programs to ensure that the Windows Explorer icon remains on the menu.

Adding Items to the Start Menu

Adding items to the Start menu is as easy as copying shortcuts from the menu. Simply drag the item to the Start button and position the item on the menu in the desired position. It is important to keep the mouse button depressed from the time you start dragging the icon until it is properly positioned. You can also use the techniques presented here to reorganize items on the Start menu.

TASK 10: TO ADD ITEMS TO THE START MENU:

1 Drag the Windows Explorer Shortcut icon to the Start button.
The Start menu opens.

> **Troubleshooting** Do not release the mouse button until the item is properly positioned.

2 Drag the icon to the top of the Start menu, as shown in this figure.

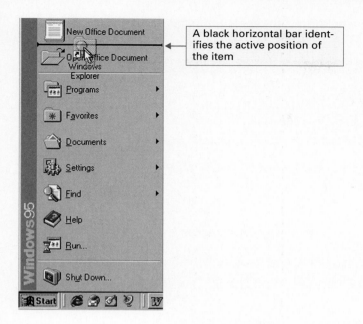

A black horizontal bar identifies the active position of
the item

3 Release the mouse button when the item is appropriately positioned.

4 Choose Start and drag the Windows Explorer from the top of the menu to the desktop.

5 Select the Windows Explorer shortcut on the desktop, and press (DEL).

Restoring the Desktop

Tasks in this preview have most likely left your desktop in a bit of a mess. You can restore the desktop to its original format using the desktop itself.

TASK 11: RESTORING THE DESKTOP:

1 Point to the Restore my desktop hyperlink on the Active Desktop, as shown in this figure.

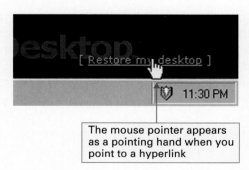

The mouse pointer appears
as a pointing hand when you
point to a hyperlink

2 Click the hyperlink, to display the dialog box shown here.

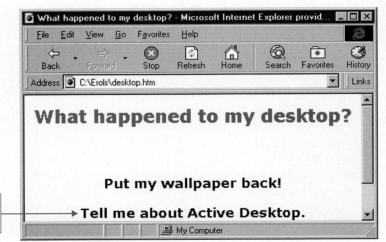

Review other features of the Active Desktop by choosing Tell me about Active Desktop

3 Choose Put my wallpaper back.
The dialog box shown in this figure appears.

4 Choose Yes.
The original wallpaper forms the desktop background.

5 Close all open programs, if necessary, and shut down Windows 95.

Conclusion

While Windows 95 Active Desktop offers the capabilities you've worked with in this Project, Windows 98 Active Desktop enables users to add new and different objects to the Desktop. For example, with Windows 98 Active Desktop, you can add Java programs such as stock market tickers to the Desktop. In addition, you can subscribe to Web services and newsgroups and add shortcuts to these features to your Desktop. When Windows 98 is available and installed on your computer, explore Windows 98 and look for these features. Then identify other features and benefits Windows 98 has available.

Spreadsheets
Using Microsoft Excel 97

Overview

Excel is a tool you can use for organizing, calculating, and displaying numerical data. You might use Excel to record your checking account transactions, plan a budget, prepare a bid, control inventory, track sales, or create an expense report. Before you can become proficient with Excel 97, however, you need to get acquainted with the program and learn how to perform some of the most basic functions. Then you will be ready to start working on the projects in this part of the book.

Objectives

After completing this project, you will be able to:

➤ **Identify Excel 97 Features**

➤ **Launch Excel 97**

➤ **Identify Excel 97 Screen Elements**

➤ **Get help**

➤ **Close a workbook**

➤ **Exit Excel 97**

Identifying Excel 97 Features

Excel 97 is the electronic equivalent of one of those green (or buff color) columnar pads that bookkeepers and accountants use. Excel calls the area in which you work a *worksheet* — other programs call this a spreadsheet. An Excel worksheet has 256 *columns* and 65,536 *rows*, for a whopping total of 16,777,216 cells. Is that big or what?

Note A *cell* is the intersection of a column and a row.

An Excel worksheet is actually a page in a ***workbook*** file. By default, a new workbook file has three worksheets, but you can add additional worksheets if you need them — as many as your computer memory allows.

You can do more than store numbers with Excel 97; you can use it to perform calculations, recalculate formulas when numbers are changed, analyze data, and create charts and maps from the data that you enter. Many of the same text features available in a word processing program are also available in Excel. For example, you can check the spelling of words, use text styles, add headers and footers, and insert graphics and other objects. Figure 0.1 shows a worksheet with numbers, calculations, text formatted with styles, a graphic, and a chart.

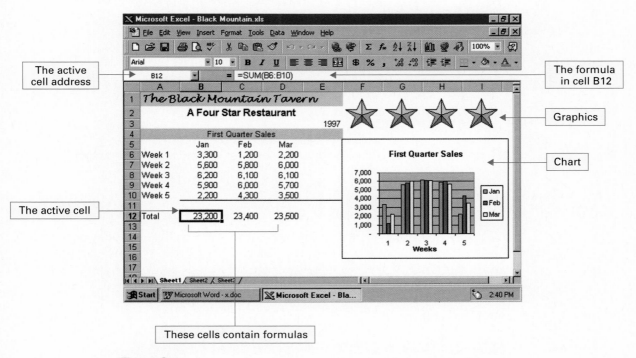

Figure O.1

Launching Excel 97

When you start your computer, you may have to log on to a network or perform some other steps before Windows 95 starts. After the Windows 95 desktop displays on the screen, you're ready to launch Excel 97.

TASK 1: TO LAUNCH EXCEL 97:

1   Click the Start ![Start] button and point to Programs.

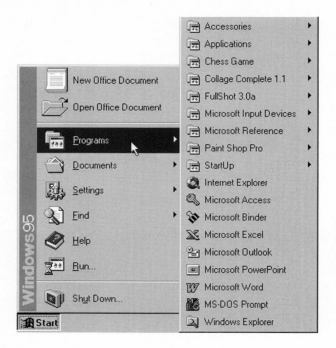

2 Point to Microsoft Excel and click.
The program opens in a window and creates a workbook called *Book1*.

Identifying Excel 97 Screen Elements

When you create a new workbook, the screen should look similar to the one shown in Figure O.2. The Excel 97 screen has many of the common elements of a Windows 95 screen as well as some elements that are unique to the Excel 97 program.

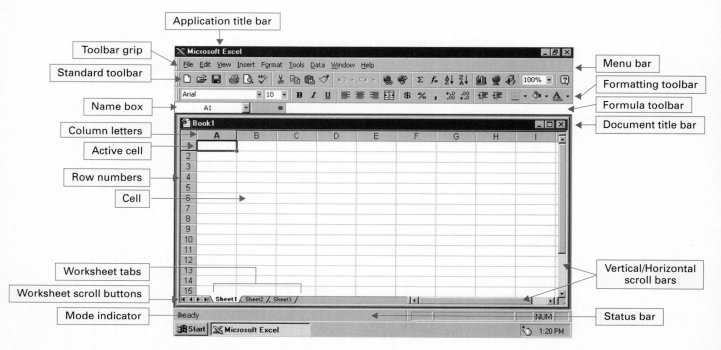

Figure O.2

Note The screen displays two Close buttons. The button in the Application title bar closes Excel 97; the button in the document title bar closes the current workbook. If the document window is maximized, the Close button for the document appears in the menu bar.

Table 0.1 lists the elements of the Excel 97 screen.

Table O.1   Elements of the Excel 97 Screen

Element	Description
Application title bar	Displays the name of the application and the Minimize, Maximize/Restore, and Close buttons. If the document window is maximized, the name of the workbook also displays in the application title bar.
Document title bar	Displays the name of the workbook file and the Minimize, Maximize/Restore, and Close buttons. If the window is maximized, there is no document title bar and the document buttons display in the menu bar.
Menu bar	Contains menu options. To use the menu, click an option to display a drop-down menu, and then click a command on the drop-down menu to perform the command, view another menu, or view a dialog box.
Standard toolbar	Contains buttons for accomplishing commands. To use the toolbar, click the button for the command you want to perform.
Formatting toolbar	Contains buttons and controls for formatting. To use the toolbar, click the button for the command you want to perform or click a drop-down list arrow to make a selection.
Name box	Displays the address of the active cell.
Formula bar	Displays the cell address and the contents of the active cell. Also used to enter and edit formulas.
Active cell	Marks the cell where data will be entered with a black border.
Scroll bars	Vertical and horizontal Scroll bars scroll the screen vertically and horizontally.
Worksheet tabs	Display the names of worksheets in the current workbook. Clicking a tab displays the worksheet.
Worksheet scroll buttons	Scroll the worksheet tabs (if you have too many worksheets to display all the tabs).
Status bar	Displays information about the current workbook. The Mode indicator displays on the far left side of the status bar. The right side of the status bar displays "NUM" if the Num Lock Key is on and "CAPS" if the Cap Lock key is on.
Row numbers	Indicate the numbers associated with the rows.
Column letters	Indicate the letters associated with the columns.
Cell	The intersection of a column and a row, referred to with an address that combines the column letter(s) with the row number, such as A1, AA223, and so on.
Mode	Displays on the left side of the status bar and shows a word that describes the current working condition of the workbook. For example, the word *"Ready"* means that the worksheet is ready to receive data or execute a command. Other modes include *Edit*, *Enter*, *Point*, *Error*, and *Wait*.

> **Note** Although you can turn off the display of certain screen elements (toolbars, the Formula bar, and the Status bar), generally all the screen elements are displayed in Excel 97 because they are used so often.

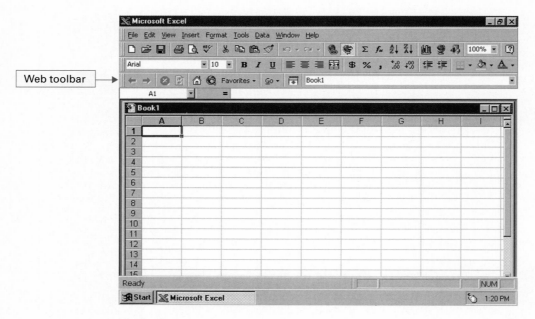

Figure O.3

Working with Toolbars

Toolbars contain buttons that perform functions. Usually the tools grouped together on a toolbar perform tasks that are all related. For example, the buttons on the Chart toolbar all perform tasks related to creating and modifying charts.

The Standard toolbar and the Formatting toolbar are the default toolbars, the ones that Excel 97 automatically displays. You can display or hide as many toolbars as desired. You also can move toolbars to different locations on the screen. When a toolbar is displayed, Excel places it where it was last located.

If you use the Internet frequently, you may want to display the **Web toolbar** by clicking the Web Toolbar button ![icon] in the Standard toolbar. With the Web toolbar displayed, your screen should look like Figure 0.3. To hide the Web toolbar, click the Web Toolbar button again.

TASK 2: TO WORK WITH TOOLBARS:

1   Choose View, Toolbars.

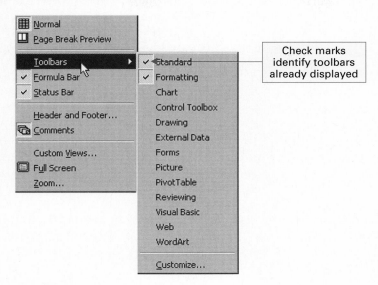

2   Choose Chart.

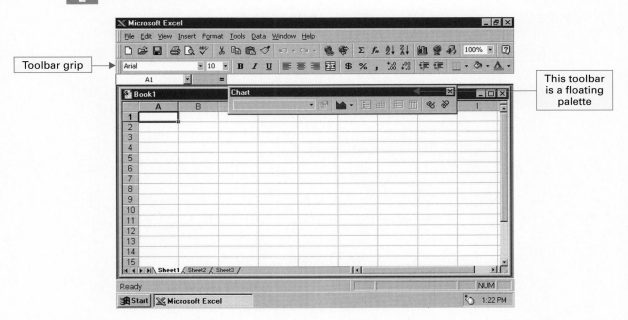

3   Point to the title bar of the Chart toolbar and drag the toolbar to a new location. If the toolbar doesn't appear as a palette, drag the toolbar by grabbing the grip.
The toolbar moves.

4   Choose View, Toolbars, Chart.
The toolbar no longer displays.

Getting Help

Excel 97 provides several ways to get help. You can use the standard help dialog box that contains the Contents, Index, and Find pages and the What's This Help feature. Additionally, you can use the Office Assistant and Microsoft on the Web, both of which are help features unique to Office 97.

Using the Office Assistant

The Office Assistant offers help on the task you are performing, often referred to as *context-sensitive help*. If the Office Assistant doesn't display the help you want, you can type a question to obtain the desired help.

> **Note** Sometimes the Office Assistant offers unsolicited help. When this happens, you can choose to read the help or just close the Office Assistant. Unfortunately, there is no way for a user to deactivate the Office Assistant.

TASK 3: TO USE THE OFFICE ASSISTANT:

1 Click the Office Assistant ⁇ button if you don't see the Office Assistant.

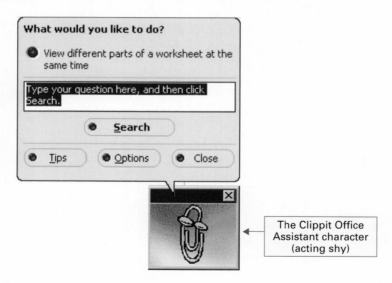

The Clippit Office Assistant character (acting shy)

2 Type **How do you enter a formula?**

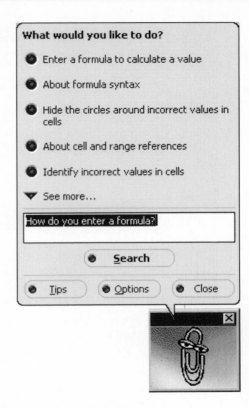

3 Click Search and then click About formula syntax.

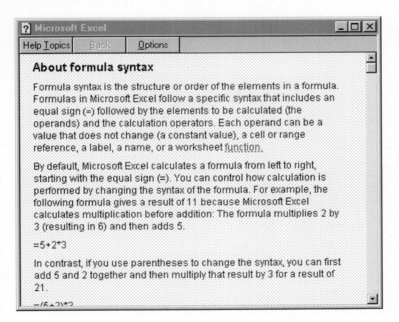

4 Read the Help dialog box and then click ☒ on the Help title bar.
The Help dialog box closes, but the Office Assistant window remains open.

5 Click the Office Assistant character in the Office Assistant window.
The Office Assistant asks what you want to do.

> **Note** The default Office Assistant is a paper clip named Clippit. Other assistants include Shakespeare, a robot, and a cat — to name a few.

6 Click Close.
The "bubble" closes.

7 Click ✖ on the Office Assistant title bar.
The Office Assistant window closes.

Getting Help from the World Wide Web

Microsoft maintains several sites on the Web that have useful information, user support, product news, and free programs and files that you can download. If your system is connected to the Internet, you can access this type of help easily. The Microsoft sites are open to all users.

> **Note** When Microsoft is beta testing a program, the company maintains "closed sites" open only to beta testers with a valid password.

TASK 4: TO READ ANSWERS TO FREQUENTLY ASKED QUESTIONS:

1 Choose Help, Microsoft on the Web.

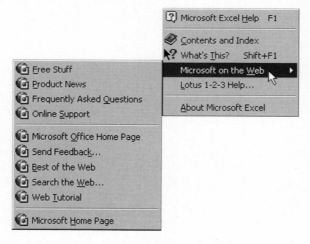

2 Choose Frequently Asked Questions.
The Internet browser program Internet Explorer starts and connects to the appropriate Web site. (You may be prompted to connect to the Internet.)

3 When you finish browsing the Web, click ✖ in the browser window. (I know you're tempted to start browsing around, but you can do that later.)

Closing a Workbook and Exiting Excel 97

Before you exit Excel, you should always save any work that you want to keep and then it's a good idea to close any open workbooks. When you exit Excel 97, the program closes, and the Windows desktop is visible unless you have another program running in a maximized window. In that case, the program will be visible, not the desktop.

> **Tip** If you forget to save a changed file before you try to exit, Excel 97 asks whether you want to save changes. You can choose Yes to save the changed file, No to exit without saving, or Cancel to cancel the exit request. If you exit without closing a file that does not need to be saved, Excel closes the file for you automatically.

TASK 5: TO CLOSE THE WORKBOOK AND EXIT EXCEL 97:

1 Click the Close ☒ button in the menu bar (if the document window is maximized) or in the document title bar (if the window is not maximized).

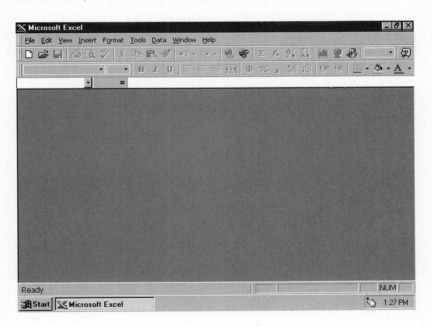

2 Click ☒ in the application title bar.
The Excel 97 program closes.

Summary and Exercises

Summary

- Excel 97 is a full-featured spreadsheet program that's easy to use.
- An Excel workbook includes three worksheets by default.
- Worksheets enable you to store numbers, perform calculations and recalculations, analyze data, and create charts and maps.
- Many features found in Word are also available in Excel 97.
- Excel 97 provides a variety of Help features.
- Excel 97 warns you if you try to exit the program without saving your work.

Key Terms and Operations

Key Terms

active cell
cell
column
column indicators
Edit mode
Enter mode
Error mode
Formatting toolbar
formula bar
menu bar
mode indicator
Office Assistant
Point mode
Ready mode
row
row indicators
scroll bars
Standard toolbar
status bar
title bar
toolbar
Wait mode
Web toolbar
What's This?
workbook
worksheet
worksheet scroll buttons
worksheet tab

Operations

exit Excel 97
get help from the Web
start Excel 97
use Office Assistant

Study Questions

Multiple Choice

1. Another name for a columnar worksheet is a
   a. workbook.
   b. spreadsheet.
   c. cell.
   d. booksheet.

2. The intersection of a column and a row is
   a. a worksheet tab.
   b. a cell.
   c. an active cell.
   d. an indicator.

3. The number of worksheets in a workbook is limited
   a. by default.
   b. to three.
   c. by memory.
   d. to 256.

4. The size of an Excel worksheet is
   a. 128 columns by 9,999 rows.
   b. 65,536 columns by 256 rows.
   c. over 256 million cells.
   d. 256 columns by 65,536 rows.

5. The name of a worksheet displays
   a. in the column letters.
   b. on the worksheet tab.
   c. in the row number.
   d. in the status bar.

6. Which of the following applications would most likely be created in Excel?
   a. a letter
   b. a budget
   c. a memo
   d. a meeting report

7. The standard Windows 95 help features used in Excel include all of the following except
   a. What's This?
   b. Contents.
   c. Index.
   d. Office Assistant.

8. Before exiting Excel 97, you should
   a. save all files and then close all files.
   b. close all files, saving only those that you want to keep.
   c. close all files without saving because Excel saves them automatically.
   d. close the Office Assistant.

9. Which of the following statements are false?
   a. The Office Assistant gives context-sensitive help and unsolicited help.
   b. The Office Assistant is an animated character.
   c. The Office Assistant can be deactivated.
   d. The Office Assistant displays help in a bubble.

10. Which of the following are false statements?
    a. The formula bar displays the cell address and the cell contents of the active cell.
    b. The formula bar is a floating palette.
    c. The formula bar is used for typing formulas.
    d. The formula bar can be hidden.

Short Answer
1. How do you start Excel?

2. What is a cell address? Give examples.

3. How are columns and rows identified?

4. How do you display the Web toolbar?

5. Why are screen elements not usually hidden in Excel?

6. Name some of the things that Excel can do.

7. Name some of the word processing features that are found in Excel.

8. Name and describe the different help features in Excel.

9. Name some of the mode indicators in Excel.

10. How many cells are in a worksheet?

For Discussion
1. Name some tasks that you could perform in Excel for your own personal use.

2. Discuss the advantages of using a program like Excel over keeping columnar records manually.

3. Name examples of situations that would benefit from having multiple worksheets in the same file.

4. Discuss the value of a chart in a worksheet.

Review Exercises

1. Starting Excel and exploring the workbook
In this exercise, you will start Excel 97 and move around in the workbook.

1. Start Excel 97.

2. Turn on the Web toolbar if it isn't displayed.

3. What text is displayed in the status bar?

4. What text is displayed in the Name box?

5. Click the tab that says Sheet2.

6. Is there any change in the status bar and in the Name box?

7. Turn the Web toolbar on if necessary and then turn it off.

2. Getting help on the Web

In this exercise, you will explore the help feature on the World Wide Web.

1. Choose Help, Microsoft on the Web.

2. Choose Product News.

3. Print the initial Web page that displays.

4. Disconnect from the Internet and exit Internet Explorer.

3. Displaying and docking toolbars and getting help from the Office Assistant

1. Launch Excel 97, if necessary.

2. Display the Control Toolbox toolbar.

3. Float the Excel 97 menu bar.

4. Display the Office Assistant and move the Office Assistant to a different location on-screen.

5. Ask the Office Assistant how to change the name of a worksheet.

6. Select a topic from among those the Office Assistant identifies about renaming a worksheet and print a copy of the topic.

7. Dock the menu bar at its original position by dragging its title bar.

8. Close the Control Toolbox toolbar and the Office Assistant.

9. Exit Excel without saving the worksheet.

Assignments

1. Getting online help

Start Excel 97 and use the Office Assistant to find and open a help topic about the Text Import Wizard. Choose Options and print the topic. When finished, close the Help dialog box.

2. Using the Web toolbar

Start Excel 97 and display the Web toolbar in the new workbook if it isn't already displayed. Go to this address: http://www.dominis.com/Zines/ and explore the site. Give a brief description of what you find. When finished, close Internet Explorer, disconnect from the Internet, and exit Excel 97.

1

PROJECT

Creating a Workbook

In order to use Excel 97 effectively, you must know how to create, save, and print workbooks. In this project, you will enter text and numbers and calculate the numbers with formulas and functions to create a simple worksheet. (This might sound like a lot, but I promise you won't have to use all 16,777,216 cells!)

Objectives

After completing this project, you will be able to:

➤ **Create a new workbook**

➤ **Move around in a worksheet and a workbook**

➤ **Name worksheets**

➤ **Enter data**

➤ **Enter simple formulas and functions**

➤ **Save a workbook**

➤ **Preview and print a worksheet**

➤ **Close a worksheet**

The Challenge

Mr. Gilmore, manager of The Grande Hotel, wants a down-and-dirty worksheet to compare the January receipts to the February receipts for both restaurants in the hotel (the Atrium Café and the Willow Top Restaurant). Since the worksheet is just for him, you won't have to worry about formatting right now.

The Solution

You will create a workbook with a page for the Atrium Café and a page for the Willow Top Restaurant as shown in Figure 1.1. (For now, don't worry about aligning headings such as Jan and Feb. You'll learn this in a later project.)

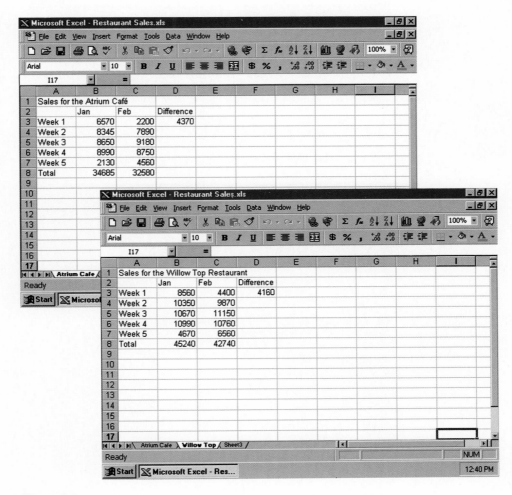

Figure 1.1

The Setup

So that your screen will match the illustrations in this chapter and to ensure that all the tasks in this project will function as described, you should set up Excel as described in Table 1.1. Because these are the default settings for the toolbars and view, you may not need to make any changes to your setup.

Table 1.1   Excel Settings

Location	Make these settings:
View, Toolbars	Deselect all toolbars except the Standard and Formatting.
View	Use the Normal view and display the Formula Bar and the Status Bar.

Creating a New Workbook

When you launch Excel 97, a new blank workbook named Book1 automatically opens for you, and you can begin to enter data.

TASK 1: TO CREATE A NEW WORKBOOK:

1 Click the Start ⊞Start button and point to Programs.

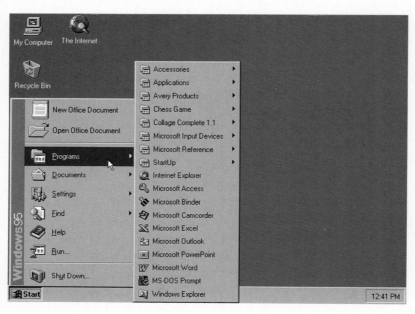

2 Choose Microsoft Excel.
The program launches and creates a workbook called Book1.

> **Note** If Excel is already started and you don't see a workbook on the screen, click the New ▯ button on the standard toolbar, and Excel will create one for you.

Moving Around in a Worksheet and a Workbook

To enter data in a worksheet like the one shown on the next page in Figure 1.2, you must move to the desired cell. The *active cell* is outlined with a black border. You make a cell the active cell by clicking in the cell or by moving to the cell with keystrokes. Table 1.2 lists the navigational keystrokes used to move to the desired cell.

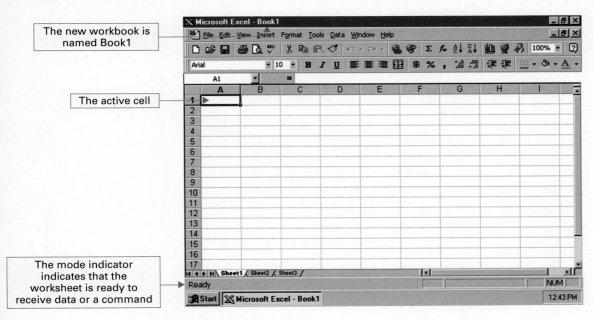

The new workbook is named Book1

The active cell

The mode indicator indicates that the worksheet is ready to receive data or a command

Figure 1.2

Note If you want to click in a cell you can't see on the screen, use the vertical or horizontal scroll bar to scroll the worksheet until you see the cell.

Table 1.2 Navigational Keystrokes

Target Location	Keystroke
Cell to the right of the active cell	→ or TAB
Cell to the left of the active cell	← or SHIFT+TAB
Cell below the active cell	↓ or ENTER
Cell above the active cell	↑ or SHIFT+ENTER
Upper-left corner of the worksheet	CTRL+HOME
Lower-right corner of the active area of the worksheet	CTRL+END
Down one screen	PGDN
Up one screen	PGUP
Right one screen	ALT+PGDN
Left one screen	ALT+PGUP

To display a different worksheet, click the worksheet tab. If you can't see the tab for the worksheet that you want to display, click the appropriate scroll button (the arrows just to the left of the worksheet tabs) to display the tab.

TASK 2: TO MOVE AROUND IN A WORKSHEET AND A WORKBOOK:

1   Press (PGDN).

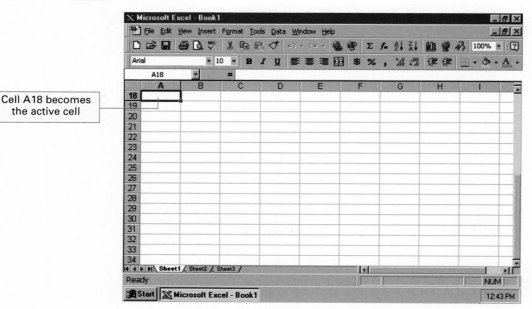

Cell A18 becomes the active cell

Note The monitor's size and resolution determine the number of columns and rows displayed on a screen. When you press (PGDN), (PGUP), (ALT)+(PGDN), or (ALT)+(PGUP), the active cell may be different from those shown in the illustrations.

2   Press ⊕ five times.

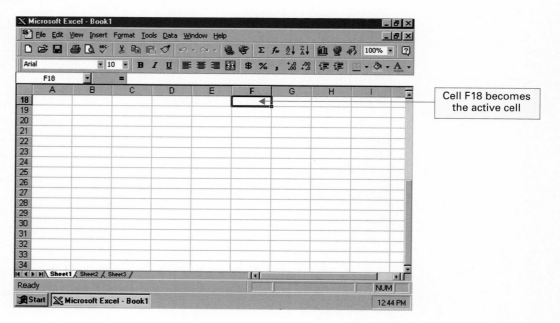

Cell F18 becomes the active cell

3   Type **88** and press (ENTER).
The number displays in cell F18, and cell F19 becomes the active cell.

> **Note**   Instead of pressing the (ENTER) key to enter data in a cell, you can press any one of the arrow keys ((↑), (↓), (←), or (→)) or any key that moves the cell pointer, such as the (PGUP) key or the (PGDN) key. When you enter data across a row, it's more efficient to use the (→) key than to use the (ENTER) key.

4   Press (CTRL)+(HOME).
Cell A1 becomes the active cell.

5   Drag the box in the vertical scroll bar until you see Row 4 in the ScrollTip box.

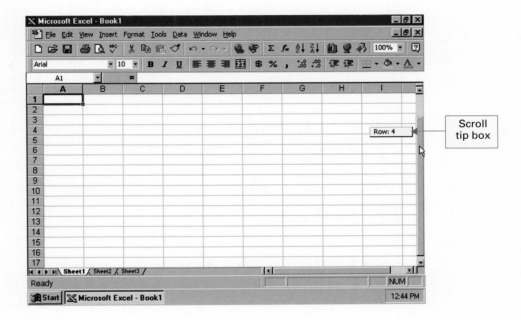

6   Click in cell D5.
Cell D5 becomes the active cell.

7   Press CTRL + END.

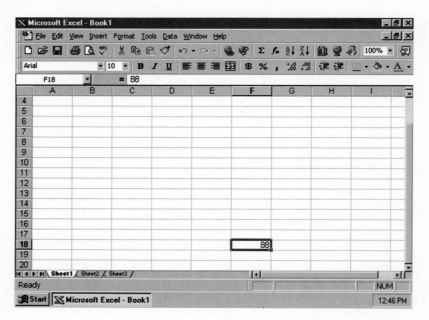

> **Note** The lower right corner of the active worksheet is always the cell at the intersection of the last row and the last column used, and it doesn't necessarily contain data.

8   Press DEL.
The number is deleted.

9   Click the Sheet2 tab.
Sheet2 displays.

Naming Worksheets

The three worksheets created by default in a new workbook are named Sheet1, Sheet2, and Sheet3. Not very imaginative or meaningful names, are they? You can give the worksheets better names to help you identify the content of the worksheet.

TASK 3: TO NAME A WORKSHEET:

1   Point to the Sheet1 tab and right-click.

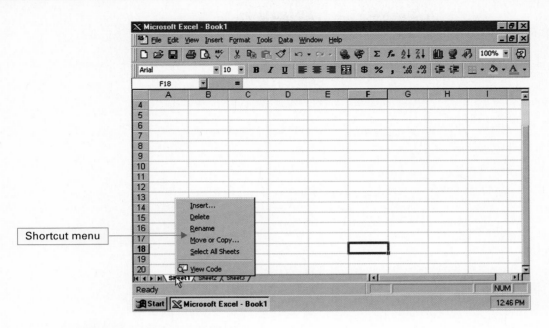

Shortcut menu

2 Choose Rename.
The current name on the tab is highlighted.

3 Type **Atrium Cafe** and press (ENTER).

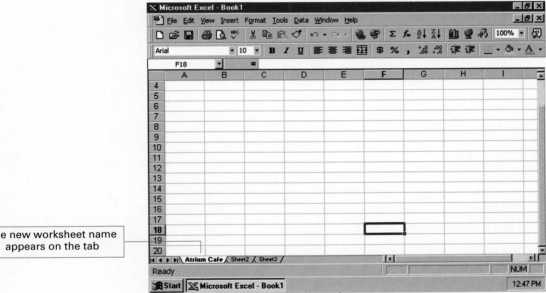

The new worksheet name
appears on the tab

4 Point to the Sheet2 tab and right-click.
The shortcut menu displays.

5 Choose Rename.
The current name on the tab is highlighted.

6 Type **Willow Top** and press (ENTER).
The name displays on the tab.

Entering Data

Excel 97 recognizes several different types of data—text, dates, numbers, and formulas. Text can include any characters on the keyboard as well as special characters such as the symbols for the British pound or the Japanese Yen. Dates can be entered with numbers separated with a slash or a dash. Numbers can include only these characters:

1 2 3 4 5 6 7 8 9 0 + − ( ) , / $ % . E

> **Tip** To enter a fraction instead of a date, precede the fraction with a zero. For example, to enter the fraction one-half, type 0 1/2 instead of 1/2 which Excel interprets as a date.

Entering Text

When you enter text in a cell, if the cell isn't wide enough to hold the text, the text will spill over into the next cell (if it's empty).

> **Tip** Any time you enter data that doesn't fit in a cell, you can widen the column and the data will display, or you can wrap the text in the cell.

TASK 4: TO ENTER DATA IN THE WORKSHEET:

1 Click the Atrium Cafe tab.
The Atrium Cafe worksheet displays.

2 Click in cell A1.
Cell A1 becomes the active cell.

3 Type **Sales for the Atrium Cafe**.
Notice that the mode changes to **Enter** because you are entering data.

4 Press (ENTER). Notice that Excel adds an accent to the "e" in "cafe" after you press the (ENTER) key to accept your data entry.

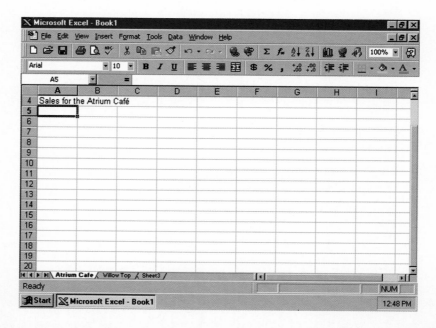

Tip If you make a mistake while typing, simply press the Backspace key and retype the text before you press (ENTER). If you change your mind about entering the data in the current cell, press (ESC) instead of pressing (ENTER).

5   Click the Willow Top tab.
The Willow Top worksheet displays.

6   Click in cell A1 if necessary.
Cell A1 becomes the active cell.

7   Type **Sales for the Willow Top Restaurant** and press (ENTER).

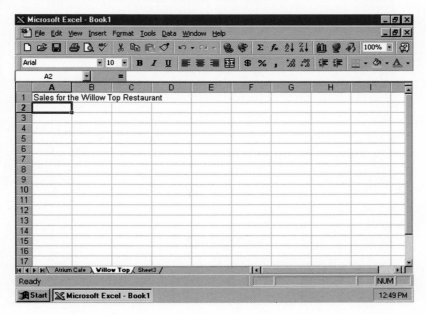

Entering Data on Multiple Worksheets

Sometimes the worksheets that you create have the same data entered several times. If the repetitive data that you are entering is text, the *Auto-Complete* feature of Excel 97 may complete the entry for you if the repetitive text appears in the same column. If the automatic completion isn't appropriate, just continue typing the text that you want.

If you are creating multiple worksheets in a workbook, you may want to use the same data for the column and row headings. To save time, you can enter the data that is the same on all worksheets at the same time.

TASK 5: TO ENTER THE SAME DATA ON MULTIPLE WORKSHEETS AT THE SAME TIME:

1   Press (CTRL) and click the Atrium Cafe tab.
Both the Atrium Cafe worksheet and the Willow Top worksheet are selected.

2   Click in cell B2 and type **Jan**.

Note The Group indicator displays in the title bar when multiple worksheets are selected.

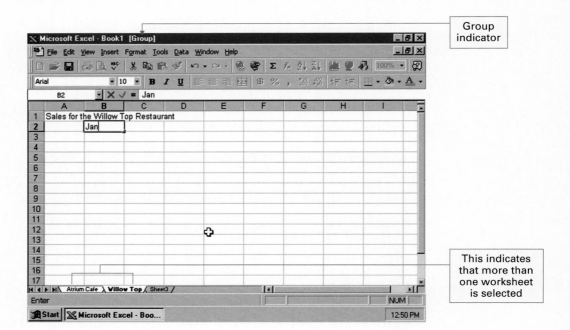

Group indicator

This indicates that more than one worksheet is selected

3 Press → and type **Feb**.

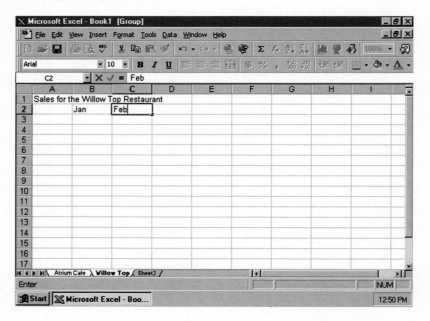

4 Press ⊕ and type **Difference**.

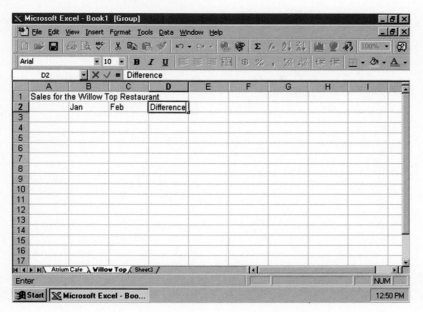

5 Click in cell A3 and type **Week 1**.

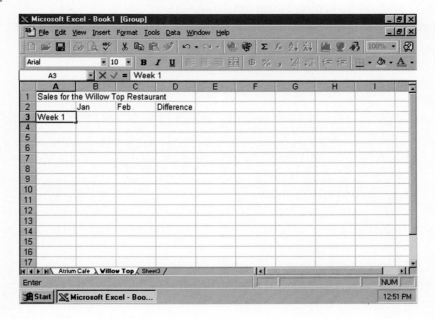

6 Press (ENTER) and type **Week**.
The AutoComplete feature completes the entry as Week 1.

7 Continue typing so that the entry is "Week 2" and then press (ENTER).

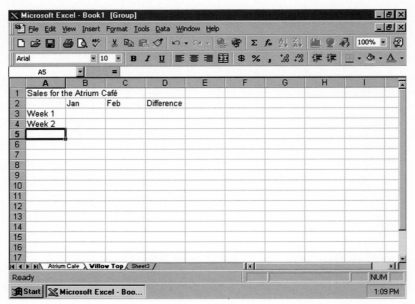

8 Click in cell A4.
Cell A4 becomes the active cell.

9 Point to the handle in the lower right corner of the cell.

> **Note** The pointer appears as a plus when you point to the handle.

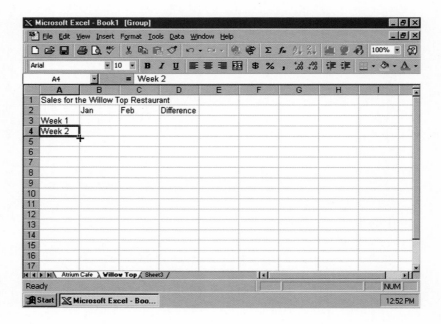

10   Drag the handle to cell A7.

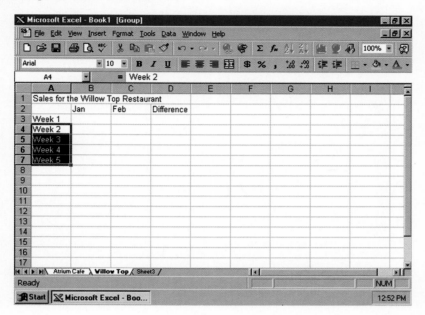

Tip You can use the dragging technique to enter almost any type of series (except the World Series, of course).

11   Click in cell A8, type **Total** and press ⒠ENTER).

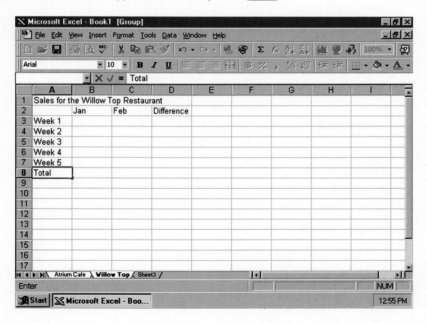

12   Click the Atrium Cafe tab to verify that the information appears on both worksheets.

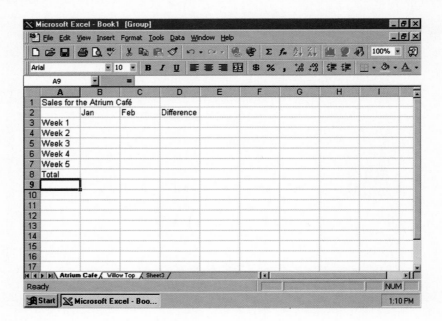

Entering Numbers

If you enter a number that doesn't fit in a cell, Excel 97 either converts the number to *scientific notation* or displays pound signs (#) in the cell. If you enter a date that doesn't fit in a cell, Excel 97 displays pound signs.

> **Note** Scientific notation is a number format used for very large numbers and very small decimal numbers. For example, the scientific notation for 1,000,000,000 is 1E+09 which means 1 times 10 to the ninth power. Perhaps our government should consider using scientific notation to express the national debt; maybe it wouldn't look so bad.

TASK 6: TO ENTER NUMBERS IN THE WORKSHEETS:

1 Press (CTRL) and click the Willow Top tab.
The Willow Top worksheet is deselected and the Group indicator no longer displays in the title bar.

2 Enter the following numbers in columns B and C on the Atrium Cafe worksheet, as shown in the illustration that follows.

COLUMN B	COLUMN C
6570	2200
8345	7890
8650	9180
8990	8750
2130	4560

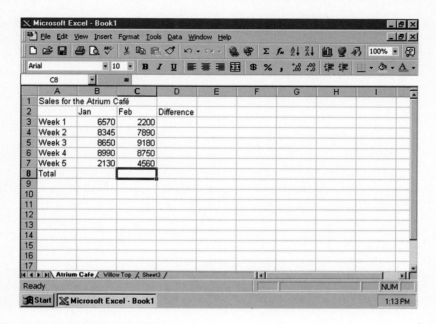

3 Click the Willow Top tab.
The Willow Top worksheet displays.

4 Enter the following numbers in columns B and C on the Willow Top worksheet:

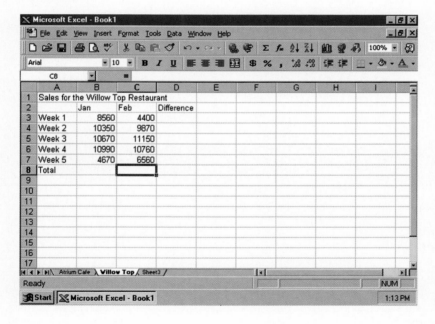

Entering Simple Formulas and Functions

Formulas and *functions* are mathematical statements that perform calculations. Formulas are made up and entered by the user to perform the specific calculation needed. Functions are formulas that are included in Excel 97. They perform calculations that are commonly used such as calculating a sum or an average. Functions require specific information, called *arguments*, to perform the calculations. Formulas and functions must start with the equal sign (=), and they can contain cell addresses, numbers, and *arithmetic operators.* Table 1.3 describes the arithmetic operators and gives examples. Table 1.4 lists some of the commonly used functions.

> **Tip** Some formulas and functions refer to a block of cells, called a *range.* The address of a range includes the first and last cells in the range separated by a colon. For example, the address of the range from cell A1 through cell B10 is A1:B10.

Table 1.3   Arithmetic Operators

Operator	Meaning	Example	Result (if A1 = 20 and A2 = 2)
+	Addition	=A1+A2	22
−	Subtraction	=A1−A2	18
*	Multiplication	=A1*10	200
/	Division	=A1/A2	10
%	Percent	=A1%	.2
^	Exponentiation	=A1^A2	400

Table 1.4   Commonly Used Functions

Function	Meaning	Example	Result (if A1 = 1, A2 = 2 and A3 = 3)
=SUM(*argument*)	Calculates the sum of the cells in the argument	=SUM(A1:A3)	6
=AVERAGE(*argument*)	Calculates the average of the cells in the argument	=AVERAGE(A1:A3)	2
=MAX(argument)	Finds the largest value in the cells in the argument	=MAX(A1:A3)	3
=MIN(*argument*)	Finds the smallest value of the cells in the argument	=MIN(A1:A3)	1
=COUNT(*argument*)	Counts the number of cells in the argument that have a numeric value	=COUNT(A1:A3)	3

TASK 7: TO ENTER FORMULAS AND FUNCTIONS:

1 Press (CTRL) and click the Atrium Cafe tab.
Both worksheets are selected, and the data you enter will display on both worksheets. Notice that the Group indicator displays in the title bar.

2 Click in cell D3 and click the equal sign in the formula bar. (If the Office Assistant opens, choose No, don't provide help now.)

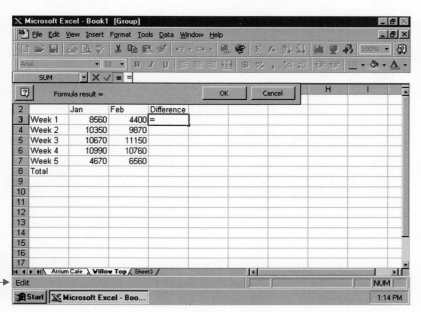

The mode changes to Edit because the data is being entered in the formula bar

3 Click in cell B3.
The mode changes to **Point** because you are pointing to cells to build the formula.

4 Type a minus sign (−).

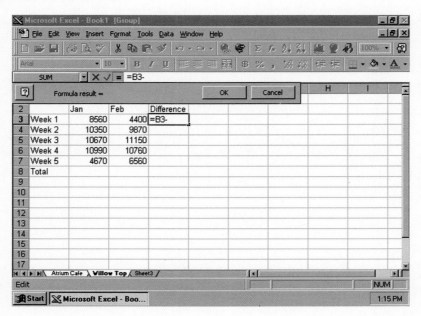

5 Click in cell C3 and then click the Enter ✓ button in the formula bar.

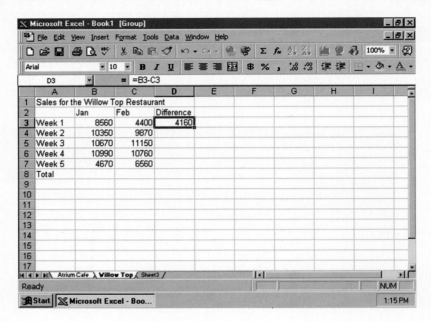

6 Click in cell B8 and type **=sum(**

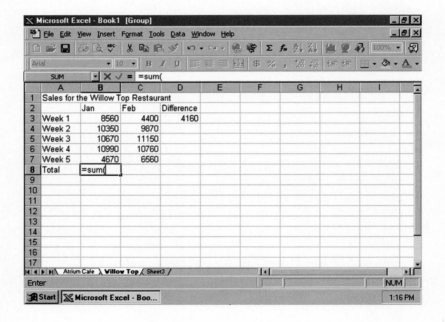

7   Drag the cursor from cell B3 through cell B7.

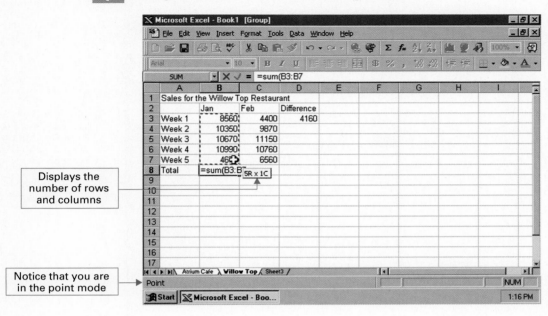

Displays the number of rows and columns

Notice that you are in the point mode

8   Press ENTER.

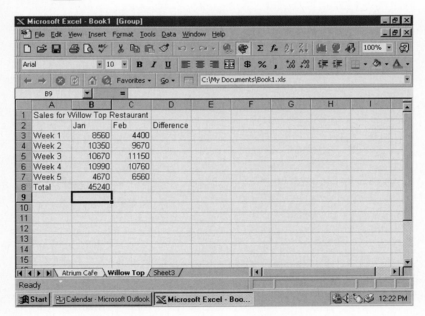

9   Click in cell C8 and click the AutoSum Σ button on the Standard toolbar.

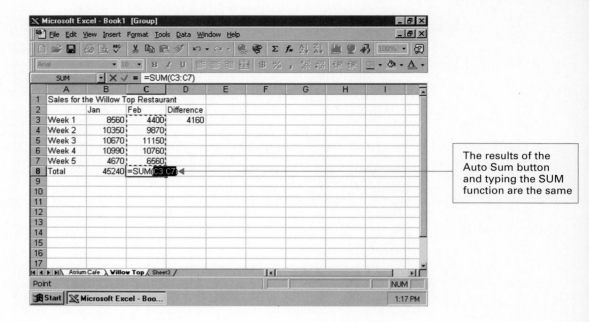

The results of the Auto Sum button and typing the SUM function are the same

10 Press ENTER.
The numbers in column C are totaled.

> **Note** If you change a number in a cell, Excel 97 automatically recalculates all formulas or functions that might be affected.

> **Key Concept** When a formula has more than one operation, Excel 97 follows an **order of precedence** to determine the sequence in which each operation should be performed. The order is as follows: exponentiation first, then multiplication or division (from left to right), and finally addition or subtraction (from left to right). If the formula has parentheses, the operation(s) in the parentheses are performed first. You can use the phrase "Please excuse my dear Aunt Sally" to remember "p" for parentheses, "e" for exponent, "m" for multiplication, "d" for division, "a" for addition, and "s" for subtraction.

Saving a Workbook

If you want to keep the data that you have entered in a workbook, you must save the file. When saving the file, you specify a name for the document and a location where it will be stored.

> **Tip** Because Excel 97 a 32-bit program, the name of a workbook can be a *long filename.* Long filenames (including the full path of the file) can use up to 255 characters. Although you can use as many spaces and periods in the filename as you want, you can't use ? or : or *. Older versions of Excel prior to Excel 7.0 do NOT use long filenames and will convert a long filename to eight characters (plus the extension).

TASK 8: TO SAVE A WORKBOOK:

1   Click the Atrium Cafe tab if it isn't the displayed worksheet.
The Atrium Cafe worksheet displays.

2   Press (CTRL) and click the Willow Top tab.
The Willow Top worksheet is deselected.

> **Tip** When you are ready to save and close a workbook and you
> have more than one worksheet selected, you might want to deselect
> all but one worksheet by pressing (CTRL) and clicking the tabs you
> want to deselect. If you don't deselect worksheets, the next time you
> open the workbook, the worksheets will still be selected and any
> changes you make will be made on all worksheets if you don't notice
> the Group indicator.

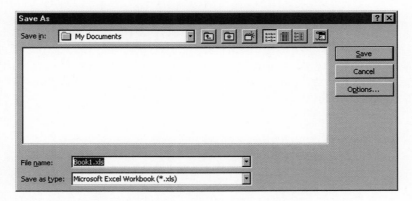

3   Click the Save 💾 button.

4   Type **Restaurant Sales** in the File Name text box.
Excel 97 adds the default extension xls to the filename when the file is saved.

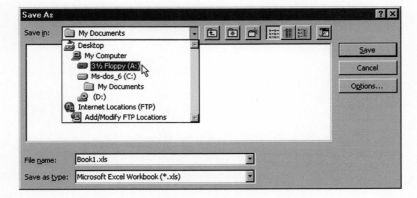

5   Click the down arrow in the Save In text box and choose drive A: (or the
drive and folder designated by your professor or lab assistant).

6   Click Save.
The dialog box closes, the file is saved on the disk, and the title bar displays
the name of the file.

EX-38

> **Tip** After saving a file for the first time, you should save the document periodically as you continue to work on it in case your system goes down for some reason. After a file has a name, you can save the file again simply by clicking the Save button.

> **Note** To save a file in a different location or with a different name, choose File, Save As.

Previewing and Printing a Worksheet

Before you print a file, you should preview it to see if it looks like what you expect. (You don't want any surprises.) The ***Print Preview*** shows the full page of the current worksheet and allows you to zoom in on the worksheet so you can actually read the data, if necessary.

You can print a worksheet in the Print Preview mode or in Normal view. Clicking the Print button prints one copy of the complete workbook. If you want to print only part of the workbook or more than one copy, you should use the Print command from the File menu because it allows you to make selections from the Print dialog box.

TASK 9: TO PREVIEW AND PRINT A WORKSHEET:

1   Click the Print Preview button on the Standard toolbar.

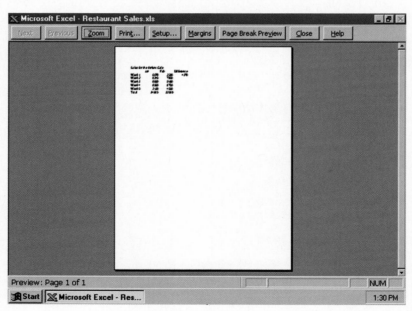

2   Click the pointer, now shaped like a magnifying glass, at the top of the worksheet.

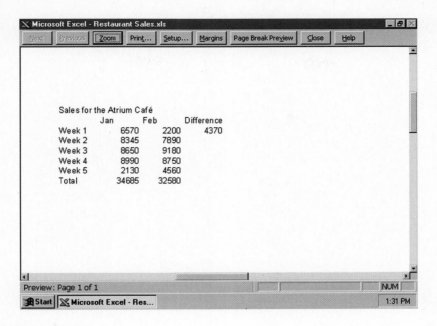

3   Click again.
The full page displays again.

4   Click Close in the Print Preview toolbar.
The Print Preview mode closes and the worksheet screen displays.

5   Ensure that the computer you are using is attached to a printer and that the printer is online.

6   Choose File from the menu bar.

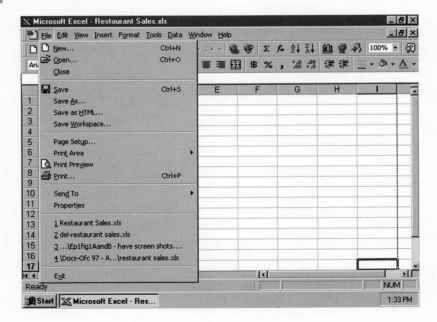

7 Choose Print.

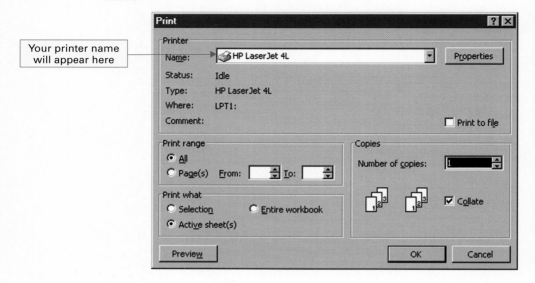

Your printer name will appear here

8 Click OK.
The workbook prints.

Closing a Workbook

When you are finished with a workbook, you can close it. If you have made changes that you want to keep, you should save the workbook before closing it. If you forget to save a workbook before closing, Excel 97 asks if you want to save changes.

TASK 11: TO SAVE AND CLOSE A FILE:

1 Click 🖫.
The worksheet is saved.

2 Click ✕ on the Menu bar.
The file closes.

The Conclusion

You can exit Excel 97 now by clicking ✕ on the application title bar, or you can work on the Review Exercises and Assignments.

Summary and Exercises

Summary

- When you launch Excel 97 a workbook named Book1 is created automatically.
- To enter data in a worksheet, the cell pointer must be positioned in the desired cell.
- By default, a new workbook has three worksheets.
- Excel 97 recognizes several different types of data: text, dates, numbers, and formulas.
- Formulas and functions are mathematical statements that perform calculations.
- Files can be saved with long filenames.
- Before you print a worksheet, you can preview it to see if it looks acceptable.
- When you close a file, if you haven't saved changes to the file, Excel 97 asks if you want to save the changes.

Key Terms and Operations

Key Terms	Operations
active cell	close a workbook
arithmetic operators	create a workbook
AutoComplete	enter data
Edit mode	enter formulas and functions
Enter mode	move in a workbook
formula	name a workbook
function	name a worksheet
order of precedence	preview a worksheet
Point mode	print a worksheet
Print Preview mode	save a workbook
range	
scientific notation	

Study Questions

Multiple Choice

1. Using the order of precedence, solve the formula 5–2*(8+2). What is the answer?
   a. 26
   b. −15
   c. −9
   d. 30

2. To move to the cell below the active cell, press
   a. (ENTER).
   b. (PGDN).
   c. (TAB).
   d. (CTRL)+⊕.

3. Which of the following is a range address?
   a. D1;D10
   b. D1,D10
   c. D1 D10
   d. D1:D10

4. Which of the following cannot be included in numeric data?
   a. 1
   b. 2
   c. E
   d. =

5. Which of the following is an example of scientific notation?
   a. 1.5E+11
   b. 1^10
   c. 7.8!
   d. $A$2

6. If A1 is 10, A2 is 15, and A3 is 20, what is the result of =SUM(A1:A2)?
   a. 10
   b. 15
   c. 25
   d. 45

7. If A1 is 10, A2 is 15, and A3 is 20, what is the result of =AVERAGE(A1:A3)?
   a. 10
   b. 15
   c. 25
   d. 45

8. If A1 is 10, A2 is 15, A3 is 20, and A4 says "Total," what is the result of =COUNT(A1:A4)?
   a. 3
   b. 15
   c. 45
   d. 4

9. The Preview mode shows
   a. all pages of a workbook.
   b. the current page of the workbook.
   c. the formulas.
   d. the formulas and functions.

10. When you press CTRL+END, what cell becomes the active cell?
   a. IV65536
   b. The last cell in the current column.
   c. The cell in the lower right corner.
   d. The cell in the lower right corner of the active area of the worksheet.

Short Answer

1. What happens when you change a number in a cell that is included in a formula?

2. What should you do before you close a workbook?

3. How do you rename a worksheet?

4. What is the order of precedence?

5. What displays in a cell if you enter 1/10?

6. How can you make 1/10 display as a fraction in a cell?

7. Write the formula to add the numbers from cell A1 through cell A5.

8. Write the function to add the numbers from cell A1 through cell A5.

9. How do you enter the same data on more than one worksheet?

10. What function finds the smallest value?

For Discussion

1. Describe a situation in which you would use several worksheets in the same workbook.

2. The cell displays #######. What caused the problem and how can you solve it?

3. Discuss the reasons you might rename worksheets in a workbook.

4. What is a range and how is it addressed?

Review Exercises

1. Creating an expense account

Your good friend Karl Klaus, the head chef at the 4-star restaurant in *The Grande Hotel*, has asked you to create an expense report for him because he can't type. In this exercise, you will create a worksheet that lists the expenses Karl had on a recent trip for the hotel.

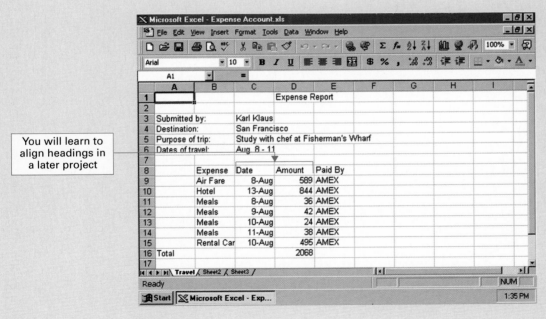

You will learn to align headings in a later project

Figure 1.3

1. Create a new workbook.

2. Rename Sheet1 to Travel.

3. Enter the data shown in Figure 1.3 except for Row 16.

Note The format for dates might be different on your computer.

4. Use the AutoSum button to calculate the total expenses.

5. Save the workbook as *Expense Account.xls*.

2. Calculating savings

In this exercise, you will use a worksheet to calculate the amount of money you will have in twenty years, based on different variables such as the amount you can save each year and the rate of interest you earn.

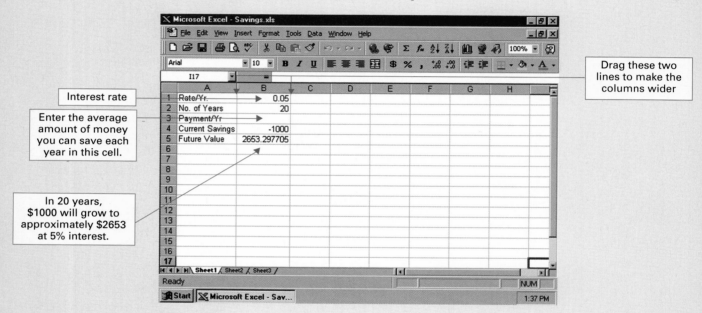

Interest rate

Enter the average amount of money you can save each year in this cell.

In 20 years, $1000 will grow to approximately $2653 at 5% interest.

Drag these two lines to make the columns wider

Figure 1.4

1. Go to this address on the Web:
http://www.finaid.org/finaid/calculators/finaid_calc.html.

2. Select the Savings Plan Designer.

3. If you currently have $1000 in savings and you can get 5 percent interest, how much will you have to save each month to have $200,000 in 20 years?

4. Create a new worksheet and enter the data for A1, A2, A3, A4, A5, B1, B2, and B4 as shown in Figure 1.4. Be sure to enter the data in the same cells shown in the figure.

Note The values for current savings is a negative number due to the use of debits and credits in standard accounting procedures.

5. In cell B5, type this function: =FV(B1,B2,B3,B4,1).

6. In cell B3, enter the number that is 12 times the answer you got in step 3. Precede the number with a minus sign. The answer in cell B5 should be approximately 200,000.

7. Change the Payment/Yr amount to −2000 and change the Rate/Yr to .15.

8. Save the worksheet as *Savings.xls*.

3. Creating a sales analysis worksheet

1. Launch Excel 97, if necessary, or create a new blank workbook.

2. Create the worksheet displayed in Figure 1.5.

Tip The product description of rows 5–7 contains the word cardboard.

	A	B	C	D	E	F
1	Multi-Size Container Corporation					
2	Sales Analysis					
3						
4	Product #	Product	Actual	Expected	Actual-Expected	
5	3-453	3" Cardboa	145300	156900		
6	3-455	5" Cardboa	132900	186700		
7	3-457	7" Cardboa	865330	163300		
8	5-852	2" Glass	655900	567000		
9	5-854	4" Glass	754980	641500		
10						

Figure 1.5

3. Name the worksheet *<Current year> Sales*, substituting the current year as indicated.

4. Save the workbook using the filename *Container Corporation Sales xxx* (where *xxx* represents your initials).

5. Add a formula to Column E that calculates the difference between the actual sales and the amount expected.

6. Add a formula to Row 10 that calculates the total actual sales, the total expected sales, and the total difference.

7. Save the changes to the workbook and print a copy of the worksheet.

8. Close the workbook and exit Excel.

Assignments

1. Creating a timesheet

Create a workbook with a worksheet for each of your classes. List the dates and the number of hours that you spend for each class (including class time, lab time, and homework) in a week. Total the number of hours. Save the worksheets and workbook, using an appropriate filename.

2. Creating a worksheet that compares menu prices

Go to http://www.metrodine.com and follow links to find restaurant menus that list entrees and prices. Search for "menu." Create a worksheet that lists the entrees and prices for at least two restaurants. Use the MIN and MAX functions to show the lowest and highest priced entree for each restaurant. Save the worksheets and workbook, using an appropriate filename.

Editing a Workbook

Moving a title to a different location, deleting last week's totals, copying this month's totals to the summary worksheet, adding comments to a cell, checking the spelling — an Excel user's work is never done! In this project, you will edit a workbook and modify the data using some basic editing tasks.

Objectives

After completing this project, you will be able to:

➤ **Open a workbook**

➤ **Find data**

➤ **Edit data**

➤ **Work with data**

➤ **Add comments**

➤ **Check spelling**

The Challenge

Mr. Gilmore was impressed at how quickly you created his "down-and-dirty" worksheet, but he wants a few changes made to it. Specifically, he wants you to add some comments and create a new worksheet that includes the January sales figures from both restaurants.

The Solution

To make the changes Mr. Gilmore wants, you will open the Restaurant Sales workbook, revise some of the data, move and copy some of the cells, add comments, and check the spelling. The finished workbook will look like Figure 2.1.

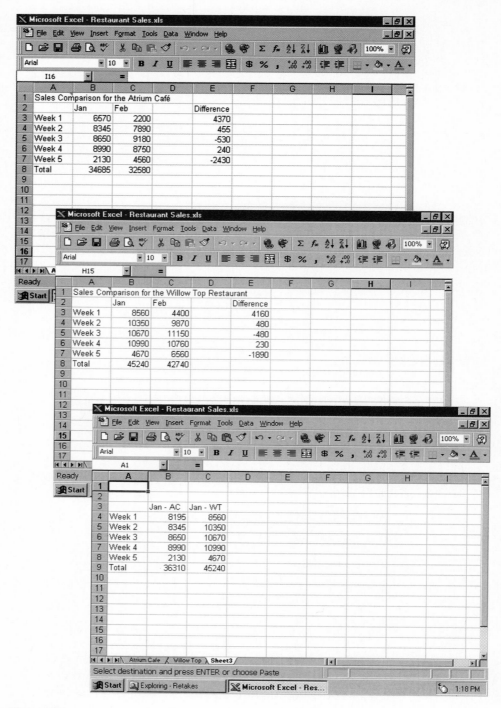

Figure 2.1

The Setup

So that your screen will match the illustrations in this chapter and to ensure that all the tasks in this project will function as described, you should set up Excel as described in Table 2.1. Because these are the default settings for the toolbars and view, you may not need to make any changes to your setup.

Table 2.1   Excel Settings

Location	Make these settings:
View, Toolbars	Deselect all toolbars except Standard and Formatting
View	Use Normal and display the Formula Bar and the Status Bar.

Opening a Workbook

When you want to view or revise a workbook that you have saved, you must open the workbook first. The worksheet and cell that were active when you last saved and closed the workbook are active when you open the workbook.

> **Tip** If the workbook is one that you have opened recently, you may see it listed at the bottom of the File menu. To open the file, simply select it from the menu.

TASK 1: TO OPEN A WORKBOOK:

1 Click the Open 📂 button.

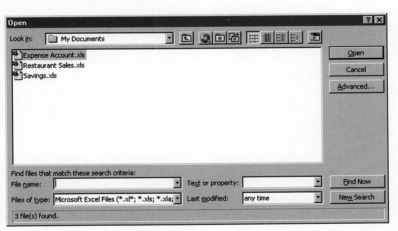

2 Click on the arrow in the Look in text box to display the drop down list if the desired folder does not display automatically.

3 Select the correct path and folder.
The folder name appears in the Look in text box.

4 Double-click *Restaurant Sales.xls.*

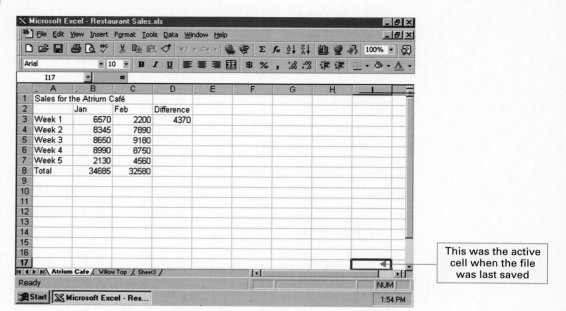

This was the active cell when the file was last saved

When you open a workbook, it opens to the location where you were when you last saved and closed it.

5 Click the Atrium Cafe tab if necessary.
The Atrium Cafe worksheet displays.

Finding Data

The Find command helps you find specific text or values in a worksheet. The command is very useful if the worksheet is large, but it also can be useful in small worksheets to find text and values that aren't shown on the screen. For example, you can use the Find command to find a word, number, or cell address that is in a formula.

TASK 2: TO FIND DATA:

1 Press (CTRL)+(HOME).

2 Choose Edit.

3 Choose Find.

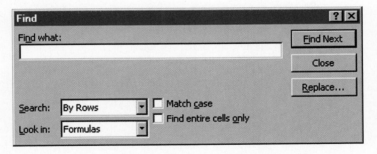

4 Type **Sum** in the Find what text box and ensure that Formulas is selected in the Look in text box.

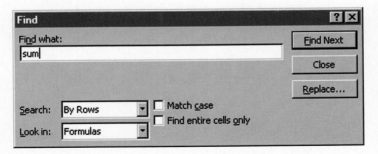

5 Click Find Next.
Cell B8 becomes the active cell.

6 Click Find Next.
Cell C8 becomes the active cell.

7 Click Find Next.
Cell B8 becomes the active cell again even though the next worksheet has a SUM function.

> **Tip** The Find command searches only the current worksheet.

8 Click Close.
The Find dialog box closes.

Editing Data

If you want to change the data that is entered in a cell, just click in the cell and type the new data. If the data is lengthy, it is more efficient to edit the existing data unless the new data is completely different. If the cell that you edit is used in a formula or function, Excel 97 recalculates automatically to update the worksheet.

TASK 3: TO EDIT DATA IN A CELL:

1 Click in cell A1 in the Atrium Cafe worksheet.
Cell A1 becomes the active cell.

2 Click in the formula bar before the "f" in "for."

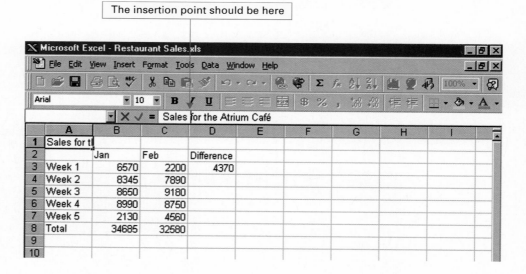

The insertion point should be here

3   Type **Comparison** and then press ⌴SPACE BAR⌴.

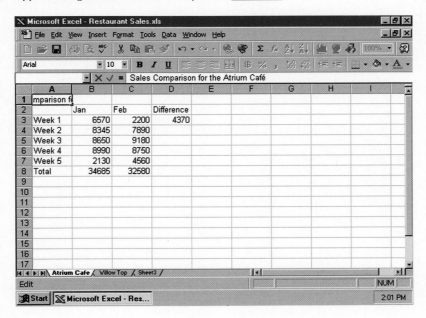

4   Press ⌴ENTER⌴.

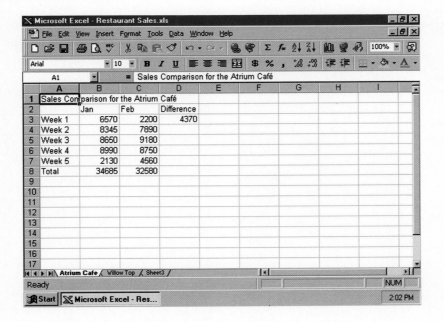

5   Click the Willow Top tab.
The Willow Top worksheet displays.

6   Click in cell A1.
Cell A1 becomes the active cell.

7 Click in the formula bar before the "f" in "for."

The insertion point should be here

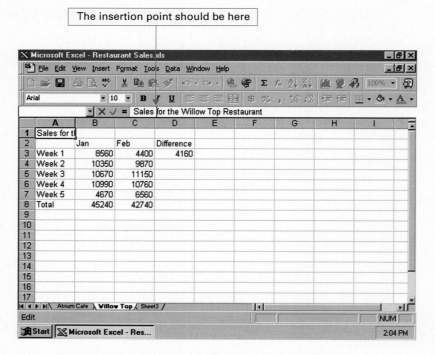

8 Type **Comparison**, press (SPACE BAR), and press (ENTER).

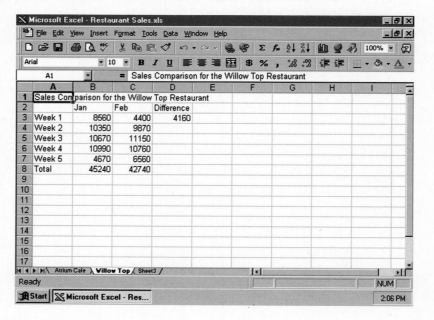

9 Click in cell B3.
Cell B3 becomes the active cell.

10   Type **8195** and press (ENTER).

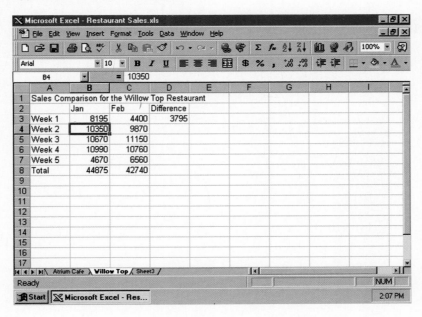

Working with Data

After you have entered data in a worksheet, you may find that you need to make some changes. You may have to copy, delete, or move the data. All of these types of revisions require selecting cells.

Selecting Cells

When you select cells, they are highlighted. In most cases, the easiest way to select cells is to drag the mouse pointer over the cells, but Table 2.2 describes other ways of selecting cells that are appropriate in many situations.

Table 2.2   Selection Methods

Selection	Method
Entire column	Click the column letter at the top of the column.
Entire row	Click the row number at the left of the row.
Entire worksheet	Click the blank button above the row numbers and to the left of the column letters.
Adjacent columns	Drag the pointer through the column letters.
Adjacent rows	Drag the pointer through the row numbers.
Non-adjacent ranges	Select the first range (the range can be an entire column or row) and then press (CTRL) while you select additional ranges.

TASK 4: TO SELECT RANGES:

1 Click the column letter above column A.

Mouse pointer

All cells in column A are selected

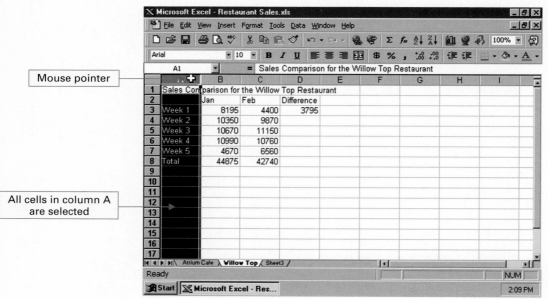

2 Drag the pointer through row numbers 3 and 4.

Rows 3 and 4 are selected

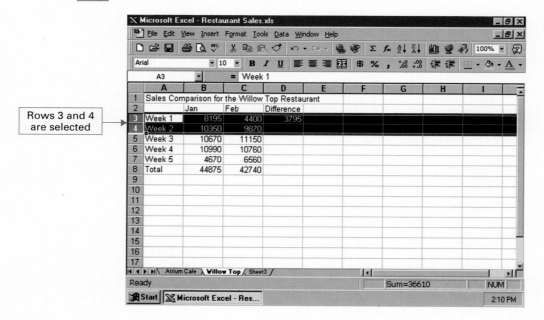

3 Select column C and then press (CTRL) while you select column F, row 8, and the range from cell H6 through cell I9.

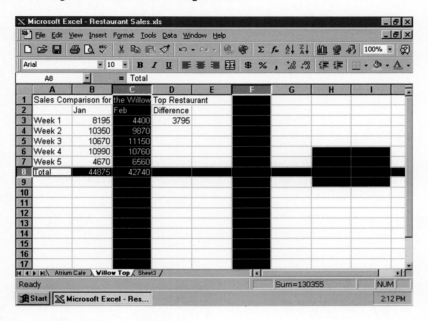

4 Select cell B3 through cell B7.

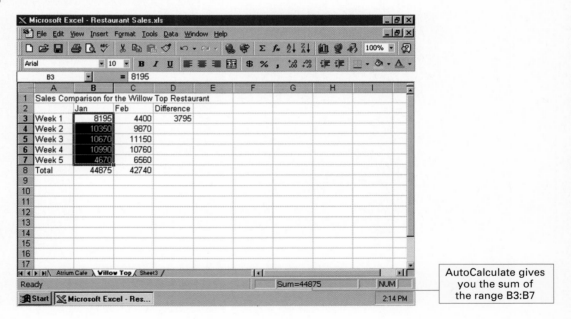

AutoCalculate gives you the sum of the range B3:B7

Tip When you select a range with values, the *AutoCalculate* feature displays a calculation in the status bar. To change the type of calculation, right-click the calculation and choose a different one.

Copying Data

When you copy data, Excel 97 stores the data in a memory area called the *Clipboard*. Data in the Clipboard can be pasted in any cell, or range of cells in any worksheet or any workbook. If you copy or cut additional data, the new data replaces the existing data in the Clipboard. Pasting data from the Clipboard does not remove data from the Clipboard; therefore, you can paste it repeatedly.

TASK 5: TO COPY DATA:

1 Press (CTRL) and click the Atrium Cafe tab.
The Atrium Cafe worksheet and the Willow Top worksheet are both selected, and the Willow Top worksheet still displays.

2 Click in cell D3.
Cell D3 becomes the active cell.

3 Click the Copy button.

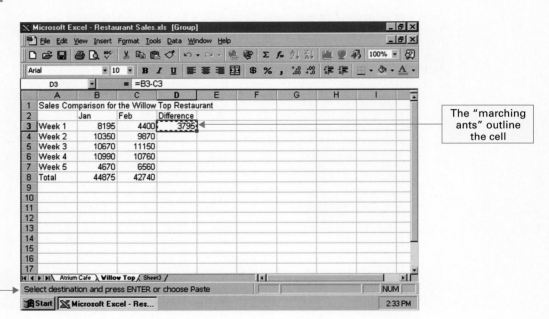

The "marching ants" outline the cell

The status bar tells you what to do next

4   Select the range from cell D4 through cell D7.

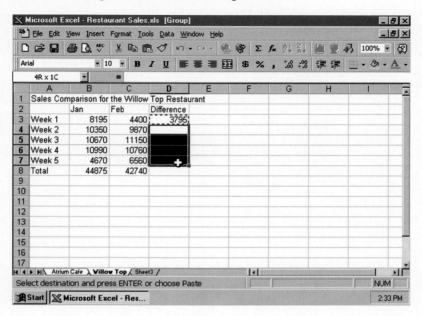

5   Click the Paste button.

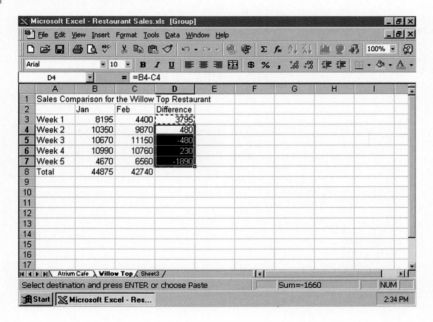

6   Click the Atrium Cafe tab.
The Copy command has been executed on this worksheet, too.

7   Press (CTRL) and click the Willow Top tab.
The Willow Top worksheet is deselected.

8 Select the range from cell B2 through cell B8.

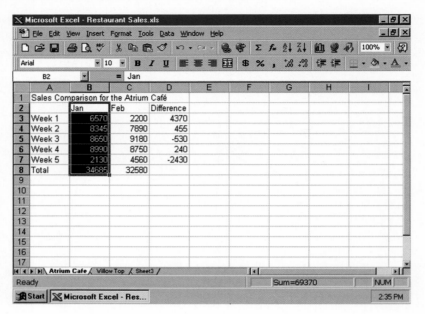

9 Click 🖺.
The cells are copied to the Clipboard.

10 Click the Sheet3 tab.
The Sheet3 worksheet displays.

11 Click in cell A3.
Cell A3 becomes the active cell.

12 Click 🖺.

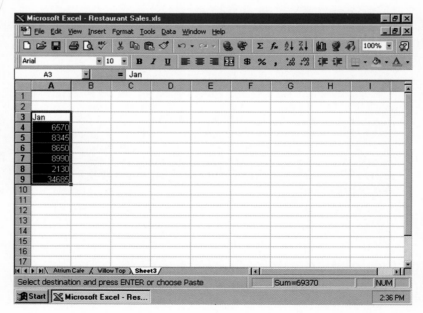

> **Caution** Pasting data into cells automatically replaces data already contained in the cells — without notice. Use the Undo feature to restore data, if necessary.

13 Copy and paste the same range from the Willow Top worksheet to cell B3 in Sheet3.

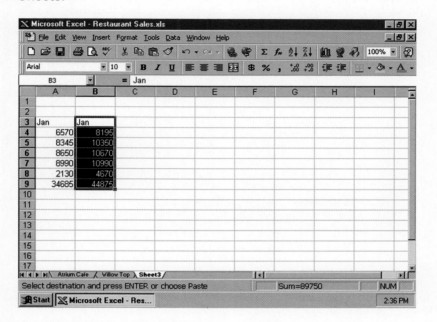

14 Rename Sheet3 to "January."
The name January appears on the tab.

Deleting Data

To erase the data in a cell or a range of cells, simply select the cells and press the Delete key. If you change your mind, click the Undo button.

> **Warning** Some users try to erase cells by passing the space bar. Although the cell looks blank, it really isn't; it contains the character for a space. You should never use this method to erase a cell; you could get arrested by the SSP (Special Spreadsheet Police).

> **Note** The Edit, Clear command accomplishes the same as pressing the (DEL) key.

TASK 6: TO DELETE DATA:

1   Select cell A8 through cell B8 on the January worksheet.

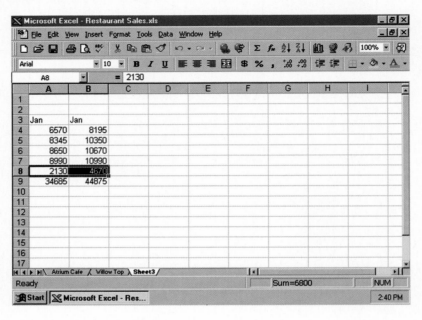

2   Press (DEL).

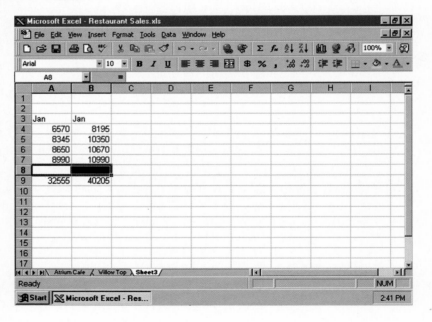

3   Click the Undo button.
The data appears again.

Tip When you delete text with the (DEL) key, the text isn't stored in the Clipboard and therefore it can't be pasted in another location. You can press (SHIFT)+(DEL) if you want deleted text placed in the Clipboard.

Moving Data

You can move data to a different location in the same worksheet or to a location in a different worksheet.

TASK 7: TO MOVE DATA:

1 Click on the Atrium Cafe tab.
The Atrium Cafe worksheet displays.

2 Select cell D2 through cell D7.

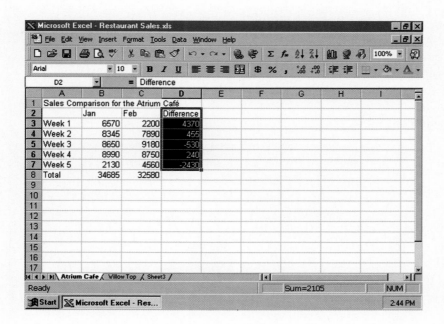

3 Click the Cut ✂ button.

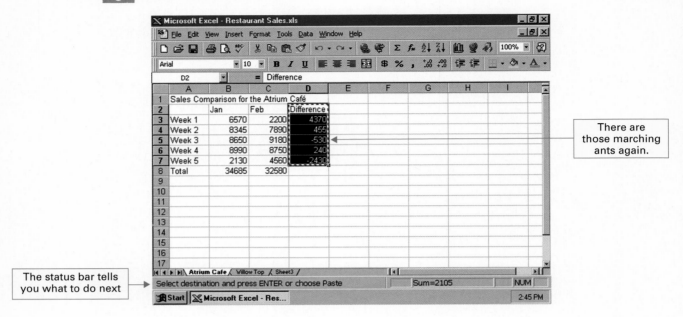

There are those marching ants again.

The status bar tells you what to do next

4 Click in cell E2.
Cell E2 becomes the active cell.

5 Click 📋.

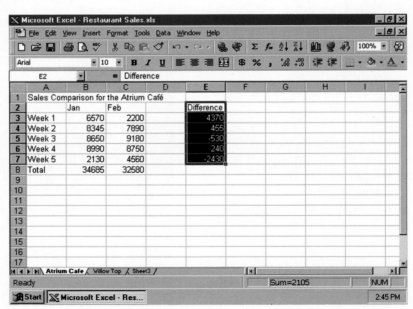

Warning Pasting anything that has been cut (or copied) to a new location that contains data overwrites the data.

6   Display the Willow Top worksheet and move the range D2 through D7 to cell E2.

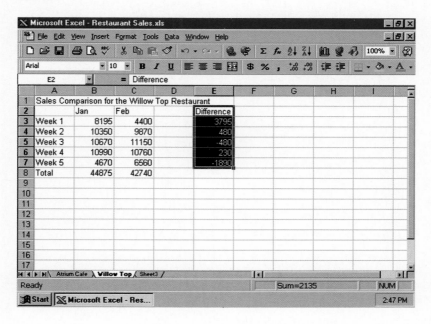

Adding Comments

You can attach **comments** to cells in a worksheet to provide additional information. The comment will contain the user name that is specified on the General page of the Options dialog box accessed from the Tools menu. The text in a comment displays on the screen and it can be made to print as well.

TASK 8: TO ADD COMMENTS:

1   Click in cell A1 on the Willow Top worksheet.
Cell A1 becomes the active cell.

2   Choose Insert from the Menu bar.

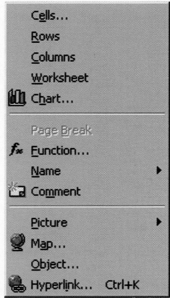

3 Choose Comment.

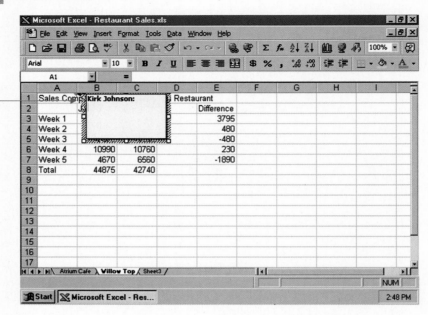

The user name precedes the comment

4 Type **Open for dinner only.**

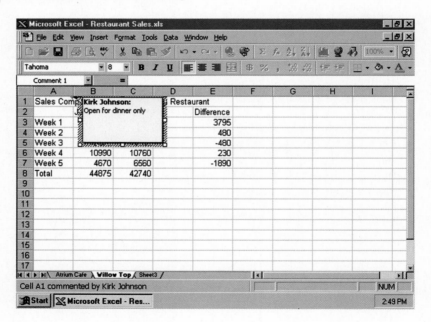

5   Click anywhere outside the comment box.

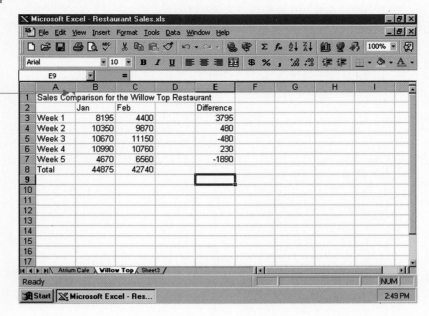

The red mark denotes a comment

6   Click the Atrium Cafe tab.
The Atrium Cafe worksheet displays.

7   Click in cell A1.
Cell A1 becomes the active cell.

8   Choose Insert, Comment, and type **Open for breakfest, lunch, and dinner.**
Do not correct the spelling of "breakfast."

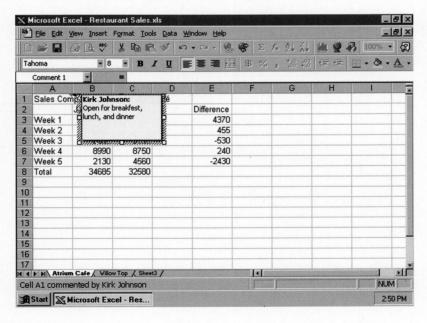

9   Click anywhere outside the comment box.
A red mark appears in cell A1.

If you want to see the comments on a worksheet, you can point to the cell that has a red mark and the comment box will pop up, or you can turn on the Comment view and all the comments will be visible.

TASK 9: TO TURN ON THE COMMENT VIEW AND TURN IT OFF AGAIN:

1 Choose View.

2 Choose Comments.

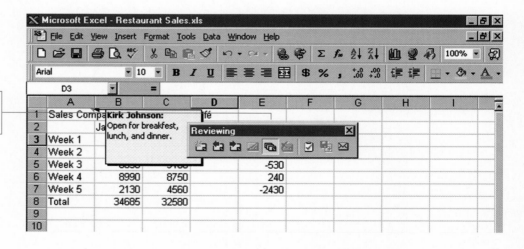

The Reviewing toolbar displays when you turn on the Comments view

3 Click the Willow Top tab.

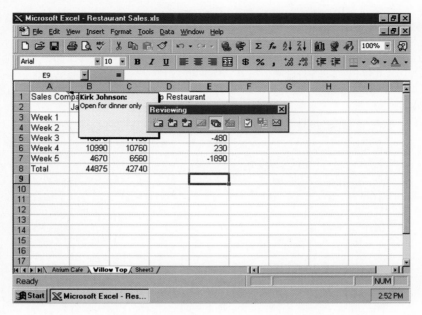

4 Click **X** on the Reviewing toolbar.
The toolbar closes.

5 Choose View, Comments.
The comments are hidden.

> **Tip** Use the Find command to find text or values in comments by selecting Comments from the Look in drop-down list.

Checking Spelling

When you have made all the revisions in a worksheet, it is a good idea to check the spelling, especially since Excel 97 doesn't underline spelling errors as you make them (as Word 97 does).

> **Note** Even though Excel 97 doesn't check your spelling as you go, it does make automatic corrections for many typing errors.

TASK 10: TO CHECK THE SPELLING:

1 Click the Atrium Cafe tab.
The Atrium Cafe worksheet displays.

2   Click in cell A1 so that Excel 97 will begin its check of the spelling with cell A1.

3   Click the Spelling button.

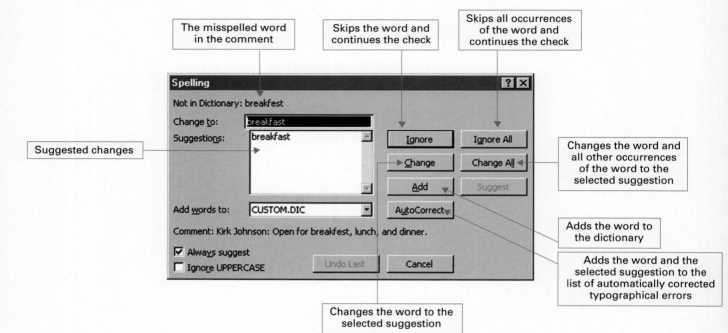

The misspelled word in the comment

Skips the word and continues the check

Skips all occurrences of the word and continues the check

Suggested changes

Changes the word and all other occurrences of the word to the selected suggestion

Adds the word to the dictionary

Adds the word and the selected suggestion to the list of automatically corrected typographical errors

Changes the word to the selected suggestion

4   Choose Change.
If there is another word not found in the dictionary, Excel 97 lists it, but if there are no more words, a message displays telling you that the spell check is complete.

5   Click OK.
The worksheet redisplays.

> **Note** If you have used multiple worksheets, you must spell check each sheet individually. Sorry!

Conclusion

If you have time, you may want to spell check the other worksheets. Then save the file and close it.

Summary and Exercises

Summary

- The Find command finds specific text or values in a worksheet.
- You can edit the data in a cell or simply reenter the data.
- Excel 97 automatically recalculates formulas if the numbers in the cells change.
- When you copy data it is stored in the Clipboard.
- Comments provide additional information in a workbook.
- You can check the spelling of worksheets in a workbook.

Key Terms and Operations

Key Terms
AutoCalculate
Clipboard
comment

Operations
add comments
copy data
delete data
edit data
find data
move data
open a workbook
paste data
select cells
spell check a worksheet

Study Questions

Multiple Choice

1. A workbook's name may appear at the bottom of the File menu,
   a. if it is in the current path.
   b. if the workbook has multiple worksheets.
   c. unless it is on a floppy disk.
   d. if it has been opened recently.

2. To edit a cell, first
   a. select the cell.
   b. click in the formula bar.
   c. activate the edit mode.
   d. press (F4).

3. The easiest way to select the entire worksheet is to
   a. triple-click in any cell.
   b. click the button above the row numbers and to the left of the column letters.
   c. drag the pointer through all the cells in the worksheet.
   d. select all the rows in the worksheet.

4. The Find command can find
   a. only text.
   b. only numbers.
   c. only cell addresses.
   d. text in comments.

5. The Spell Checker will
   a. not check all worksheets at once.
   b. not check comments.
   c. only start in the first cell of a worksheet.
   d. not add words to the dictionary.

6. When you press (DEL), the
   a. contents of the selected cells are erased.
   b. selected cells are removed from the worksheet.
   c. contents of the selected cells are stored in the Clipboard.
   d. same result is achieved as when you choose Edit, Delete.

7. The Find command
   a. searches only the current worksheet.
   b. searches all worksheets in the workbook.
   c. searches only formulas.
   d. is useful only in large worksheets.

8. Which of the following do not require pressing the (CTRL) key?
   a. non-adjacent columns
   b. non-adjacent rows
   c. adjacent columns
   d. selecting non-adjacent ranges.

9. To move data, use the
   a. Cut and Paste buttons.
   b. Copy and Paste buttons.
   c. Move and Paste buttons.
   d. Cut and Insert buttons.

10. A comment
   a. is attached to the worksheet.
   b. is attached to a cell.
   c. is only visible when you point to the cell.
   d. displays when you click a cell.

Short Answer

1. When you open a workbook, what is the location of the active cell?

2. How do you use the AutoCalculate feature?

3. What happens if you copy data to a range that already contains data?

4. What toolbar displays when you turn on the Comments view?

5. How would you select both Column C and the range A1 through A10?

6. How do you move data?

7. What happens to the data in the Clipboard when you copy new data?

8. What happens to the data in the Clipboard when you exit Excel 97?

9. How do you select several consecutive rows?

10. How do you insert a comment?

For Discussion

1. What do you do if you need to find all the formulas that reference cell B3?

2. Discuss the two methods of changing data in a cell and when you use each method.

3. Describe several scenarios in which comments are useful.

4. Describe several scenarios in which the AutoCalculate feature could be used.

Review Exercises

1. Revising the restaurant sales worksheet

In this exercise, you will revise the Restaurant Sales worksheet, revising data and adding a comment.

1. Open the workbook named *Restaurant Sales.xls,* unless it is already open.

2. Make the revisions (highlighted in yellow) shown in Figure 2.2.

3. Add a comment to cell A7 in the Atrium Cafe worksheet that says "This

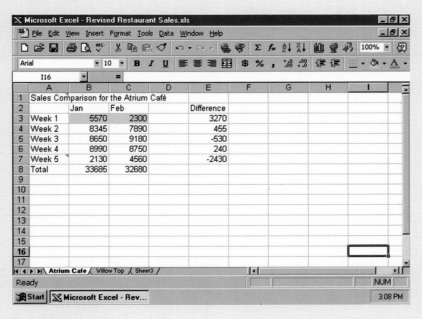

Figure 2.2

week had 4 days in January and 3 days in February."

4. Make sure the numbers on the January worksheet match the numbers on the Atrium Cafe and Willow Top worksheets.

5. Save the file as *Revised Restaurant Sales.xls* and close it.

2. Revising a timesheet

In this exercise, you will revise a timesheet workbook.

1. Ask your instructor how to obtain the file *Tmsheet.xls.* (If you have Internet access, you can download this file from the Addison Wesley Longman website at http://hepg.awl.com/select and follow the appropriate links).

2. Open the file and find the word "sum" in a formula in the Smith worksheet. Copy the formula to the next six cells on the right.

3. Delete the text in row 4.

4. Move the data in cell B1 to cell D1.

5. Copy A1:H9 to the same location in the Jones worksheet.

6. Save the file as *Times.xls* and close it.

3. Moving and copying data in a worksheet

1. Launch Excel and open *Container Corporation Sales xxx.xls* (where *xxx* represents your initials).

Note If you do not have a workbook named *Container Corporation Sales xxx.xls*, ask your instructor for a copy of the file you should use to complete this exercise.

2. Make the following changes to the workbook:
- Delete *Multi-Size* from the name of the container company in Cell A1.
- Move the data in Columns C, D, and E and place the data in Columns D, E, and F.
- Copy the data in Columns A, B and F to the second and third worksheets in the workbook.
- Copy the data in Rows 4 and 10 to the second and third worksheets.
- Rename Sheet2 *<Last Year> Sales*, substituting last year's date as indicated.
- Rename Sheet3 *Sales Increase*.

3. Add a comment note that contains your name and the current date to Cell A1.

4. Spell check the workbook and make appropriate corrections.

5. Save the workbook using the filename *2 Container Corporation Sales xxx*.

6. Print a copy of each worksheet in the workbook and then close the workbook and exit Excel.

Assignments

1. Creating and revising a budget
Create a worksheet that lists expenses for your personal budget. List expense items in column A starting in row 4. List the projected amounts for the next three months in columns B through D. Total each month at the bottom of the column. Save the worksheet as *My Budget.xls*. Revise the amounts so they are more conservative. Move the totals to row 3. Add comments for expenses that need further explanation. Save the revised worksheet as *Lower Budget.xls*.

2. Tracking the American Stock Exchange (Optional Exercise)
Go to the web site http://www.amex.com and explore the site. Create a worksheet to track individual stocks or the market summary. Save the worksheet as *Amex.xls*. Check the site on several different days and add the information to the worksheet.

Enhancing the Appearance of a Workbook

Now that you can create and edit a worksheet, it's time for you to add a little pizzazz to the worksheet with various formatting techniques. In this project you will use borders and colors to give the worksheet a classy look.

Objectives

After completing this project, you will be able to:

➤ **Format text**

➤ **Change cell alignment**

➤ **Format numbers**

➤ **Format dates**

➤ **Format numbers as text**

➤ **Add borders and fill**

➤ **View and change a page break**

➤ **Use AutoFormat**

The Challenge

Mr. Williams, the manager of the golf and tennis property at The Willows, has created a worksheet named *Income.xls* that estimates the income for the upcoming Pro-Celebrity Tournament. He has entered all the data and formulas, but he wants you to format the worksheet so it looks better and is easier to read.

The Solution

You will open the workbook, format the numbers and dates, add a border to the important information and emphasize the totals with shading. Additionally, you will format and align the data in some of the cells and use AutoFormat to format a group of cells automatically. The formatted worksheet will look like Figure 3.1 when you are finished. (The Full Screen view is used in Figure 3.1.)

Before you can begin you must download *Income.xls* from the Addison Wesley Longman web site. The file can be found at http://hepg.awl.com/select. (Follow the appropriate links.). If you are unable to download, obtain the file from your instructor.

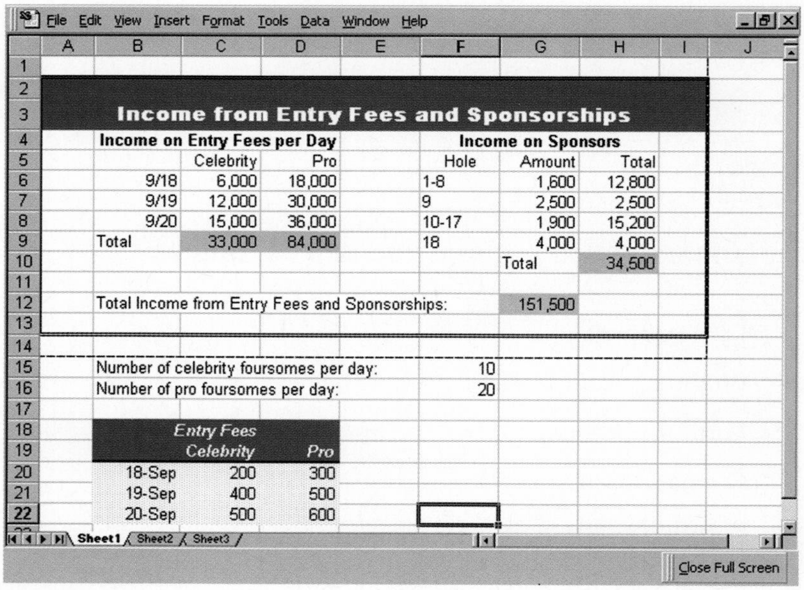

Figure 3.1

The Setup

So that your screen will match the illustrations in this chapter and to ensure that all the tasks in this project will function as described, you should set up Excel as described in Table 3.1. Because these are the default settings for the toolbars and view, you may not need to make any changes to your setup.

Table 3.1   Excel Settings

Location	Make these settings:
View, Toolbars	Deselect all toolbars except Standard and Formatting.
View	Use the Normal view and display the Formula Bar and Status Bar.

Formatting Text

You can format text in a number of ways. You can make it bold, italic, or underlined, or change the font, the font size, and the font color. The Formatting toolbar includes buttons for many of the text formatting options. Before you begin formatting the worksheet, you will save it as *Income2.xls* so you can use the original again later.

TASK 1: TO FORMAT TEXT:

1   Open *Income.xls* and choose File, Save As. Select the drive or folder, type *Income2.xls* in the filename text box and click Save.

2   Select cells D3, B4, and F4.

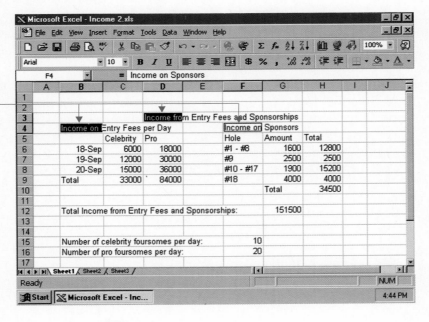

Click the first cell to select it and then press Ctrl when you click the other cells

3   Click the Bold **B** button.
The text in all three cells changes to bold.

4   Select cell D3. Click the drop-down arrow for Font Size and choose 12.
The text in the cell changes from 10 point to 12 point.

5 Click the drop-down arrow bar Font and choose Arial Black.

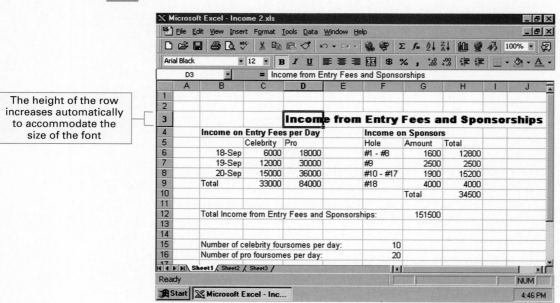

The height of the row increases automatically to accommodate the size of the font

Income from Entry Fees and Sponsorships				
Income on Entry Fees per Day			Income on Sponsors		
	Celebrity	Pro	Hole	Amount	Total
18-Sep	6000	18000	#1 - #8	1600	12800
19-Sep	12000	30000	#9	2500	2500
20-Sep	15000	36000	#10 - #17	1900	15200
Total	33000	84000	#18	4000	4000
				Total	34500
Total Income from Entry Fees and Sponsorships:				151500	
Number of celebrity foursomes per day:			10		
Number of pro foursomes per day:			20		

Changing Cell Alignment

Data in a cell can be aligned on the left, in the center, or on the right. Each type of data that you enter uses a default alignment—text is left aligned and numbers and dates are right aligned.

You can change the alignment of data in a selected cell by clicking on one of the alignment buttons in the Formatting toolbar. Sometimes you may want to align data across several cells; for example, you might want to center a title in the first row so that the title spans the columns used in the worksheet. In this case, you can merge the cells into one wide cell, and then center the data in the wide cell.

TASK 2: TO CHANGE THE CELL ALIGNMENT:

1 Select A3:I3.
The cells are highlighted.

2   Choose Format.

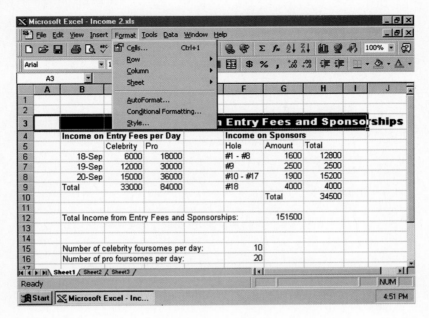

3   Choose Cells.

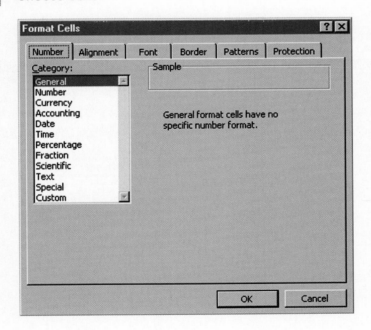

4 Click the Alignment tab.

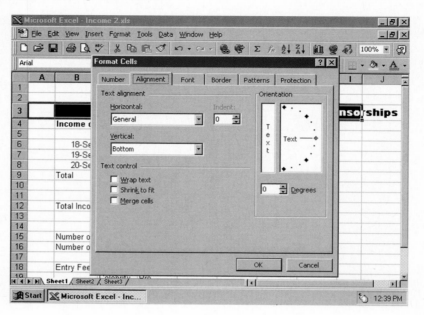

5 Choose Merge cells and click OK.
The cells become one cell.

6 Click the Center ▤ button on the Formatting toolbar.

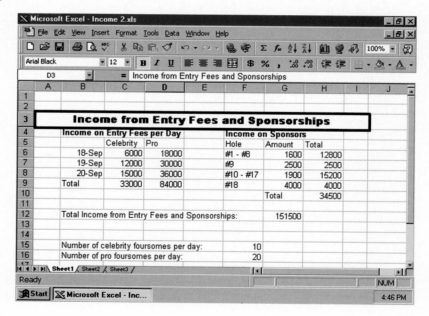

Tip To merge and center at the same time, select the cells and click the Merge and Center button ⊞.

7 Merge and align the remaining cells:
Merge the cells B4:D4 into one cell and center the text in the cell. Merge the cells F4:H4 into one cell and center the text in the cell. Center the text in cell F5. Select cells C5, D5, G5, and H5 and click the Align Right ≡ button.

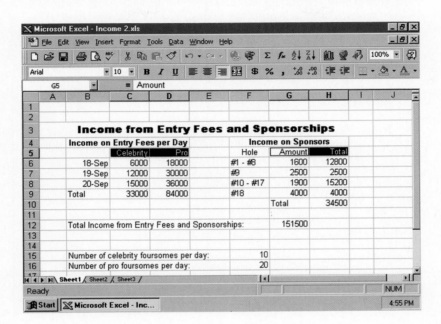

Formatting Numbers

The numbers you enter in a workbook can be "dressed up" with several different formats. As with text, you can make numbers bold, italic, change the font size, and font color. But there are other formatting options available for numbers. Table 3.2 describes the formats that are available in Excel and Figure 3.2 shows some examples.

Table 3.2   Number Formats

Format	Description
General	Numbers appear as entered except for fractions in the form of 1/2 which must be entered as 0 1/2. Commas and decimal points can be entered with the numbers. If commas are not entered, they will not display automatically as in other formats. You can enter a minus or parentheses for negative numbers.
Number	Numbers have a fixed number of decimal places, comma separators can be displayed automatically, and negative numbers can be displayed with a minus, in red, with parentheses, or in red with parentheses.
Currency	Numbers have thousands separators and can have a fixed number of decimal places, a currency symbol, and negative numbers can be displayed with a minus, in red, with parentheses, or in red with parentheses.
Accounting	Numbers have thousands separators, a fixed number of decimal places, and can display a currency symbol. Currency symbols and decimal points line up in a column.
Date	Dates can display with numbers, such as 3/4/97 or 03/04/97, or with numbers and text, such as March 4, 1997 or March-97. Some date formats also display the time.
Time	Times can display as AM or PM or use the 24-hour clock, as in 13:15 for 1:15 PM. Some Time formats also display dates.
Percentage	Numbers are multiplied by 100 and display a percent sign.
Fraction	Numbers display as one, two, or three digit fractions.
Scientific	Numbers display as a number times a power of 10 (represented by E).
Text	Numbers display exactly as entered but are treated as text; therefore, the number would not be used in a calculation.
Special	These formats are used for zip codes, phone numbers, and social security numbers.
Custom	Numbers display in a format created by the user.

	A	B	C	D	E
1	This column is formatted with the **General** Format which is the default.	This column is formatted with the **Number** format with two decimal places.	This column is formatted with the **Currency** format, two decimal places, a dollar sign, and negative numbers in red.	This column is formatted with the **Accounting** format and two decimal places.	This column is formatted with the **Scientific** format with two decimal places.
3	1.37512349	1.38	$1.38	$ 1.38	1.38E+00
4	1000000000	1000000000.00	$1,000,000,000.00	$ 1,000,000,000.00	1.00E+09
5	-98	-98.00	$98.00	$ (98.00)	-9.80E+01
6	12345.6	12345.60	$12,345.60	$ 12,345.60	1.23E+04
7	10	10.00	$10.00	$ 10.00	1.00E+01

Figure 3.2

TASK 3: TO FORMAT NUMBERS:

1 Select cells C6:D9, G6:H9, H10, and G12.
The cells are highlighted.

2 Choose Format, Cells, click the Number tab, and select Currency from the
Category list.

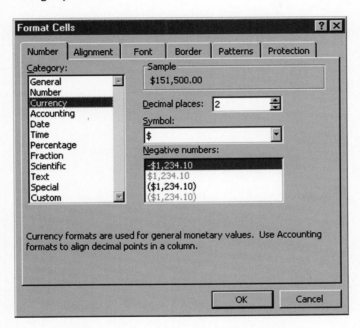

3 Select 0 for Decimal places and None for Symbol.

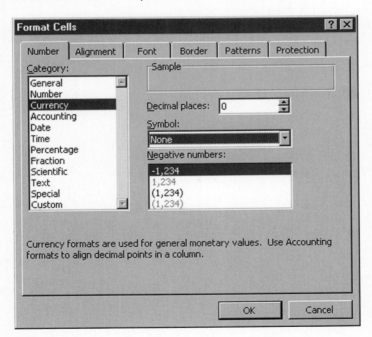

4 Click OK.
The format is applied.

Formatting Dates

The date format is included in the number formats because Excel stores dates as numbers. You can format dates in several ways. For example, if you enter the date 3/4/98, you can format it to look like any of the following:

3/4	Mar-98
3/4/98	March-98
03/04/98	March 4, 1998
4-Mar	M
4-Mar-98	M-98
04-Mar-98	

Some numbers that you enter are really text. For example, in Figure 3.1, shown on page 77 and again below, the range of 1–8 refers to holes 1 through 8 on the golf course. If you do not format "1–8" as text, Excel will interpret the entry as a date. You will learn how to format dates in Tasks 4 and 5.

Figure 3.1

TASK 4: TO FORMAT DATES:

1 Select B6:B8.
The cells are highlighted.

2 Choose Format, Cells, and click on the Number tab (if necessary).
The default Date format is selected.

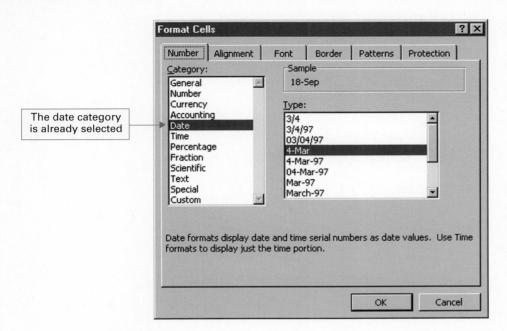

The date category is already selected

3 Select the first option from the Type list (3/4) and click OK.

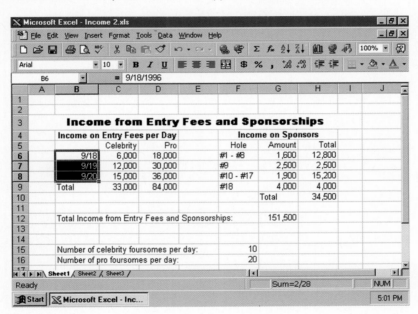

Formatting Numbers as Text

When you enter numbers with dashes or slashes in a worksheet, as we did in golf course holes 1–8 and 10–17 shown below, Excel interprets the entry as a date. To avoid this, you must format the numbers as text.

TASK 5: TO FORMAT NUMBERS AS TEXT:

1 Reenter the data in cells F6:F9 exactly as shown:
F6: **1 - 8**
F7: **9**
F8: **10 - 17**
F9: **18**

Excel has interpreted the text in these two cells as dates

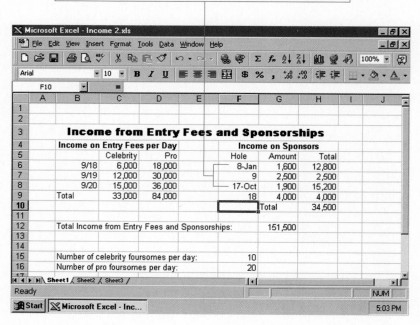

2 Select cells F6:F9.
The cells are highlighted.

3 Choose Format, Cells, and click on the Number tab (if necessary). Select Text for the Category and click OK.

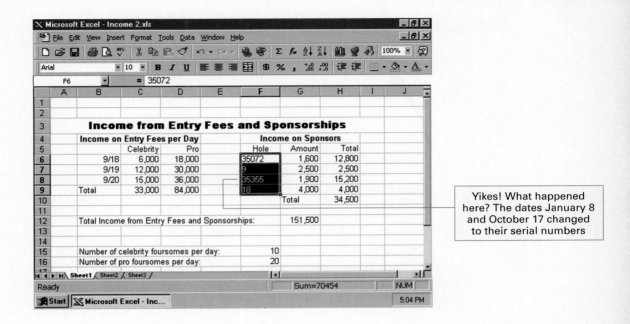

Note A serial number is a sequential number given to every day of every year since the turn of the century. So the number 35072 means that January 8, 1997 is the 35,072nd day of the 20th century.

4   Type **1 - 8** in cell F6. Type **10 - 17** in cell F8.

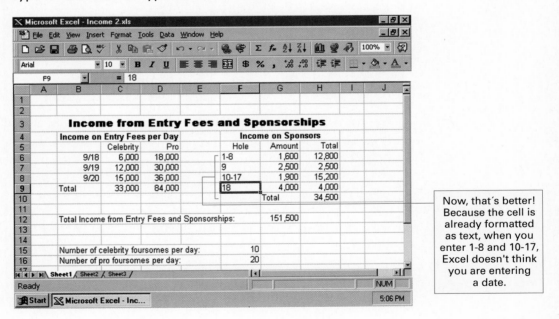

Adding Borders and Fill

A **border** is a line that displays on any side of a cell or group of cells. You can use borders in a variety of ways: to draw rectangles around cells, to create dividers between columns, to create a total line under a column of numbers, and so on.

Fill, also called **shading** or **patterns**, is a color or a shade of gray that you apply to the background of a cell. Use fill carefully if you do not have a color printer. Sometimes it doesn't look as good when it prints in black and white as it does on screen.

TASK 6: TO ADD A BORDER AND FILL:

1   Select cells A2:I13.
The cells are highlighted.

2   Choose Format, Cells, and click the Border tab.

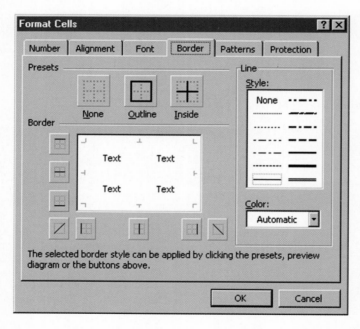

3   Select the double line in the Style box, click the Outline button, and click OK.

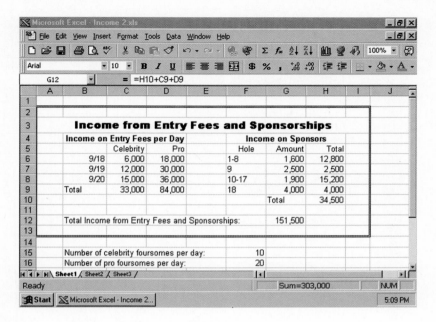

4   Select cells C9:D9, H10, and G12.
The cells are highlighted.

5   Choose Format, Cells, and click the Patterns tab.

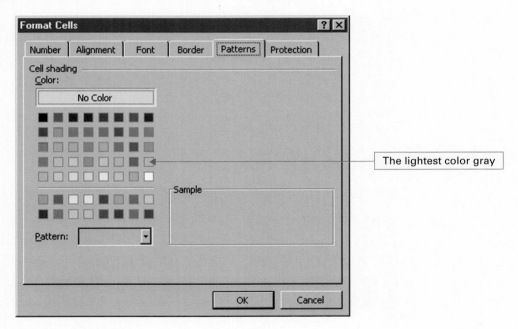

The lightest color gray

6   Select the lightest color gray and click OK.

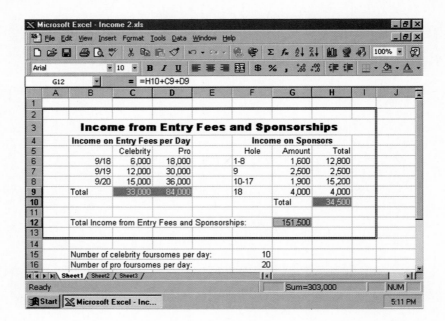

7   Select cells A2:I3 and format them with the first color on the second row of the color chart on the Patterns page.

The cells are shaded with the selected color, but you cannot tell because the cells are still selected.

> **Tip** You also can apply color by clicking the down arrow on the Fill Color 🖍️▾ button on the Formatting toolbar and selecting a color from a smaller palette.

8   Select cell A3.

The cell is highlighted.

9   To change the text color, click the down arrow in the Font Color 🅰️▾ button and click the white rectangle in the color palette.

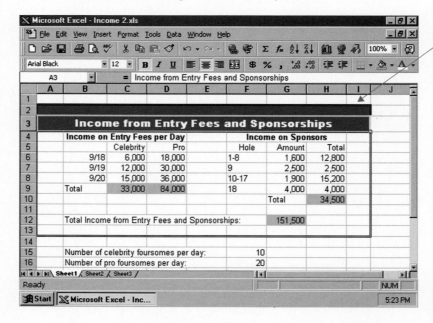

The border is in the same place, but it is hard to see because of the selected cells

Viewing and Changing a Page Break

Unlike word processing documents, worksheets are not represented on the screen by pages. The complete worksheet, all 16,777,216 cells of it, is one big page on the screen. So that you can see where the pages will break when the worksheet prints, Excel provides a *Page Break view*. You can adjust the location of the *page breaks* in this view.

TASK 7: TO VIEW THE PAGE BREAK IN THE INCOME WORKSHEET AND CHANGE IT:

1   Click the Print Preview ⬚ button.

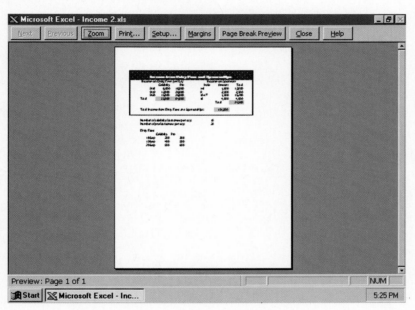

2   Click the Page Break Preview button. (Click OK if a message displays.)

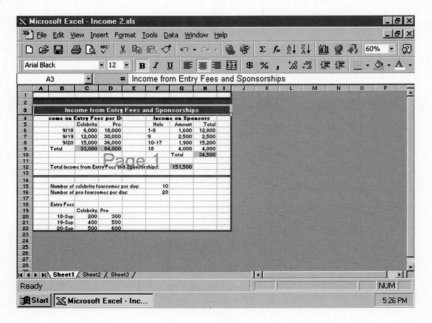

3 Drag the blue line at the bottom to just below row 14.

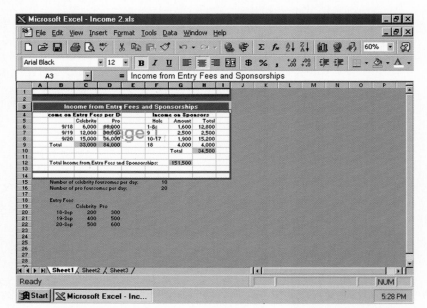

4 Click .
Now, only the bordered text displays in the print preview for page 1.

5 Click the Normal View button.
The worksheet displays in Normal view. Notice that the page break location is indicated with a dotted line.

Using AutoFormat

Excel provides several formats that you can apply to a complete work-sheet or to a single range. The **AutoFormat** feature enables you to apply many formatting features automatically, creating very professional look-ing worksheets without much effort on your part. (Excel works hard so you don't have to.)

> **Note** AutoFormats are designed for worksheets or ranges that have row headings in the first column and column headings in the first row.

TASK 8: TO APPLY AN AUTOFORMAT:

1 Select B18:D22.
The cells are highlighted.

2   Choose Format, AutoFormat.

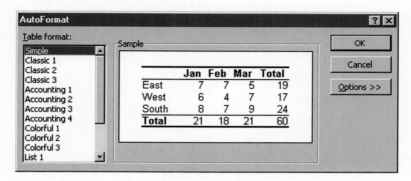

3   Select Colorful 2. Click Options, deselect Width/Height, and click OK. Click in a cell outside the selected range to see the true colors.

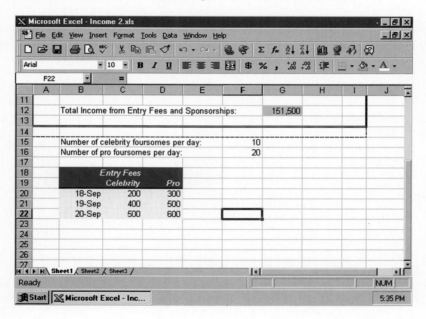

The Conclusion

If you have access to a printer, print page 1 of the worksheet. Save the workbook and close it.

Summary and Exercises

Summary

- You can format text with bold, italic, underline, different fonts and font sizes, and so on.
- Data in a cell can be left, right, or center aligned.
- Excel provides many formats for displaying numbers.
- You can apply a border to any side of a cell.
- You can apply a background color to a cell.
- You can apply a color to text.
- The Page Break view shows where page breaks are located.
- You can rearrange page breaks in the Page Break view.
- An AutoFormat can be applied to a worksheet or a range.

Key Terms and Operations

Key Terms	Operations
border	add a border
fill	add fill
page break	align cells
Page Break view	AutoFormat
pattern	change a page break
shading	format dates
	format numbers
	format text
	view a page break

Study Questions

Multiple Choice

1. If you type text in cell A1 and you want to center the text across cells A1 through A5,
   a. merge the cells and click the Center button.
   b. select A1:A5 and click the Center button.
   c. select A1:A5 and choose Format, Cells, Alignment, Center, and click OK.
   d. merge the cells, and choose Format, Align, Center.

2. You can apply an AutoFormat
   a. to a cell.
   b. only to a complete worksheet.
   c. to a single range.
   d. to noncontiguous ranges.

3. To make text bold,
   a. click in the cell, type the text, click the Bold button, and press Enter.
   b. select the cell and click the Bold button.
   c. select the cell and choose Format, Bold.
   d. All of the above.

4. Borders can be applied to
   a. any side of a range.
   b. all sides of a range.
   c. the top and bottom sides of a range.
   d. All of the above.

5. To add shading to a cell, select the cell and
   a. click the drop-down arrow on the Shading button and choose the color.
   b. choose Format, Cells, Shading, select the color, and click OK.
   c. choose Format, Cells, Patterns, select the color, and click OK.
   d. choose Format, Shading, select the color, and click OK.

6. A page break is marked with
   a. a dotted line in the worksheet.
   b. a blue line in the Print Preview.
   c. a dotted line in the Page Break Preview.
   d. a blue line in the worksheet.

7. Which of the following format(s) (if any) would be used to achieve this format: $ 1,200.00?
   a. general format with a dollar sign symbol and two decimal places
   b. accounting format with a dollar sign symbol and two decimal places
   c. currency format with a dollar sign symbol and two decimal places
   d. number format with a dollar sign symbol and two decimal places

8. When you increase the point size of text,
   a. you must first increase the height of the row.
   b. the text may wrap in the cell if the cell is not wide enough to accommodate the new size.
   c. the row height increases automatically to accommodate the size of the text.
   d. the cell width increases automatically to accommodate the size of the text.

9. The option to rotate text in a cell is found
   a. on the Orientation page of the Format Cells dialog box.
   b. on the Format menu.
   c. on the Rotate button in the Formatting Toolbar.
   d. on the Alignment page of the Format Cells dialog box.

10. Excel stores a date as
    a. a number.
    b. a date.
    c. text.
    d. a mixture of text and numbers.

Short Answer

1. How are numbers aligned in a cell?

2. How can you enter 1–2–97 and make it appear as January 2, 1997?

3. How do you change the font of the text entered in a cell?

4. How do you change the color of the text entered in a cell?

5. Under what circumstances do you have to format a cell as text?

6. How do you merge cells?

7. How are dates aligned in a cell?

8. The entry 1.2E103 is an example of what number format?

9. What is a serial number?

10. What is the default alignment for text in a cell?

For Discussion

1. Describe the AutoFormat feature and discuss the advantages of using it.

2. How can you designate where the pages will break when the worksheet prints?

3. Compare the Page Break Preview with the Print Preview view.

4. Give examples of ways you could use borders.

Review Exercises

1. Enhancing the restaurant sales worksheet

In this exercise, you will enhance the worksheet with border, shading, and number formats.

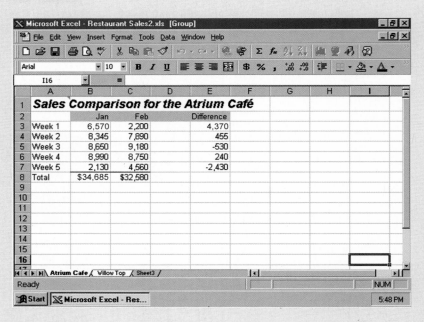

Figure 3.3

1. Open *Restaurant Sales.xls*, the file you saved at the end of Project 2.

2. Right align cells B2 and C2 on both worksheets.

3. Format all numbers on both worksheets (except for cells B8 and C8) with the Currency format, using no decimal places and no dollar sign. Format B8 and C8 on both worksheets with Currency, no decimal places, and a dollar sign.

4. Format cell A1 on both worksheets with bold, italic, 14 point.

5. Add a border to the bottom of cells B7 and C7 on both worksheets.

6. Add light gray fill to cells B2:E2 on both worksheets.

7. Save the file as *Restaurant Sales2.xls* and close it.

2. Creating a concert list

In this exercise, you will create a workbook for a list of concerts and enhance the worksheet with formatting.

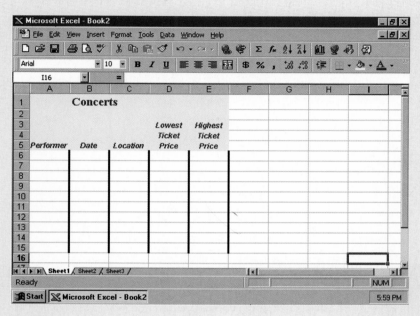

Figure 3.4

1. Go to http://www.ticketmaster.com and follow the link to the Box Office.

2. Search for at least 10 concerts by groups or performers that you like. Obtain information about when and where the concert will be and how much the tickets cost.

3. Create a worksheet based on Figure 3.4, with these column headings: Performer, Date, Location, Lowest Ticket Price, Highest Ticket Price.

4. Format the title with 14 point Times New Roman.

5. Format the column headings in bold, italic, 9 point and center them.

6. Use a thick border between each column.

7. Fill the range A1:E5 with light blue and change the color of the text in the range to dark blue.

8. Save the file as *Concerts.xls* and close it.

3. Enhancing the Container Corporation sales worksheet

1. Launch Excel and open *2 Container Corporation Sales xxx.xls* (where *xxx* represents your initials).

Note If you do not have a workbook named *2 Container Corporation Sales xxx.xls*, ask your instructor for a copy of the file you should use to complete this exercise.

2. Make the following changes to all three worksheets in the workbook:
   - Center the data contained in Cells A1 and A2 across Columns A through F.
   - Change the color of text in Cells A1 and A2.
   - Format the text in Cell A1 to 26-point bold.
   - Format the text in Cell A2 to 16-point italics.
   - Format cells containing dollar values as Currency with 0 decimal points.
   - Center the column headings in Row 4 and add a fill color to cells containing data in Row 4.
   - Center the Produce #s in Column A and add a different fill color to cells containing product numbers.
   - Center the data contained in Column B across Columns B and C.

3. Save the workbook using the filename *3 Container Corporation Sales xxx* and print a copy of each worksheet.

Assignments

1. Reformatting the *Income.xls* File

Open the Income.xls file. Move the data in cells B15:F22 to cell A1 Sheet2. Format the data on Sheet1 using your own ideas for borders, shading, fonts, and so on. When finished, save the file as *Income 3.xls*.

2. Using AutoFormat

If you have Internet access, download *Revenues.xls* from http://hepg.awl.com/ select. If you are unable to download this file, ask your instructor how to obtain it. Experiment with different AutoFormats. Choose one of the formats you like and save the file as *Revenues2.xls*. Open *Revenues.xls* again and save it with another format that you like as *Revenues3.xls*. Open *Revenues.xls* and save it with another format that you like as *Revenues4.xls*.

4

Editing the Structure of a Worksheet and a Workbook

Think of yourself as an Excel architect. You design workbooks using the Excel "materials" — cells, columns, rows, and worksheets. When you want to edit the structure of a worksheet or a workbook, you have to request that materials be added to or removed from the file. Sometimes the design you want calls for different-sized materials or special materials — such as headers and footers. This project introduces you to the tools you'll need to modify the structure of a worksheet.

Objectives

After completing this project, you will be able to:

➤ **Insert, delete, and arrange worksheets**

➤ **Change the size of columns and rows**

➤ **Insert columns, rows, and cells**

➤ **Delete columns, rows, and cells**

➤ **Create headers and footers**

The Challenge

You have a workbook that contains March and April restaurant sales information that you have been preparing for the hotel manager, Mr. Gilmore.

You need to delete some information, add some information, make some adjustments in the columns and rows, and add a header and footer.

The Solution

You will begin your edits by deleting one of the worksheets, inserting a new worksheet, and rearranging worksheets. Then you will adjust the width of columns and the height of rows as needed. Next, you will insert and delete columns, rows, and cells, and, finally, you will add the headers and footers. Figure 4.1 shows the first worksheet in the workbook.

To obtain the files you need for this project, download them from the Addison Wesley Longman web site (http://hepg.awl.com/select or obtain them from your instructor.

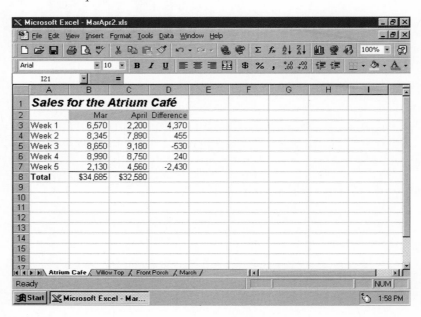

Figure 4.1

The Setup

So that your screen will match the illustrations and the tasks in this project will function as described, make sure that the Excel settings listed in Table 4.1 are selected on your computer. Because these are the default settings for the toolbars and view, you may not need to make any changes to your setup.

Table 4.1: Excel Settings

Location	Make these settings:
View, Toolbars	Deselect all toolbars except Standard and Formatting.
View	Use the Normal view and display the Formula Bar and Status Bar.

Inserting, Deleting, and Arranging Worksheets

As you remember (if you don't remember, just keep it to yourself and no one will be the wiser), a workbook starts out with three worksheets. You can add more worksheets or delete up to two of the three. You also can re-arrange the order of worksheets.

TASK 1: TO INSERT AND DELETE PAGES:

1 Open *MarApr.xls.*

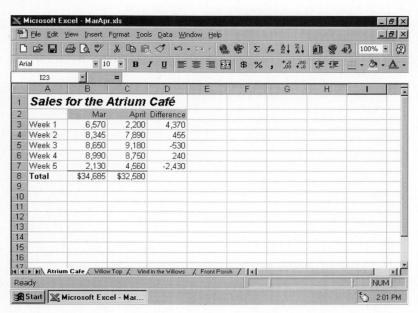

2 Click each worksheet tab to see each page of the workbook.

3 Right-click the tab for Wind in the Willows.

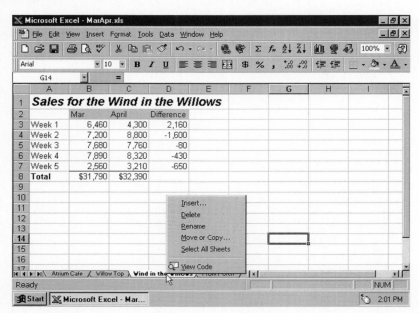

4　Choose Delete from the shortcut menu.

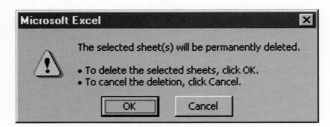

5　Click OK.
The worksheet is permanently deleted from the workbook, and no amount of clicking the Undo button will bring it back.

6　Right-click the Atrium Café tab and choose Insert from the shortcut menu.

Worksheet is selected by default →

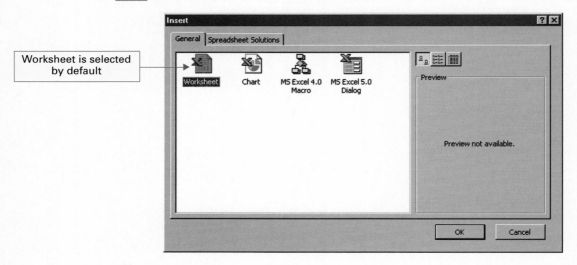

7　Click OK.
A new blank worksheet is inserted before the selected worksheet.

8　Rename the new worksheet **March**.

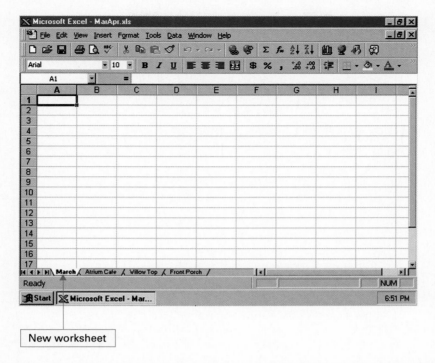

New worksheet

9   Drag the March tab between the Atrium Café tab and the Willow Top tab, but don't release the mouse button yet.

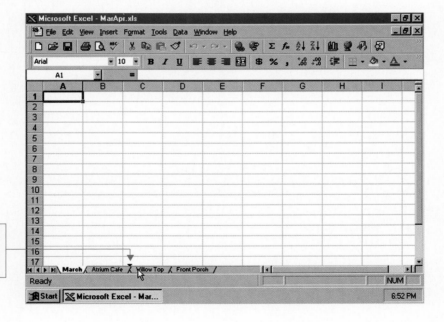

The black triangle marks the location where the new worksheet will be positioned

10   Continue dragging to the end of the tabs and then release the mouse button.

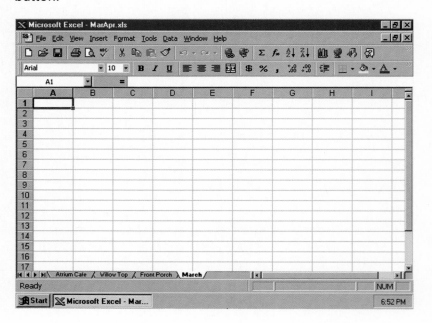

Changing the Size of Columns and Rows

When you create a new workbook, all the columns are the same width, and all the rows are the same height. When you add data to a worksheet, you often must change the row heights and column widths to accommodate the data. As you have already seen in a previous project, the height of a row increases or decreases automatically when you change the point size of the data; however, you may want to change the height of a row just to improve the spacing.

TASK 2: TO CHANGE THE WIDTH OF COLUMNS BY DRAGGING:

1   Type the following in the designated cells of the March worksheet:
A1: **March Sales**
A2: **Atrium Café**

> **Note** Excel will add the accent to the "e" in "café" automatically.

A3: **Willow Top Restaurant**
A4: **Front Porch Restaurant**

2   Point to the line that divides column letters A and B in the Column heading row.

The pointer changes to a double-headed arrow

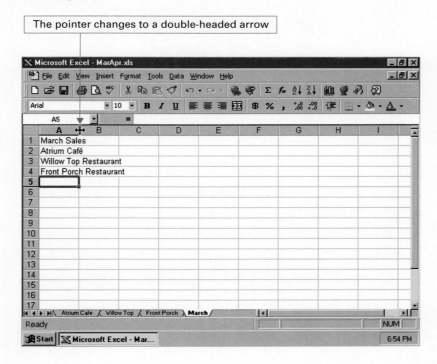

3   Drag the line to the right until the column is wide enough to hold the text.

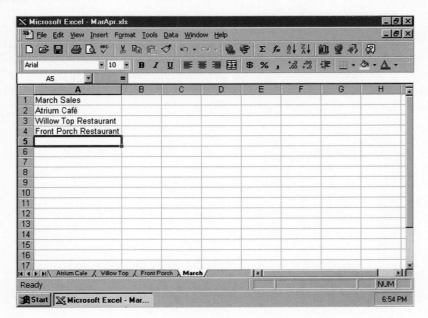

4 Drag the column until it is too wide as shown:

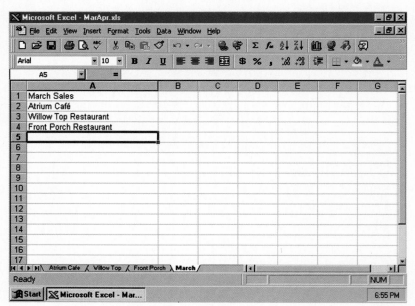

5 Type the following in the designated cells:
B2: **34685**
B3: **45240**
B4: **30835**

6 Drag the line between column letters B and C until column B is too wide as shown:

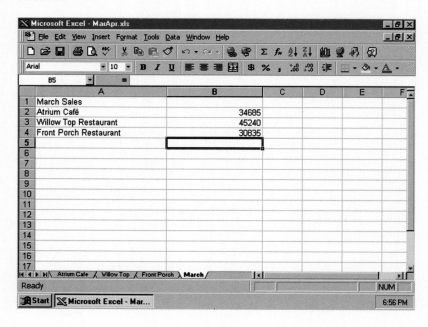

Using AutoFit

Another way to change the width of a column is to use AutoFit. **AutoFit** automatically adjusts columns to be just wide enough to accommodate the widest entry and can adjust the widths of several columns at once.

TASK 3: TO CHANGE THE WIDTH OF COLUMNS BY USING AUTOFIT:

1   Select columns A and B by dragging the mouse pointer through A and B at the top of the columns.
The columns are highlighted.

2   Choose Format, Column.

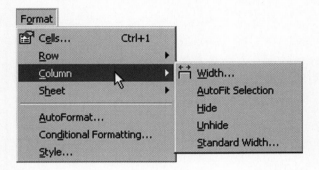

3   Choose AutoFit Selection.

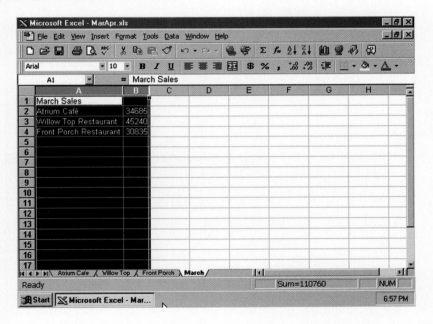

Tip You can select multiple columns and double-click the line between the column letters to AutoFit the selections.

Adjusting Row Height

If you want to control the spacing in a worksheet, you can make rows taller or shorter by dragging them to the desired height.

TASK 4: TO CHANGE THE HEIGHT OF ROWS:

1 Point to the line that divides row numbers 1 and 2 in the row indicators column.

The pointer changes to a double-headed arrow

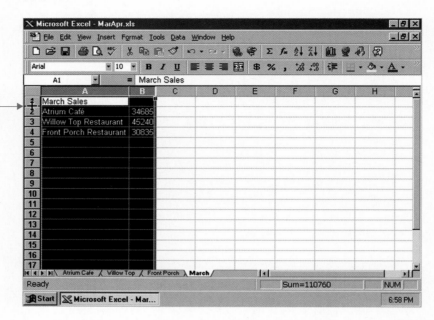

It doesn't matter if columns are selected when you change the row height because you don't have to select anything to change the height.

2 Drag down to make the row taller.

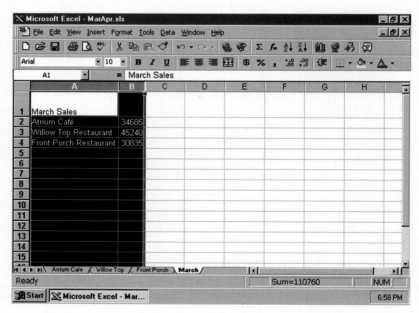

Tip You also can size rows with AutoFit. As you probably can guess, the command is under Format, Row or you can select the rows and double-click the line between the row numbers.

Inserting Columns, Rows, and Cells

When you insert a column, all the other columns move to the right to give the new column room. When you insert rows, all the other rows move down, and when you insert cells, the other cells move to the right or move down. Excel is so polite!

TASK 5: TO INSERT A COLUMN, A ROW, AND A CELL:

1 Click anywhere in column A.
The cell is selected.

2 Choose Insert.

3 Choose Columns.

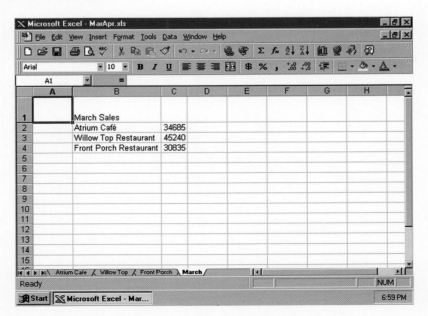

4 Click anywhere in row 2.
The cell is selected.

5 Choose Insert, Rows. (The new rows take on the dimensions of the row above.)

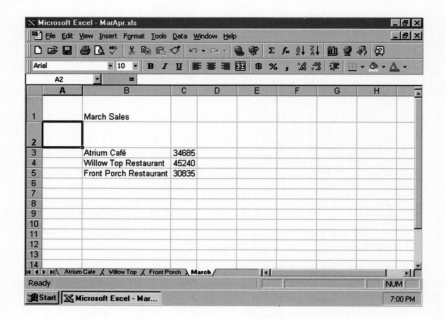

6   Type the following in the designated cells:
D1: **March Banquets**
D3: **D.A.R.**
D4: **L.W.V.**
D5: **B.S.A**
E3: **2560**
E4: **1500**
E5: **900**

7   Select cells D4 and E4.

8   Choose Insert, Cells.

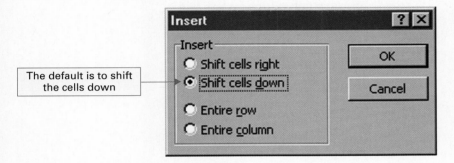

The default is to shift the cells down

9   Click OK.

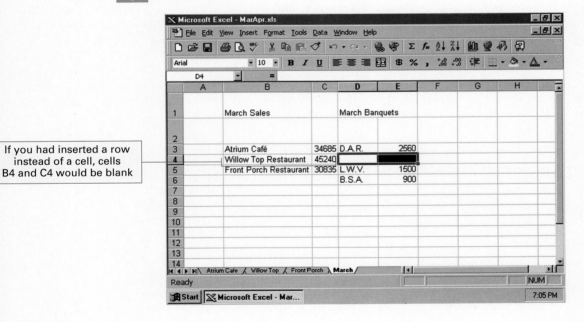

If you had inserted a row instead of a cell, cells B4 and C4 would be blank

10 Type **G.S.A.** in cell D4, press ➝, type **950**, and press ⟨ENTER⟩.

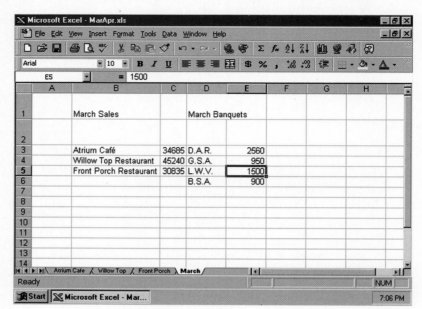

Deleting Columns, Rows, and Cells

When you delete columns, rows, or cells, you actually cut the space they occupy out of the worksheet. You don't just delete the data they contain.

> **Caution** When you delete a column or row, the entire column or the entire row is deleted. Before deleting, be sure that the column or row doesn't contain data in a location that is off screen.

TASK 6: TO DELETE A COLUMN, A ROW, AND A CELL:

1 Select row 2 by clicking the row 2 button — at the left of the row. The row is highlighted.

2 Choose Edit, Delete.

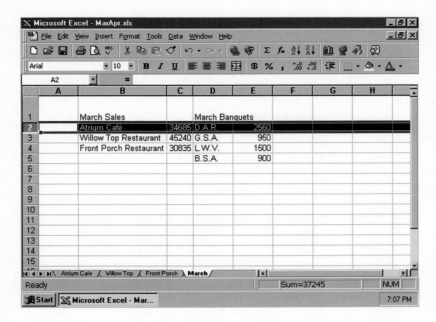

3 Select column A by clicking the column button A above the column. The column is highlighted.

4 Choose Edit, Delete.

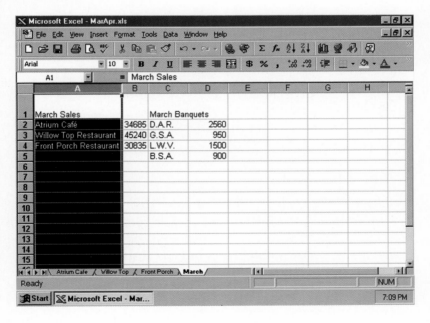

5 Select cells C2 and D2 and choose Edit, Delete.

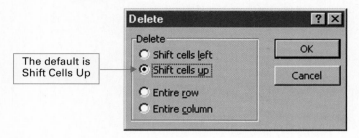

The default is
Shift Cells Up

6 Click OK.

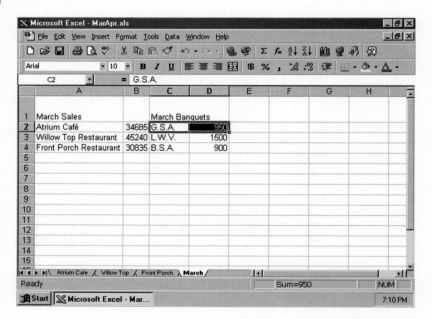

Creating Headers and Footers

A **header** prints at the top of every page of a worksheet, and a **footer** prints (you guessed it) at the bottom of every page. If the workbook has multiple worksheets, you can create headers and footers for each worksheet. A header or footer created for one worksheet doesn't print on any other worksheets in the same workbook.

TASK 7: TO CREATE A SIMPLE HEADER AND A FOOTER:

1 Choose View.

2 Choose Header and Footer.

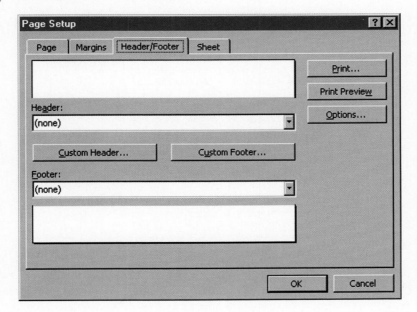

3 Click the down arrow for the Header list and choose Page 1.

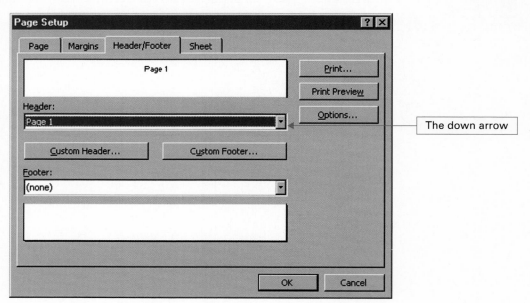

The down arrow

4 Click the down arrow for the Footer list and choose MarApr.xls.

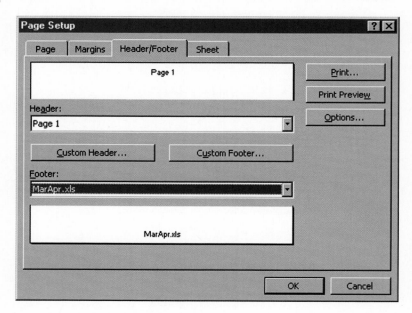

5 Click Print Preview.

Header

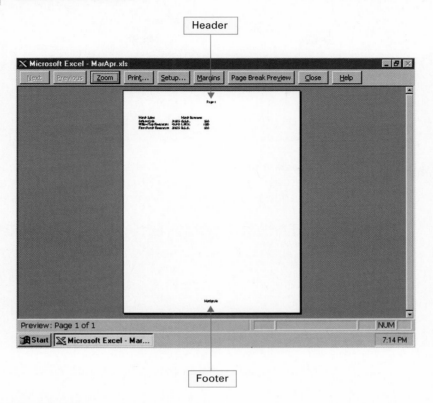

Footer

6 Click Close.
The preview closes, and the worksheet displays in Normal view.

Creating a Custom Header and Footer

If you don't want to use the text supplied for a simple header or footer, you can create a custom header or footer and type the text that you want. Custom headers and footers are divided into three typing areas. The area on the left is left-justified, the area in the middle is centered, and the area on the right is right-justified.

TASK 8: TO CREATE A CUSTOM HEADER AND FOOTER:

1 Click the Atrium Café tab.
The Atrium Café worksheet displays.

2 Choose View, Headers and Footers. The Page Setup dialog box displays.

3 Click Custom Header.

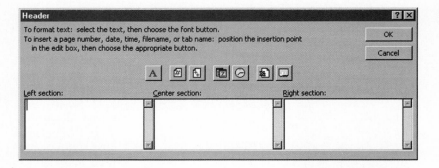

4   Type **Sales Report** in the left section, press (TAB) twice, and click the Date
    button. (When you click the Date button instead of typing the date, Excel
    adjusts the date to the current date each time the workbook is used.)

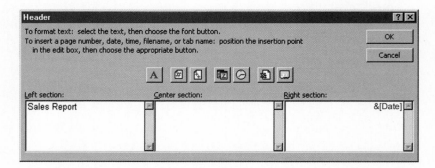

5   Click OK.
    The Header dialog box closes and the Page Setup dialog box reappears.

6   Click Custom Footer.

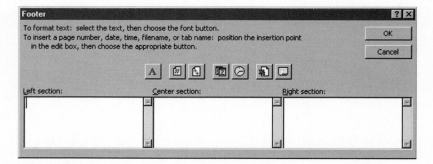

7   Press (TAB) and type **Prepared by Accounting** in the center section.

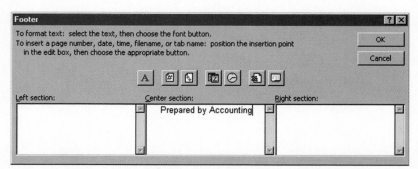

8   Click OK.
The Footer dialog box closes.

9   Click Print Preview.

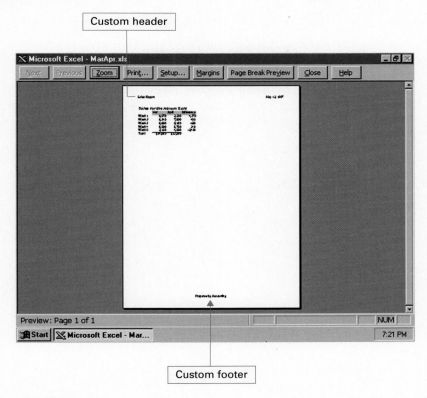

Custom header

Custom footer

10   Click Close.
The Print Preview closes, and the worksheet displays in Normal view.

The Conclusion

Save the worksheet as *MarApr2.xls* and close the file.

Summary and Exercises

Summary

- You can insert and delete worksheets, as well as rearrange them.
- You can change the width of columns and the height of rows.
- You can insert columns, rows, and cells.
- You can delete columns, rows, and cells.
- You can create a header that prints at the top of the page and a footer that prints at the bottom of a page. Headers and footers do not appear on screen in Normal view.

Key Terms and Operations

Key Terms	Operations
AutoFit	change the height of a row
footer	change the width of a column
header	create a footer
	create a header
	delete a cell
	delete a column
	delete a row
	delete a worksheet
	insert a cell
	insert a column
	insert a row
	insert a worksheet
	move a worksheet

Study Questions

Multiple Choice

1. A header prints at the
   a. top of every page in a workbook.
   b. bottom of every page in a workbook.
   c. top of every page in a worksheet.
   d. bottom of every page in a worksheet.

2. When you delete a column,
   a. the data in the column is deleted but the cells remain in the worksheet.
   b. the data in the column is deleted and so are the cells.
   c. the column is really just hidden.
   d. the column is moved to the end of the worksheet.

3. When you insert a cell, the other cells move
   a. down.
   b. to the left.
   c. to the right.
   d. down or to the right, as specified by the user.

4. A footer prints at the
   a. top of every page in a workbook.
   b. bottom of every page in a workbook.
   c. top of every page in a worksheet.
   d. bottom of every page in a worksheet.

5. AutoFit can adjust the width of
   a. only one column at a time.
   b. only a row.
   c. columns or rows.
   d. the page.

6. A custom header
   a. is divided into three typing areas.
   b. is created by choosing Format, Header and Footer.
   c. isn't visible in Print Preview mode.
   d. only uses default data, such as the page number or the name of the file.

7. If you delete a cell,
   a. the data is deleted.
   b. the cell is deleted and the data displays in the next cell.
   c. the data and the cell are deleted.
   d. None of the above.

8. When you delete a cell, the other cells move
   a. up.
   b. down.
   c. to the left.
   d. up or to the left, as specified by the user.

9. When you drag to change the column width, the pointer displays as
   a. a four-headed arrow.
   b. an arrow.
   c. a two-headed arrow.
   d. a hand.

10. To insert a column, first
    a. select the column where you want the new column to go.
    b. click in the column where you want the new column to go.
    c. A or B
    d. None of the above.

Short Answer

1. How do you insert multiple rows?

2. How do you insert multiple columns?

3. What is a custom header?

4. How do you delete a worksheet?

5. How do you delete a row?

6. How do you delete a cell?

7. How do you create a header with the filename in the center?

8. If the row height adjusts automatically, why would you need to change the height of a row?

9. How do you move a worksheet?

10. How do you see a header or footer without actually printing the worksheet?

For Discussion

1. When would it be an advantage to use AutoFit instead of dragging columns to change the width?

2. Discuss the advantages of using a custom header or footer.

3. Describe a circumstance in which it would be preferable to insert a cell instead of a row.

4. What precautions should you take before deleting a column or a row?

Review Exercises

1. Editing the *MarApr2* workbook

In this exercise you will enhance the worksheet and create a footer.

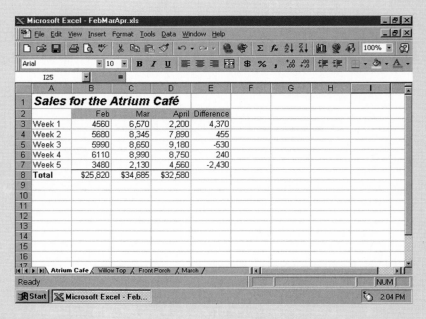

Figure 4.2

1. Open *MarApr2.xls* and click the Atrium Café tab, if necessary.

2. Insert a column before column B and type this information:

    B2: **Feb**

    B3: **4560**

    B4: **5680**

    B5: **5990**

    B6: **6110**

    B7: **3480**

    B8: **=SUM(B3:B7)**

3. Apply a gray fill to cell B2, apply a border to the bottom of cell B7, and format cell B8 with a Currency format (no decimal places) and remove the bold.

4. Create a footer for the Willow Top worksheet that says "Located in The Grande Hotel" and center the footer.

5. Save the file as *FebMarApr.xls* and close it.

2. Creating a sales workbook for the sandwich shops and snack bars
In this exercise, you will create a workbook that can be used to track the sales of all the sandwich shops and snack bars at The Willows Resort.

1. Download the file *Willows.doc* from the Addison Wesley Longman web site (http://hepg.awl.com/select), or ask your instructor for this file. Open the file and find the list of sandwich shops and snack bars.

2. Create a workbook with a worksheet for each of the nine shops and name each worksheet with the name of the shop.

3. Type a title on each worksheet that says "Sales for *xxx*," where *xxx* is the name of the sandwich shop or snack bar. In column A, starting in cell A3, list the weeks in the month (Week 1, Week 2, and so on) and the word "Total" (as in Figure 4.2). In cells B2, C2, and D2, list the first three months of the year (Jan, Feb, and Mar).

4. Create a footer with a centered page number for each worksheet.

5. Save the file as *ShopSales.xls*.

3. Editing and enhancing the Container Corporation sales worksheet

1. Launch Excel and open the workbook *3 Container Corporation Sales xxx.xls*.

> **Note** If you do not have a workbook named *3 Container Corporation Sales xxx.xls*, ask your instructor for a copy of the file you should use to complete this exercise.

2. Make the following changes to the Sales Increase worksheet:
   - Move the *Sales Increase* worksheet so that it appears as the first worksheet in the workbook.
   - Search for the word Actual and replace it with the current year.
   - Search for the word Expected and replace it with the last year.

3. Copy the *<Last Year> Sales* worksheet to create a new worksheet at the end of the workbook.

4. Rename the worksheet *Projected <Next Year> Sales*.

5. Delete the *Sales Increase* worksheet.

6. Make the following changes to all worksheets in the workbook:
   - Change the data in Cell B4 to *Product Description*.
   - Change the width of Column C to accommodate the new column heading.
   - Change the height of Row 5 and Row 10 so that there is more room between Row 4 and Row 5 and between Row 9 and 10.

- Add a bottom border to Cells D9, E9, and F9 and center the word *Total* in bold in Cell A10.

- Change the fill color for cells in Row 10 to the same color added to Cells A5–A9.

7. Save the workbook using the filename *4 Container Corporation Sales xxx*.

8. Add a header that contains your name right aligned to the workbook and print a copy of each worksheet in the workbook.

Assignments

1. Creating a banquet workbook

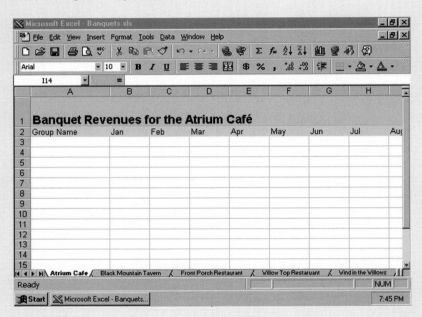

Figure 4.3

Create a workbook with five worksheets and name each worksheet as follows: Atrium Café, Willow Top Restaurant, Wind in the Willows, Front Porch Restaurant, and Black Mountain Tavern. Arrange the worksheets in alphabetical order. Add the text and formatting shown in Figure 4.3 to all the worksheets. (Remember, you can enter the same data on multiple worksheets at the same time.) Save the file as *Banquets.xls* and close it.

2. Creating a shopping list (Optional Exercise)

Take an international shopping trip via the Planet Shopping Network (http://www.planetshopping.com). Create a workbook that lists the items you would like to buy, their prices (including any shipping, handling, taxes, and duties), and their Web addresses. Use the SUM formula to total the prices and other costs. Create a worksheet for each shopping category (apparel, books, music, jewelry, automobiles, and so on). Save the workbook as *ShopTilYouDrop.xls*.

Creating a More Complex Workbook

Well, you're getting pretty good at this, so you're probably ready for something more challenging. This project provides both challenge and fun.

Objectives

After completing this project, you will be able to:

➤ **Copy data from another workbook**
➤ **Sort data**
➤ **Enter formulas with relative references**
➤ **Use headings in formulas**
➤ **Enter formulas with absolute references**
➤ **Create and modify a chart**

The Challenge

Ruth Lindsey, the manager of most of the gift shops at The Willows Resort, would like for you to work on an inventory of the ten top selling items and create some charts for the first quarter sales.

The Solution

You will copy data from an existing workbook into the inventory workbook, enter new data, and create formulas to calculate the number of items that you need to order and the wholesale prices of the items. Additionally, you will create a chart for the first quarter sales and a chart for the January sales. Figure 5.1 shows the results.

You can download the files needed for this project from the Addison Wesley Longman web site (http://hepg.awl.com/select) or you can obtain them from your instructor.

The Setup

So that your screen will match the illustrations in this chapter and to ensure that all the tasks in this project will function as described, you should set up Excel as described in Table 5.1. Because these are the default settings for the toolbars and view, you may not need to make any changes to your setup.

Table 5.1: Excel Settings

Location	Make these settings:
View, Toolbars	Deselect all toolbars except Standard and Formatting.
View	Use the Normal view and display the Formula Bar and Status Bar.

Copying Data from Another Workbook

You have copied data from one range to another on the same worksheet, and you have copied data from one worksheet to another in the same workbook. Now you will copy data from one workbook to another. The procedure is very similar to what you have already learned.

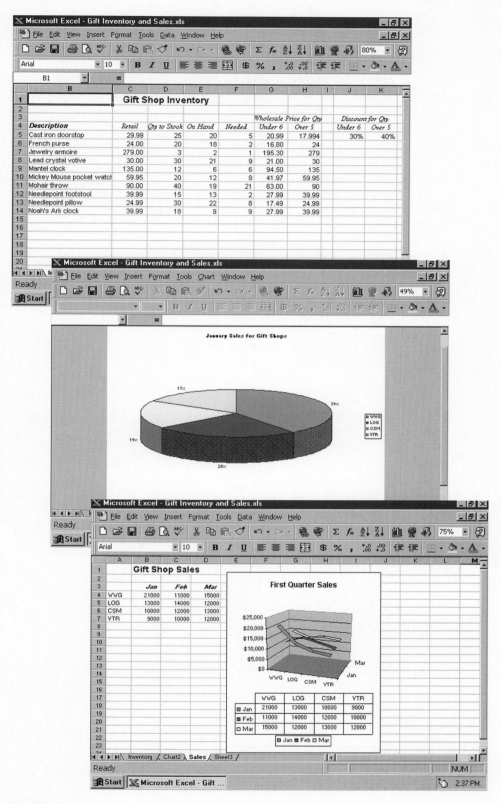

Figure 5.1

TASK 1: TO COPY DATA FROM ANOTHER WORKBOOK:

1   Open *Giftinv.xls*.

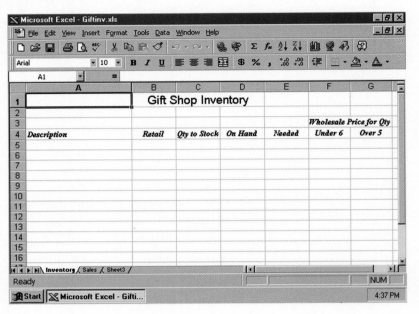

2   Open *TopTen.xls* and select the range A4:B13.

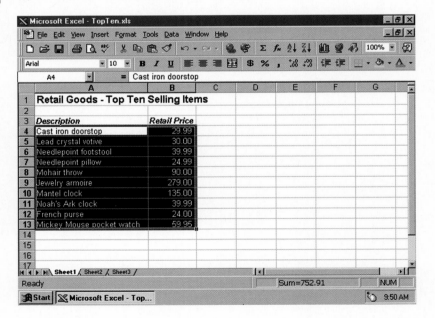

3   Click .
The data is copied to the Clipboard.

4   Choose Window from the menu bar and then choose Giftinv.xls.
The *Giftinv.xls* workbook displays.

5 Click in cell A5 and click 🖺.

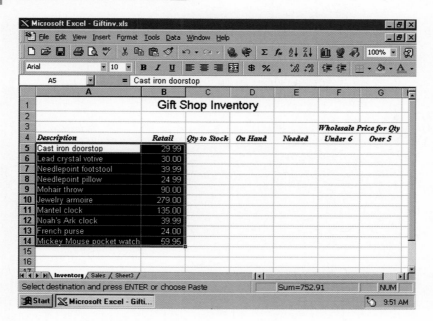

6 Choose Window, TopTen.xls.
The *TopTen.xls* workbook displays.

7 Click ☒ in the menu bar.
The *TopTen.xls* workbook closes, and the Giftinv.xls workbook displays.

Sorting Data

You can sort columns of data in an Excel worksheet in ascending order or descending order. The Standard toolbar has a button for each function.

TASK 2: TO SORT DATA:

1 Make sure that the range A5:B14 is still selected.
When you sort data, you must be careful to select all the columns that should be included in the sort. When selecting the rows to include, don't include the row with the column headings.

2 Click the Sort Ascending ![Sort Ascending icon] button.

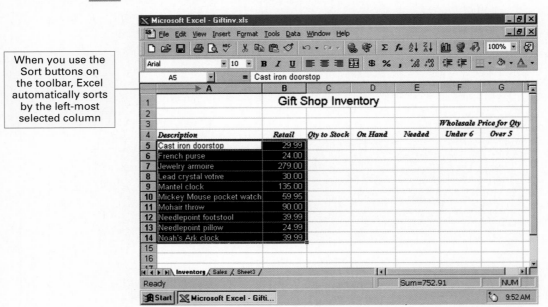

> When you use the Sort buttons on the toolbar, Excel automatically sorts by the left-most selected column

Tip If you want to sort a range by any column other than the first column, you must use the Sort command on the Data menu. This command displays a dialog box that allows you to specify the column you want to sort on and the order of the sort. You also can specify two other columns to sort on after the first column is sorted. Check it out. Choose Data, Sort to see the dialog box.

Entering Formulas with Relative References

All the formulas you have used so far have included cell addresses that are relative references. A **_relative reference_** is an address that Excel automatically changes when the formula is copied to another location to make it true for its new location. For example, if the formula =A1+A2 is in cell A3 and you copy it to cell B3, Excel changes the formula in column B to refer to the corresponding cells in column B, and the formula becomes =B1+B2. Generally, this is precisely what you want, and you are happy that Excel can make such intelligent decisions on its own.

Perhaps you are wondering how this works. Here's the scoop: Excel doesn't interpret a relative cell address in a formula as the actual cell address but rather as a location relative to the location of the formula. For example, Excel interprets the formula =A1+A2 in cell A3 as "Add the cell that is two rows above the formula in the same column to the cell that is one row above the formula in the same column." Therefore, when you copy the formula to any other column, the formula will add the cells that are two rows and one row above the location of the formula.

TASK 3: TO ENTER AND COPY A FORMULA WITH RELATIVE ADDRESSES:

1 Enter the following data in the *Qty to Stock* column and the *On Hand* column so that you can write a formula to calculate the value for the *Needed* column.

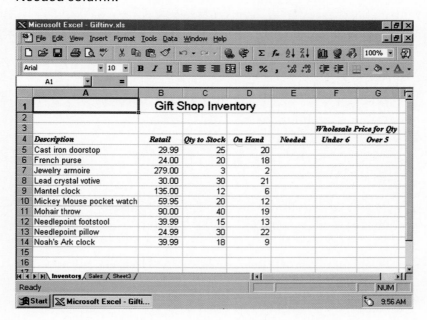

2 Click in cell E5, type **=C5–D5**, and press (ENTER).

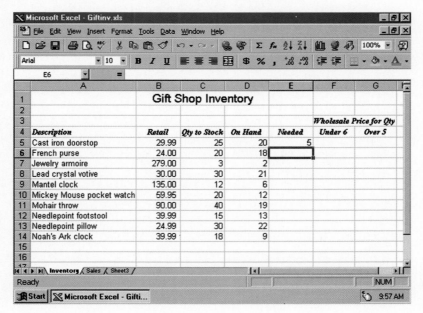

3   Copy cell E5 to the range E6:E8.

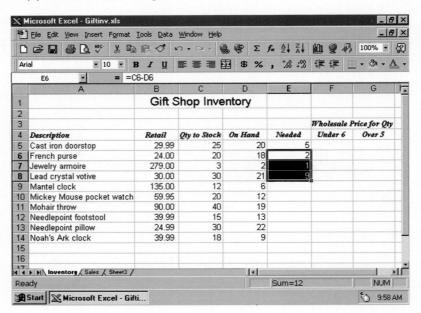

4   Click in cell E6 and notice the formula in the formula bar.

Excel changed the formula from =C5−D5 to =C6−D6

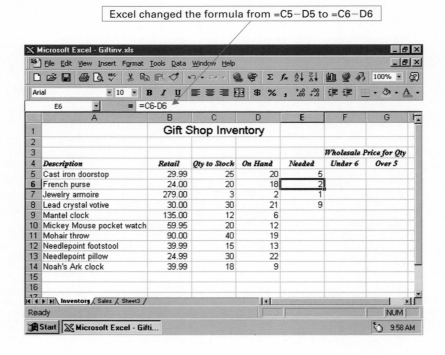

Using Headings in Formulas

Using headings in formulas instead of cell addresses is a new feature in Excel 97. The **headings** feature is helpful in two ways: when you create a formula, you can think in logical terms (such as "quantity times cost") and you can easily recognize the purpose of the formula. When you see the formula "Quantity*Cost," you know immediately what it does, but the formula A1*B1 gives you very little information.

TASK 4: TO ENTER A FORMULA THAT USES HEADINGS:

1 Click in cell E9, type **=qty to stock−on hand**, and press (ENTER).
The cell displays the correct calculation.

> **Tip** You do not have to capitalize the headings in formulas, but spelling and spaces must be exact.

2 Copy cell E9 to the range E10:E14.
The range also displays the correct calculations relative to the rows.

3 Click in cell E10 and look at the formula in the formula bar.
The formula in cell E10 is the same as in E9.

Entering Formulas with Absolute References

As you have already seen, when formulas with relative references are copied, the cell addresses change appropriately; however, sometimes formulas refer to a cell or range that should never be changed when the formula is copied. To prevent the cell or range address from changing, you must make the address an **absolute reference**. An absolute reference is denoted with the dollar sign symbol, as in $A$1.

TASK 5: TO ENTER AND COPY A
FORMULA WITH AN ABSOLUTE REFERENCE:

1 Scroll the worksheet so that columns B through J are visible.

2 Click in cell F5, type **=B5−(B5*I5)**, and press (ENTER).
This formula calculates the wholesale price of the item using the discount that applies if you are ordering a quantity of less than six. The wholesale price is the retail price minus the discount (which is determined by multiplying the retail price by 30%).

3 Copy cell F5 to F6.
The answer is obviously not correct.

4   Click in cell F6 and look at the formula in the formula bar.

> Excel changed the formula to =B6−(B6*I6).
> The reference to B6 is correct, but the reference to I6 isn't.

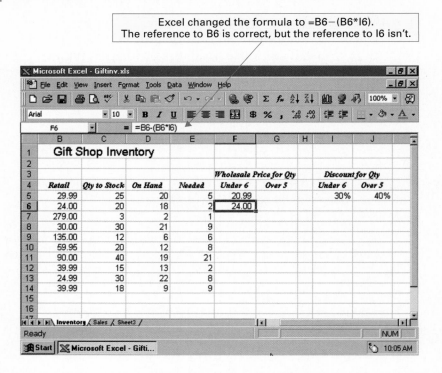

5   Edit the contents of cell F5 and insert dollar signs before and after "I" so the formula looks like **=B5−(B5*$I$5)** and press (ENTER).
The result in cell F5 is the same as before, but watch what happens when you copy it.

6   Copy cell F5 to the range F6:F13.

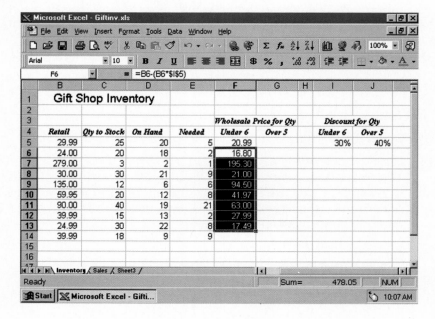

Pointing to Enter Absolute References

In the previous task, you typed the complete formula in the cell, but, as you have seen in other projects, you can enter a formula with the pointing method. When you use this method, you can designate an absolute reference with the F4 key.

TASK 6: TO ENTER A FORMULA WITH AN ABSOLUTE REFERENCE USING THE POINTING METHOD:

1   Click in cell F14, type an equal sign (=), move to cell B14 using ←, and then type a minus sign followed by an open parenthesis.

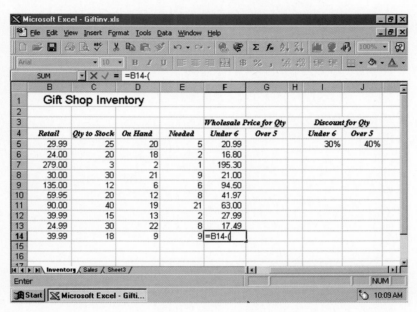

2   Move to cell B14 again, type an asterisk (*),move to cell I5, and then press F4.

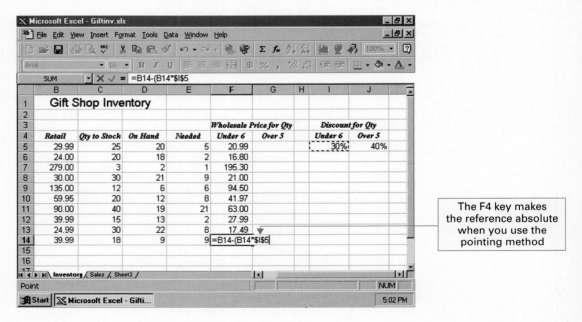

The F4 key makes the reference absolute when you use the pointing method

3   Type a closing parenthesis and press (ENTER).
The correct calculation (27.99) displays in the cell.

Using Headings with Absolute References

The heading feature in Excel 97 also works with absolute references. When designating an absolute reference for a heading, only one dollar sign is used, and it precedes the heading.

TASK 7: TO ENTER AND COPY A FORMULA WITH AN ABSOLUTE REFERENCE USING HEADINGS:

1   Copy cell J5 to the range J6:J14.

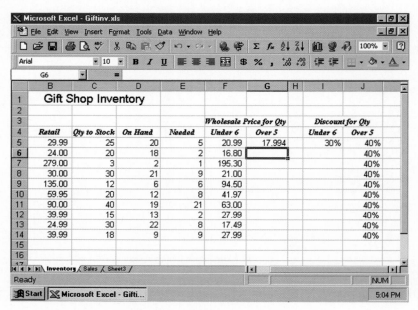

2   Click in cell G5, type **=retail−(retail*$over 5)**, and press (ENTER).

3   Copy cell G5 to the range G6:G14.
The cells display the correct computations.

Creating and Modifying a Chart

Charts present data in a worksheet in a way that numbers never can — visually. Seeing trends and data relationships is so much easier when you look at a chart than when you read numbers. To put a new spin on a tired, old saying, you might say, "A chart is worth 16,777,216 cells." The *Chart Wizard* helps you create charts in Excel.

TASK 8: TO CREATE A COLUMN CHART:

1 Click the Sales tab.

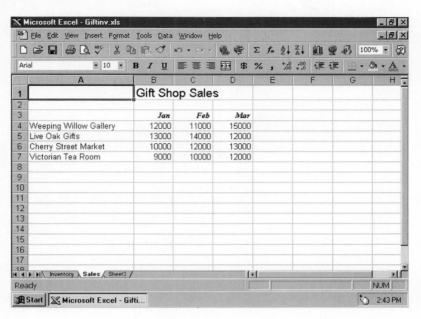

2 Select the range A3:D7 and click the Chart Wizard 📖 button.

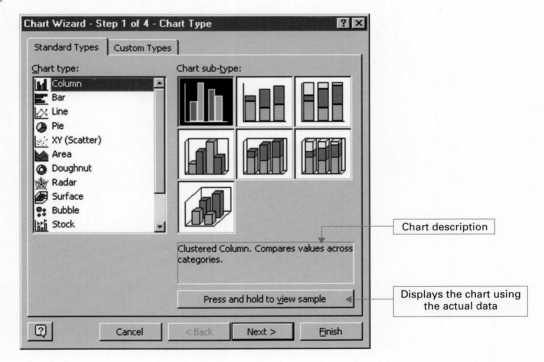

3 Click Next to accept the chart type.

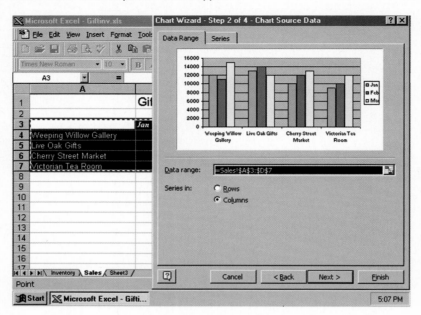

4 Click Next to accept the data range.

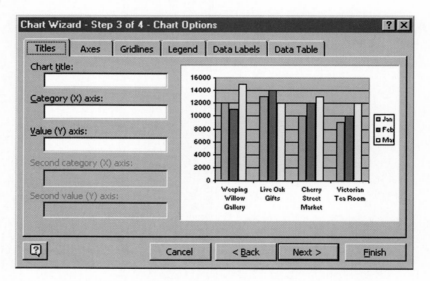

5 Type **First Quarter Sales** for the Chart title and click Next.

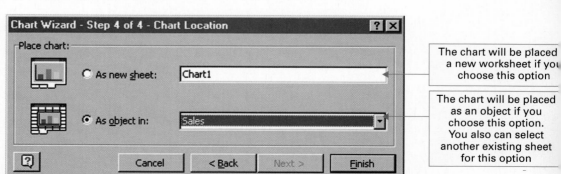

The chart will be placed a new worksheet if you choose this option

The chart will be placed as an object if you choose this option. You also can select another existing sheet for this option

6 Click Finish.
The chart displays in the current worksheet with **selection handles**. You may want to close the Chart toolbar to see the complete chart.

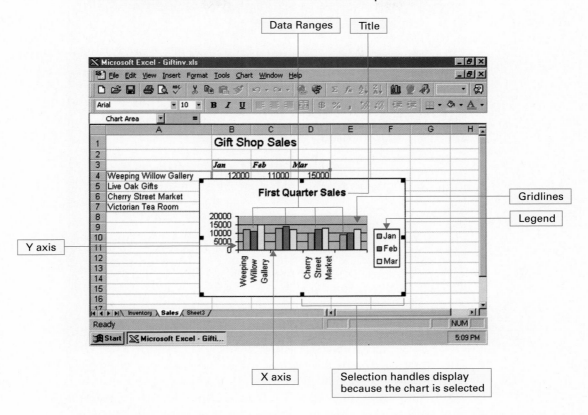

Note The Chart Wizard arbitrarily displays every other data label (in this example, Weeping Willow Gallery and Cherry Street Market), because there is too much text to show all the labels.

Moving and Sizing a Chart

When you place a chart on the same page as the worksheet, the Chart Wizard may place the chart in a location that obscures the data in the worksheet, and it may make the chart too small. Because the chart is an object, you can move it and size it however you want.

TASK 9: TO MOVE AND SIZE THE CHART:

1 Point to a blank area of the chart and drag the chart to the right of the data that created the chart.
The chart moves to the new location.

2 Point to a handle at the bottom of the chart and drag the handle down to make the chart about three rows taller.

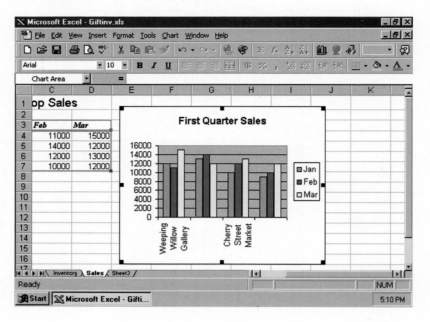

Changing Chart Data

The chart is linked to the data in the worksheet; when you change the data in the worksheet, the chart reflects the change. By the same token, when you change a value in a *data range* in the chart, the data in the worksheet reflects the change.

TASK 10: TO CHANGE CHART DATA:

1 In the worksheet, change the names of the gift shops to abbreviations as follows:
Weeping Willow Gallery: **WWG**;
Live Oak Gifts: **LOG**;
Cherry Street Market: **CSM**;
Victorian Tea Room: **VTR**.
After changing the names, make column A narrower.

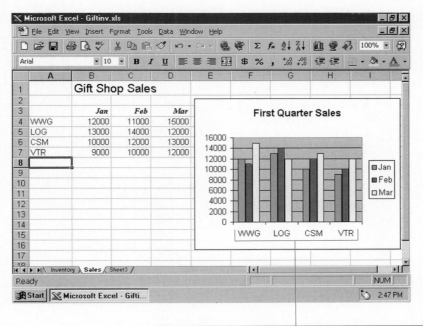

The names on the X axis reflect the change in the worksheet

2   Change the value in cell B4 to 18000 and notice the change in the chart as you press (ENTER).
The height of the first column increases when you change the value.

3   Click the first column in the chart to select the data range for January.

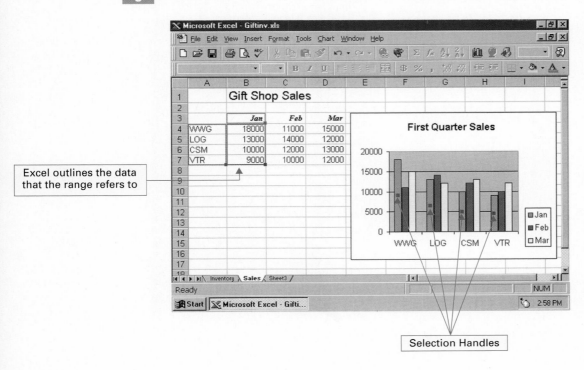

Excel outlines the data that the range refers to

Selection Handles

4 Click the first column again.

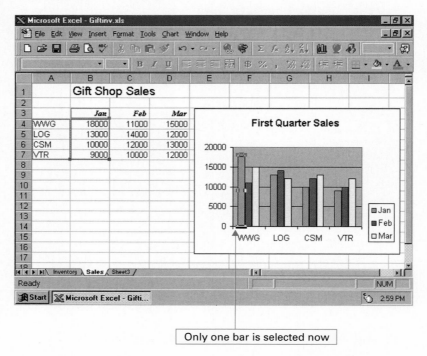

Only one bar is selected now

5 Drag the top of the column up until the value is 21000.

The data in cell B4 changes

The values in this axis and the size of the chart changes

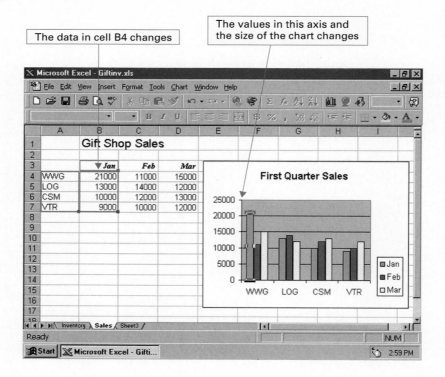

Formatting Chart Elements

When you create a chart with the Chart Wizard, the Chart Wizard decides how the chart elements will look. For example, the Chart Wizard uses the General number format for the scale on the Y axis. After the chart is created, you can format each element of a chart and use the settings that you want.

TASK 11: TO FORMAT CHART ELEMENTS:

1 Right-click the legend, choose Format Legend from the Shortcut menu, and click the Placement tab.

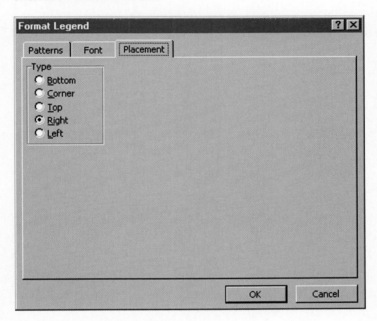

2 Select Bottom and click OK.

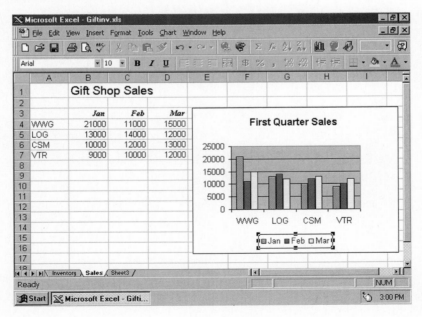

3 Right-click the numbers on the Value axis (Y axis), choose Format Axis from the Shortcut menu, and click the Number tab.

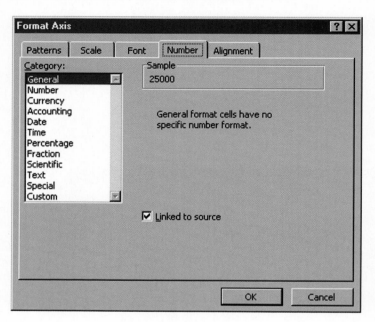

4 Select Currency, 0 decimal places, and click OK.

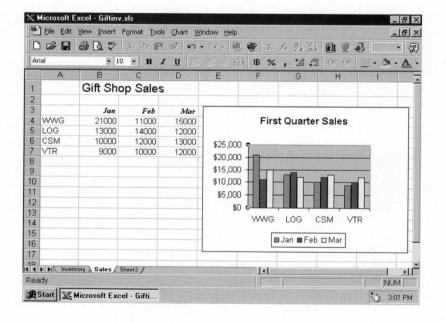

5 Right-click the text on the Category axis (X axis), choose Format Axis, and click the Font tab.

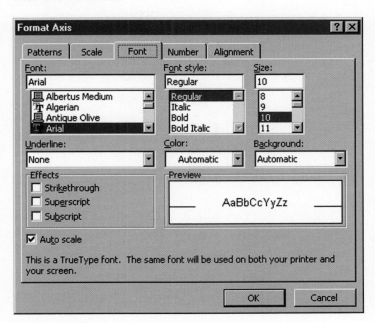

6 Select 8 for the Size and click OK.
The font size of the text is decreased.

Changing the Chart Type

Excel 97 provides many *chart types* and *chart sub-types*. Not all chart types are appropriate for the data in a workbook. Some charts are designed especially for certain types of data. For example, the Stock chart requires three series of data which must be arranged in a specific order: high, low, and close (a stock's high and low values for the day and the closing price of the stock).

TASK 12: TO CHANGE THE CHART TYPE:

1 Right-click a blank area of the chart and choose Chart type from the Shortcut menu.

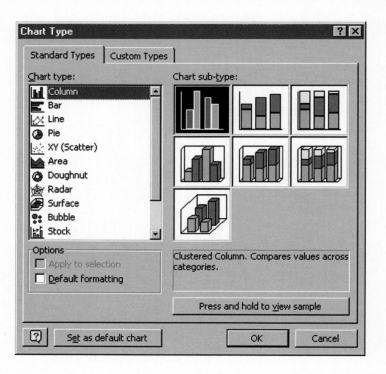

2   Select Line for Chart Type, select the 3-D line sub-type, and click OK.

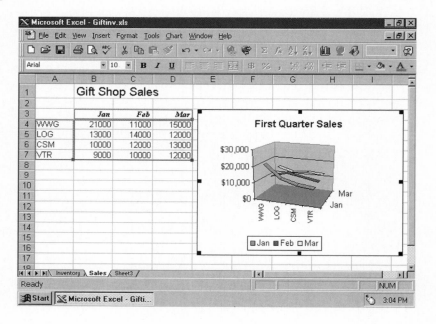

Changing the Chart Options

Settings for the chart *titles*, *X axis*, *Y axis*, *gridlines*, *legend*, *data labels*, and *data table* are all contained in the Chart Options dialog box. After you have created a chart, you can select the options that you want.

TASK 13: TO CHANGE THE CHART OPTIONS:

1 Right-click a blank area of the chart, choose Chart Options from the Shortcut menu, and click the Data Table tab.

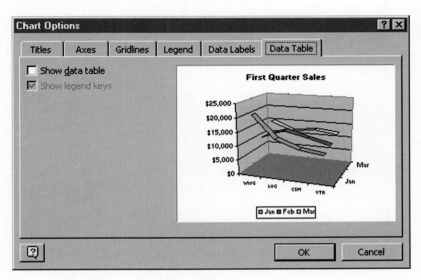

2 Select Show data table and click OK.

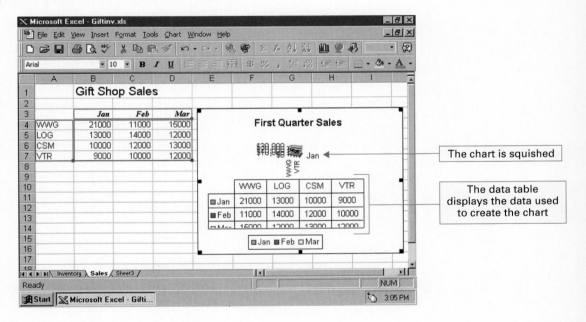

3 Make the chart about 9 rows taller.
The graph returns to its former size.

Creating a Pie Chart

A pie chart is a popular type of chart that shows the relationship of parts to the whole. When selecting data for a pie chart, you will select only one data range.

TASK 14: TO CREATE A PIE CHART:

1 Select the range A4:B7, click 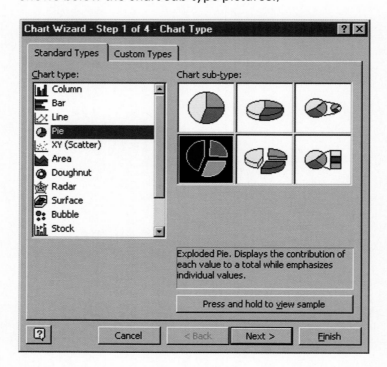, and select Pie as the Chart type and Exploded pie as the sub-type. (A description of the selected chart sub-type shows below the chart sub-type pictures.)

2 Click but don't release the button named Press and hold to view sample. A preview of the chart using your data displays in a Sample box.

3   Release the mouse button and click Next.

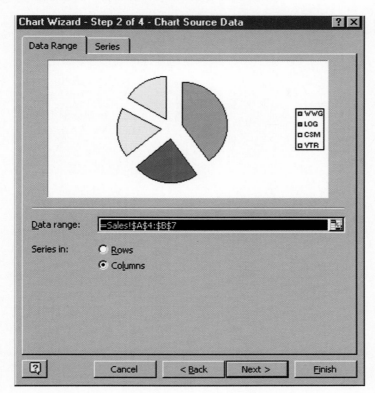

4   Click Next.

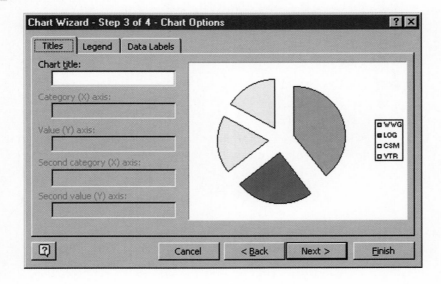

5 Type **January Sales for Gift Shops** for Chart title and click Next.

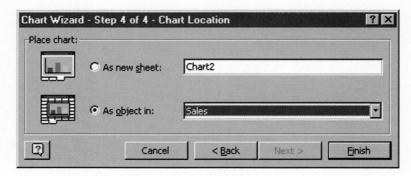

6 Select As new sheet and click Finish.

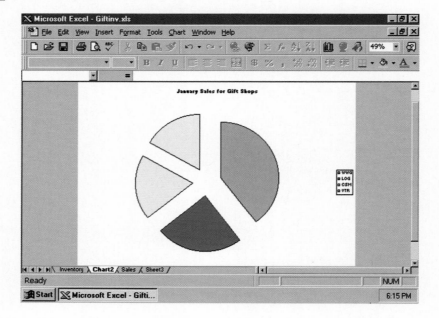

Tip You can change the name of the worksheet that the chart appears on just as you would any other worksheet name.

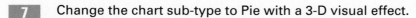

7 Change the chart sub-type to Pie with a 3-D visual effect.

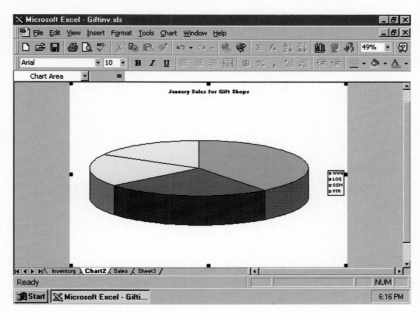

8 Right-click the pie, choose Format Data Series, and click the Data Labels tab.

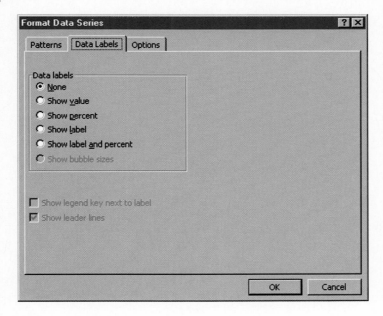

9 Select Show percent and click OK.

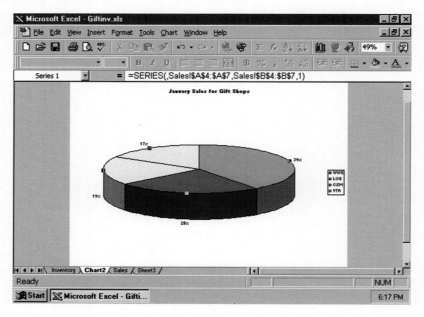

The Conclusion

Save the file as *Gift Inventory and Sales.xls*. Preview each page of the workbook and print each page if you have access to a printer. Close the file.

Summary and Exercises

Summary

- You can copy data from one workbook to another.
- You can sort data in ascending or descending order.
- Formulas use relative references, headings, and absolute references to refer to particular cells on the worksheet.
- Excel can change the address of relative references when a formula is copied, but it cannot change the address of an absolute reference.
- Charts represent the data in a worksheet visually.
- Charts can be displayed on any worksheet in a workbook.
- Once a chart has been created you can change the type, format the elements, or choose different chart options.

Key Terms and Operations

Key Terms
absolute reference
chart
chart sub-type
chart type
Chart Wizard
data labels
data range
data table
gridlines
heading
legend
relative reference
selection handles
title
X axis
Y axis

Operations
change the chart type
copy data from another workbook
create a chart
enter formulas with relative or absolute addresses
format a chart
move a chart
size a chart
sort data

Study Questions

Multiple Choice

1. Which of the following categories isn't included in the Chart Options dialog box?
   a. Data Labels
   b. Data Table
   c. Axes
   d. Pattern

2. When you sort by using the Sort Ascending button on the Standard toolbar,
   a. columns are sorted individually.
   b. you can sort on only one row.
   c. the first column must be the key column.
   d. you can sort by as many as three columns.

3. Which of the following statements about the Chart Wizard is false?
   a. The Chart Wizard creates charts by guiding you through a step-by-step process.
   b. The Chart Wizard can create only a limited number of charts that are available in Excel 97.
   c. The Chart Wizard is launched by a button on the Standard toolbar.
   d. The Chart Wizard doesn't give you an opportunity to format the chart before it is created.

4. Which of the following formulas is written in incorrect form?
   a. =A1/A10
   b. =A1/$A$1
   c. =quantity*retail
   d. =quantity*$retail$

5. A relative reference
   a. is the actual address of a cell.
   b. is the range that contains the data labels for a chart.
   c. can be changed by Excel when the formula that contains it is copied to another location.
   d. is denoted by a dollar sign.

6. When a chart is selected,
   a. it has selection handles.
   b. the outline of the chart is blue.
   c. it opens in a separate window.
   d. None of the above.

7. An exploded pie chart is a chart
   a. type.
   b. sub-type.
   c. option.
   d. element.

8. To designate a cell address as an absolute reference when entering a formula using the pointing method, press
   a. (F2).
   b. (F3).
   c. (F4).
   d. (F5).

9. If you want to show the relationship of individual values to a total, which chart type would you use?
   a. column
   b. stock
   c. line
   d. pie

10. To prevent a cell address from changing when the formula that contains it is copied to a new location,
   a. use a relative address for the cell.
   b. use an absolute address for the cell.
   c. use the value of the cell instead of the address.
   d. copy the formula with the Edit, Copy command.

Short Answer

1. When you create a chart, where are the two locations that you can place the chart?

2. What is a data table?

3. Where can a legend be placed on a chart?

4. What command do you use if you want to sort on more than one column?

5. How do you move a chart?

6. How do you size a chart?

7. What is the difference between a relative and an absolute reference?

8. Can you use an absolute reference in a formula that uses headings instead of cell addresses?

9. What happens if you change the data in a worksheet after you have created a chart that uses the data?

10. What happens in the worksheet when you select the data ranges in a chart?

For Discussion

1. Discuss the advantages of using headings in formulas.

2. Discuss the advantages of presenting information in charts as opposed to numbers.

3. Name and describe the elements of a chart.

4. Explain how Excel interprets the following formula if it were located in cell H10: =I5+I6*$A$1.

Review Exercises

1. Revising the gift inventory and sales workbook

In this exercise, you will make changes to an existing chart.

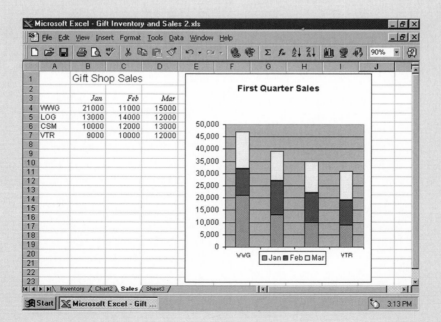

EX-156

1. Open *Gift Inventory and Sales.xls*.

2. Click the Sales tab if necessary.

3. Change the chart type to a stacked column.

4. Remove the data table.

5. Remove the dollar sign from the numbers on the Y axis.

6. Save the file as Gift Inventory and Sales 2.xls and close the file.

2. Creating a new items workbook

In this exercise, you will create a workbook that lists five possible new items and computes the discount on the items.

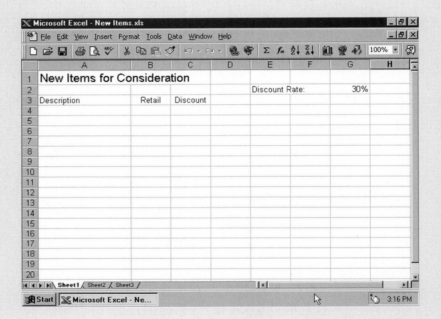

1. Create the workbook shown above.

2. Find five items on the Web that you can suggest as new items for the gift shops to carry. Enter the descriptions of the items and their retail prices in the worksheet in the appropriate columns.

3. In cell C4, enter the formula that multiplies the discount rate in cell G2 times the retail price in cell B4. Copy the formula to the range C5:C8.

4. Save the file as *New Items.xls* and close the file.

3. Sorting data and creating a sales chart in a worksheet

1. Launch Excel and open the workbook *Container Corporation Regional Sales.xls*.

2. Sort the data so that it appears in order by total sales per region with the region with the highest sales at the top.

3. Print a copy of the worksheet after sorting.

4. Create a column chart which displays a comparison of sales by quarter according to region and format the chart as follows:

   • Add a chart title *Regional Sales by Quarter*.

   • Place the chart in the workbook as a new sheet.

5. Save the workbook using the filename *Container Corporation Regional Sales xxx*.

6. Print a copy of the chart.

Assignments

1. Creating a chart of expenditures
Create a workbook that lists your expenditures for the past month. Create a pie chart for the data. Are you spending too much on pizza?

2. Completing a vacation package workbook
Download the workbook *Vacation.xls* from the Addison Wesley Longman web site (http://hepg.awl.com/select) or ask your instructor for this workbook file. Sort the data in ascending order in the range A4:C8. Enter a formula in cell D4 that multiplies the Price/Person times the appropriate discount rate (cell H4). Copy the formula to the other cells in the column. Enter appropriate formulas for the Travel Agency discounts and the Resort Club discounts. Use headings in the formulas for the Resort Club discounts.

6

Using Financial Functions

One of the advantages of electronic spreadsheets is that the user has the capability of performing "What if" analyses. The computer can easily store and retrieve data and perform calculations, so Microsoft Excel can be used to develop sophisticated models to assist in decision making.

One decision that individuals and managers often undertake involves assessing the terms under which they will borrow money. Loan payments are amortized; *amortization* is the process of distributing monthly payments over the life of a loan. The factors determining a loan's repayment include the amount of the loan, the percent interest charged by the bank or lending organization, and the length of time over which the loan will be repaid. Each of these factors has a technical name:

- The amount borrowed is the *principal*.
- The percent interest is the *rate*.
- The time period over which payments are made is the *term*.

Depending on the values associated with each factor, varying portions of each loan payment apply to the principal and the interest payment. In general, borrowers aim to pay off the principal in as short an amount of time as financially possible.

An *amortization schedule* lists the outstanding balance, monthly payment, amount of each payment that applies to the principal, and the amount of each payment that applies to the outstanding principal for the life of a loan. In this project, you will learn to use financial functions to create an amortization schedule.

EX-158

Objectives

After completing this project, you will be able to:

➤ **Define the structure of the amortization schedule**

➤ **Enter the numeric data for the loan**

➤ **Calculate the monthly payment using the PMT function**

➤ **Calculate the remaining balance using the PV function**

➤ **Calculate the principal and interest paid in each loan payment using the PPMT and IPMT functions**

➤ **Construct formulas to calculate the cumulative principal, cumulative interest, total payments, and ending balance**

➤ **Use the Fill Handle to complete the amortization schedule**

➤ **Freeze worksheet panes to assist in viewing the amortization schedule**

➤ **Create and apply a macro**

The Challenge

The Atrium Café will expand next year, so Mr. Gilmore has asked you to construct an amortization schedule so he can compare different loan scenarios. After you complete the workbook, Mr. Gilmore will determine the optimum loan scenario before contacting specific lending institutions for funding.

The Solution

Excel has a number of financial functions that will make creating this workbook a simple task! By entering four numeric constants and using the PMT, PPMT, IPMT, and PV financial functions, you can create the workbook Mr. Gilmore needs. Your completed amortization schedule will look like the one shown in Figure 6.1.

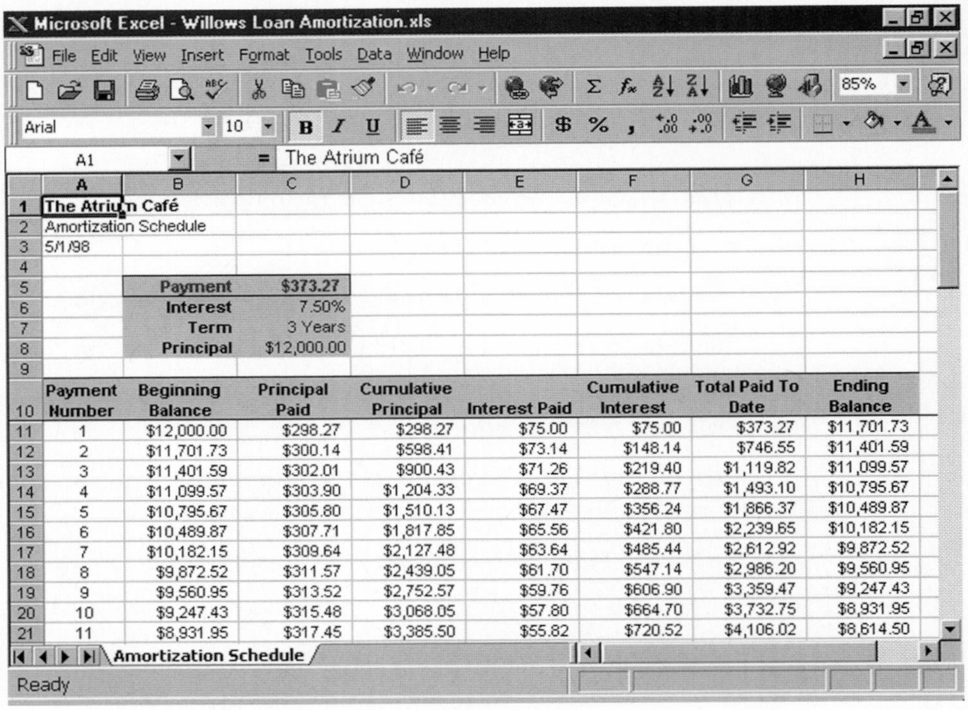

Microsoft Excel - Willows Loan Amortization.xls

A1 = The Atrium Café

The Atrium Café
Amortization Schedule
5/1/98

Payment	$373.27
Interest	7.50%
Term	3 Years
Principal	$12,000.00

Payment Number	Beginning Balance	Principal Paid	Cumulative Principal	Interest Paid	Cumulative Interest	Total Paid To Date	Ending Balance
1	$12,000.00	$298.27	$298.27	$75.00	$75.00	$373.27	$11,701.73
2	$11,701.73	$300.14	$598.41	$73.14	$148.14	$746.55	$11,401.59
3	$11,401.59	$302.01	$900.43	$71.26	$219.40	$1,119.82	$11,099.57
4	$11,099.57	$303.90	$1,204.33	$69.37	$288.77	$1,493.10	$10,795.67
5	$10,795.67	$305.80	$1,510.13	$67.47	$356.24	$1,866.37	$10,489.87
6	$10,489.87	$307.71	$1,817.85	$65.56	$421.80	$2,239.65	$10,182.15
7	$10,182.15	$309.64	$2,127.48	$63.64	$485.44	$2,612.92	$9,872.52
8	$9,872.52	$311.57	$2,439.05	$61.70	$547.14	$2,986.20	$9,560.95
9	$9,560.95	$313.52	$2,752.57	$59.76	$606.90	$3,359.47	$9,247.43
10	$9,247.43	$315.48	$3,068.05	$57.80	$664.70	$3,732.75	$8,931.95
11	$8,931.95	$317.45	$3,385.50	$55.82	$720.52	$4,106.02	$8,614.50

Amortization Schedule

Ready

Figure 6.1: Mr. Gilmore's Amortization Schedule

The Setup

Make sure that the Excel settings listed in Table 6.1 are selected on your computer. This will ensure that your screen matches the illustrations and that the tasks in this project function as described.

Table 6.1 Excel Settings

Location	Make these settings
Office Assistant	Close the Office Assistant
View, Toolbars	Display the Standard and Formatting toolbars
View, Formula bar	Display the Formula bar
View, Status bar	Display the Status bar
Maximize	Maximize the Application and Workbook windows
Tools, Options	In the General tab, set the default worksheet font to Arial, 10 point
File, Page Setup	Click the Page tab and set the orientation to landscape
Worksheet Tab for Sheet1	Double-click and rename this tab as Amortization Schedule, and delete the remaining worksheets

Defining the Structure of the Amortization Schedule

The amortization schedule's structure is defined by entering constants to specify where the payment, interest, term, and loan repayment data appear in the worksheet. Excel uses two categories of constants: *text constants* define the structure of the worksheet and *numeric constants* comprise the data upon which the *loan scenario* is based.

When you enter the constants, you format them to enhance the appearance of the worksheet.

TASK 1: DEFINE THE STRUCTURE OF THE AMORTIZATION SCHEDULE:

1 Type **The Atrium Cafe** in cell A1, and change the format to bold.

2 Type **Amortization Schedule** in cell A2.

3 Type **=NOW()** as a formula in cell A3 and click the Enter button ✔ on the Formula Bar.

> **Comment** The =NOW() function is a Date & Time function that displays the date and time according to the computer's system clock. This date is dynamic; as the system clock changes, the date is updated.

4 Select Cells from the Format menu. Select the Number tab in the Format Cells dialog box, select Date as the category, and select the date type shown in the figure below.

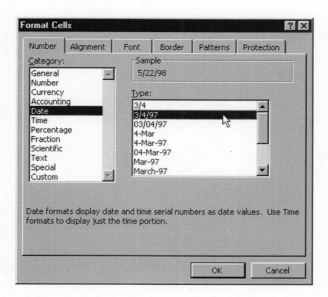

5 Set the alignment of the cell to left.

6 Click OK.

7 Type **Payment** in cell B5, **Interest** in cell B6, **Term** in cell B7, and **Principal** in cell B8. Set the alignment of these cells to right aligned.

8 Type **Payment Number** in cell A10, **Beginning Balance** in cell B10, **Principal Paid** in cell C10, **Cumulative Principal** in cell D10, **Interest Paid** in cell E10, **Cumulative Interest** in cell F10, **Total Paid To Date** in cell G10, and **Ending Balance** in cell H10.

TASK 2: APPLY ADDITIONAL FORMATS TO THE TEXT CONSTANTS:

1 Select the range A10:H10, and set the font style to bold. Using the Fill Color button ![fill icon] on the Formatting toolbar, set the fill color of the selection to 25% Gray.

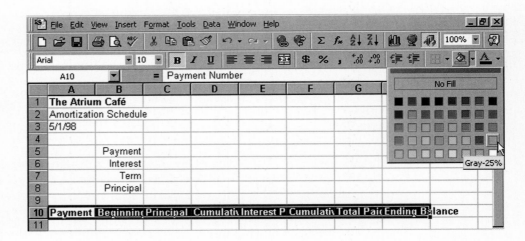

2 Select the range B5:C8. Set the fill color of the selection to 25% gray.

3 Select the range B5:C5. Using the Font Color button ![font color icon] on the Formatting toolbar, set the font color of this selection to dark red.

4 Select the Borders button ![borders icon] on the Formatting toolbar. Insert a thin border around the selection.

5 Select the range B5:B8. Set the font style of the selection to Bold.

6 Highlight the range A10 to H10, and select Cells from the Format menu. Select the Alignment tab.

7 Set the Horizontal text alignment to center, and check the option to wrap text, as shown on the next page. Click OK.

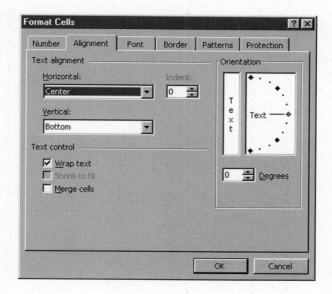

8   Select the Borders tool 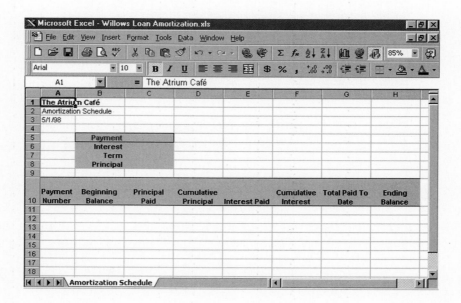 on the Standard toolbar. Select the option to add a thin border to the top and bottom of the selection.

9   Use the column headings to select columns B through H. Set the width of the selected columns to 12.00. Save your workbook to your floppy disk as *Willows Loan Amortization.xls*.

10 Change the Zoom control 85% on the Standard toolbar to 85%. Your workbook should look like the one shown below.

Entering Numeric Constants

A loan payment is calculated using three factors: the loan principal, the interest rate, and the term. These values are entered in the range C6:C8 of your worksheet. All loan repayment data is calculated using these values.

TASK 3: ENTERING NUMERIC CONSTANTS:

1 Place the cell pointer in cell C6, type **.075**, and press (ENTER).

2 Click cell C6 again to make it the active cell, select Cells from the Format menu, and click the Number tab.

3 Select Percentage as the category, and specify two decimal places. Click OK.

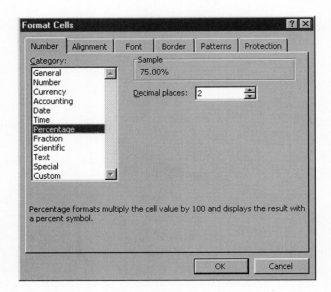

4 Make cell C7 the active cell, type the value **3**, and press (ENTER).

5 Place the cell pointer in cell C7, select Cells from the Format menu, and click the Number tab.

6 Select Custom as the category, and place the insertion point in the Type: text box.

7 Enter **## "Years"** as the custom format and click OK, as shown on the next page. This places the text string "Years" after the numeric value in the cell.

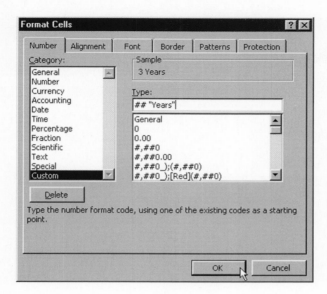

Tip   When specifying a custom format, the dialog box displays a sample of the current cell with the custom format applied.

8 Place the cell pointer in cell C8, type **12000** and press (ENTER).

9 Make cell C8 the active cell and select Cells from the Format menu. Click the Number tab, and select Currency as the category. Make sure two decimal places are specified. Click OK.

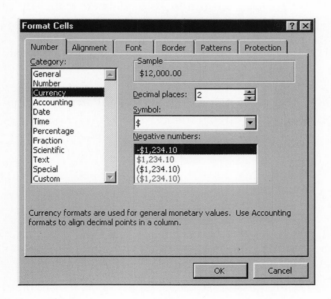

10 After entering and formatting the three numeric constants, the worksheet should look like the one on the next page.

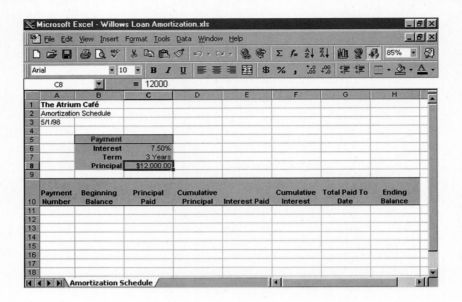

Calculating the Loan Payment

After you specify the rate, term, and principal, you can calculate the loan payment. The PMT (payment) function is a financial function used to calculate the periodic payment of a loan, assuming a constant interest rate and constant payments over the life of the loan. Functions perform calculations by using specific values, called **arguments**, in a particular order, called the syntax. The PMT function uses five arguments, three of which are required. A function's *syntax* specifies the order in which the arguments must appear. Each argument is separated from the others with a comma. The general syntax for the PMT function is:

=PMT(interest rate, number of payments, present value)

Note Search for PMT in the Help system for more information about the arguments accompanying this function.

TASK 4: CALCULATE THE LOAN PAYMENT USING THE PMT FUNCTION:

1. Place the cell pointer in cell C5 to make it the active cell. Select Function from the Insert menu.

2. In the Paste Function dialog box, select Financial as the function category and select PMT as the function name, as shown on the next page. Note that the Paste Function dialog box also displays the arguments used by the function.

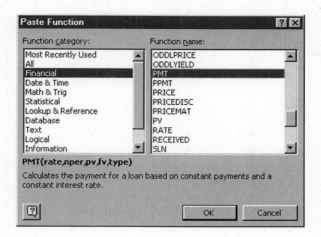

3 Click OK. The function's arguments can be entered in the box that appears.

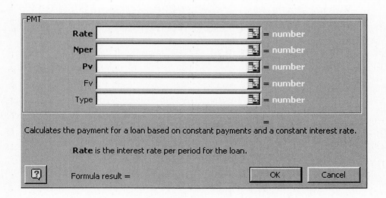

4 Click the button ![button] immediately to the right of the text box for specifying the rate.

5 Point to cell C6 and click the left mouse button, as shown in the figure below. Notice that the reference C6 appears both in the Formula bar and the text box below the Formula bar.

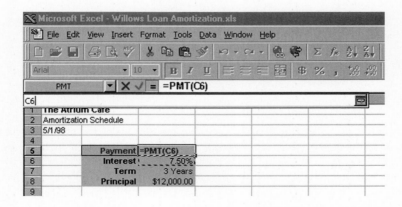

6 The interest rate specified in the worksheet is an annual interest rate. Therefore, it must be divided by 12 (the number of interest periods in one year) for the function to calculate the correct payment.

7 Place the insertion point in the text box that appears under the Formula bar, and type **/12**.

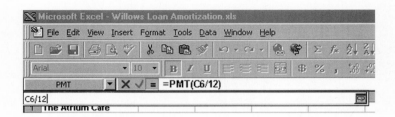

8 Press (ENTER).

The pointing method is one way of entering the arguments the PMT function needs. Because you know the term appears in cell C7 and the payment appears in cell C8, you can enter these values directly.

9 Enter the remaining required arguments, as shown below.

> **Troubleshooting** Note that the term "numeric constant" specifies years. The PMT function requires monthly payments, so you must multiply the value by 12. The PV is the present value of the loan, which is the same as the loan principal. In *annuity functions* (functions that involve payments that are constant), the cash you pay out is represented as a negative value. Therefore, you must precede the reference to cell C8 with a minus sign.

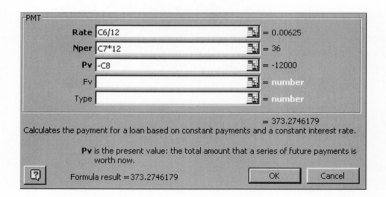

10 Click OK to enter the formula containing the PMT function in cell C5, and save your workbook. The results of the formula should appear as shown on the next page.

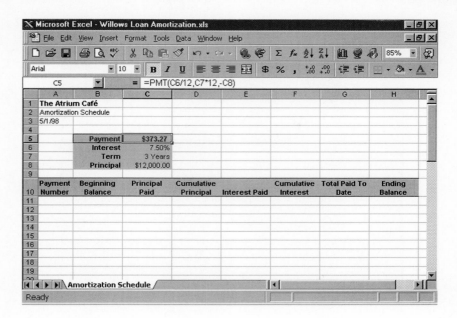

Calculating the Beginning Balance Using the PV Function

Although the beginning balance of the loan that appears in cell B11 is the same as the principal displayed in cell C8, the PV function can be used to enter a "check" into the worksheet. By using the PV function in cell B12 rather than merely including a reference to cell C5, you verify the accuracy of the worksheet.

As with the PMT function, the PV (present value of an annuity) function requires three arguments: rate, term, and payment. The general syntax for the PV function is:

=PV(interest rate, number of payments, periodic payment)

TASK 5: CALCULATE THE BEGINNING BALANCE USING THE PV FUNCTION:

1 Place the cell pointer in cell B11.

2 Type **=PV(C6/12,C7*12,–C5)** and press (ENTER).

> **Tip** As with the PMT function, the annual interest rate must be divided by the number of annual periods (12) per year. In addition, the term (in years) must be multiplied by the number of payments made each year (12), and the payment must be preceded by a minus sign.

The value displayed in cell B11 should appear as shown below.

3   Save your workbook.

Calculating the Principal Paid in Each Payment

The amount of each loan payment that applies to the loan principal (rather than the accrued interest) varies throughout the term of the loan. As with most annuity functions, the actual variance depends upon the loan's rate, term, and principal. The PPMT (periodic principal payment) returns the payment on the principal for a given period. The PPMT function requires four arguments: the rate, the specific period, the number of payments, and the present value of the annuity for the period.

In this function, the **_present value_** refers to the total amount that a series of future payments is worth now—this is the loan principal. The general syntax is:

=PPMT(interest rate, payment period, number of payments, present value)

This function, which is copied to other cells in the amortization schedule, includes both absolute cell references and one mixed cell reference. A **_mixed reference_** means that the column reference remains constant, but the row reference varies. The function also will need to reference the specific payment (by payment number) within the period. This data is supplied to the function from column A of the amortization schedule.

Tip   The term *mixed reference* is a carryover from Lotus 1-2-3 and is not used in Microsoft Excel. Therefore, this term will not be found in the Help System. It is a useful term, however, because it conveys the idea that part of the reference is relative and part is absolute. In Excel, mixed references are also referred to as absolute references.

TASK 6: CALCULATE THE PERIODIC PRINCIPAL PAYMENT USING THE PPMT FUNCTION:

1. Click cell A11 to make it the active cell.

2. Type **1** as a numeric constant representing the first periodic payment.

3. Place the insertion point in cell C11, making it the active cell.
   Type **=-PPMT($C$6/12,$A11,$C$7*12,$C$8)** and press (ENTER).

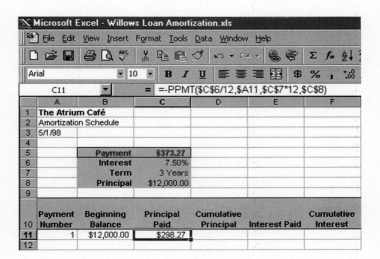

Now let's analyze this formula. The entire payment is preceded by a minus sign, because annuity payments must be specified as a negative value. The references to the rate (cell C6), term (cell C7), and present value (cell C8) are absolute, because the formula must always reference the same cells, regardless of where the formula is copied in the worksheet. Cell C11 contains a mixed reference: The row reference must change to reflect the periodic payment as the formula is copied down the amortization schedule, but column A must be referenced when the formula is copied to cell E11 to construct the IPMT function.

> **Tip** It is not mandatory that cells C6, C7, and C8 contain absolute references. Technically, these could contain mixed references to specify which part of the reference should remain constant (C$6, for example); only the row designation must remain constant as the formulas are copied. The worksheet also uses the IPMT function, which shares the same arguments as the PPMT function, so absolute references are used to assist in creating these formulas. In general, it is a good practice to use absolute references unless the column reference must change if the formula is copied to another column in the worksheet.

Calculating the Interest Paid in Each Payment

The method for calculating the portion of a loan payment that applies to the interest payment is almost identical to the method for calculating a periodic principal payment. The only difference is that the IPMT (periodic interest payment) function is used. The general syntax for the IPMT function is:

=IPMT(interest rate, payment period, number of payments, present value)

TASK 7: CALCULATE THE PERIODIC INTEREST PAYMENT:

1 Select cell C11.

2 Copy the contents of the cell.

3 Place the insertion point in cell E11.

4 Select Paste using either the Edit menu or the Standard toolbar.

5 Edit the formula in the Formula bar by changing the function from PPMT to IPMT.

Your worksheet should now look like the one shown below.

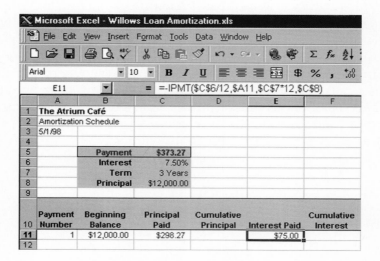

Constructing Formulas to Calculate the Cumulative Principal, Cumulative Interest, Total Payments, and Ending Balance

When building an amortization schedule, it is helpful to display not only the current principal and interest payments, but the cumulative payments as well. For the first payment, the periodic principal and interest payment equal the cumulative payments. In subsequent rows, however, the cumulative payment figures increase. The total payments to date can be calculated by adding the cumulative principal and the cumulative interest payments.

TASK 8: CONSTRUCT FORMULAS TO DETERMINE THE CUMULATIVE INTEREST, CUMULATIVE PRINCIPAL, TOTAL PAYMENTS, AND ENDING BALANCE:

1   Select cell D11 as the active cell.

2   Type **=C11**.

3   Place the insertion point in cell F11, and type **=E11**.

4   Place the insertion point in cell G11, and type **=D11+F11**.

> **Reminder**   The value displayed in cell G11 should be identical to the value in cell C5. This provides another "check" to verify the accuracy of your worksheet.

5   Place the insertion point in cell H11.

6   Type **=B11–C11**. The ending balance is the principal that must be paid to fulfill the repayment obligation. This is equal to the beginning balance minus the principal payment. Your worksheet should now look like the one shown on the next page.

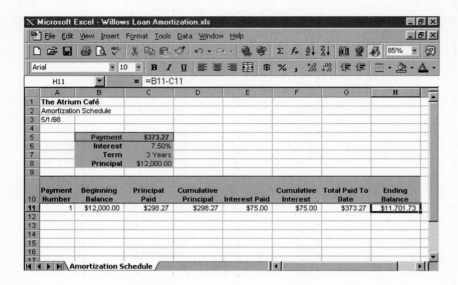

7 Save your worksheet.

Using the Fill Handle to Complete the Amortization Schedule

After you enter formulas in row 12 of the amortization schedule, you can use the Fill Handle to copy the formula to other portions of the worksheet. The default amortization schedule covers a loan with a term of three years, a principal of $12,000, and an annual interest rate of 7.50%.

TASK 9: USE THE FILL HANDLE TO COMPLETE THE AMORTIZATION SCHEDULE:

1 Place the insertion point in cell A12 to make it the active cell.

2 Type **=A11+1**.

3 Type **=H11** in cell B12. The beginning balance for this payment equals the ending balance after the last payment was made.

4 Highlight the range C11:H11. Using the Fill Handle, copy the range down to row 12, as shown on the next page.

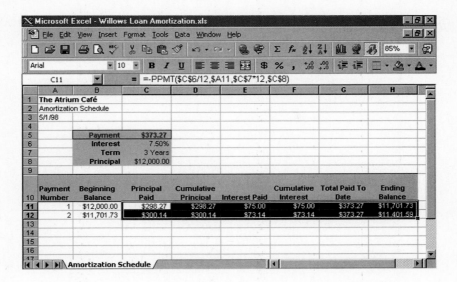

5   Highlight cell D12, and change the formula to **=D11+C12**.

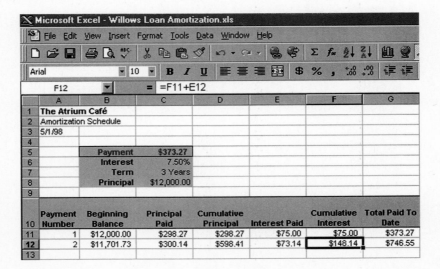

6   Highlight cell F12, and change the formula to **=F11+E12**.

7 Highlight the range A12:H12. Using the Fill Handle, copy this row of formulas through row 46, as shown below.

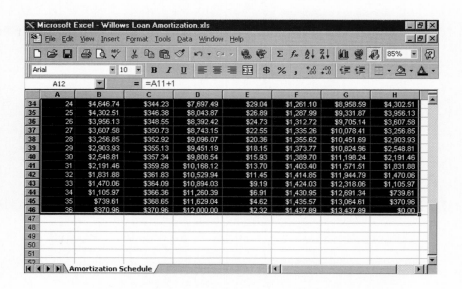

Tip Notice that the Ending Balance equals zero at payment 36. This verifies that the amortization schedule is calculating the loan repayment figures correctly.

8 Highlight Column A and set the alignment of the selection to center.

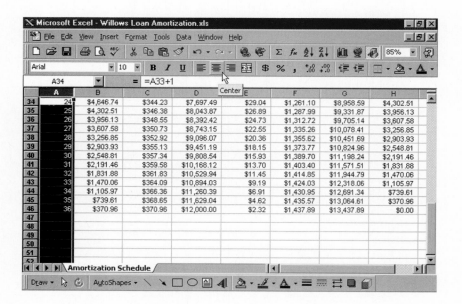

9   Highlight the range A1:A3. Set the alignment to left.

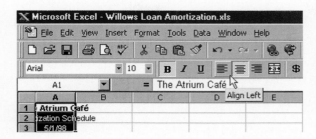

10   Save your changes. Your workbook should now look like the one shown in the figure below.

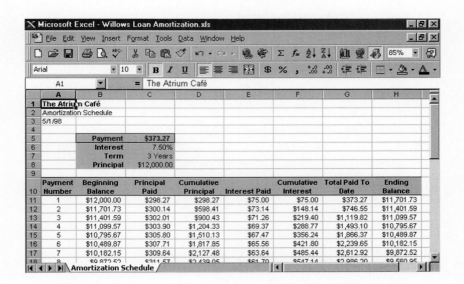

Freezing Worksheet Panes to Assist in Viewing Large Worksheets

Your amortization schedule is now fully functional. Take a moment to note the power of Microsoft Excel. By using financial functions and copying these formulas down the worksheet, the entire loan repayment table is based upon four numeric constants—even though your worksheet presently contains almost 300 formulas.

Viewing large worksheets can be problematic because the heading rows scroll out of view as you move down the worksheet. To alleviate this problem, certain rows can be "frozen" so they always appear on the screen. In the next task, you will freeze the worksheet headings so the entire amortization schedule can be viewed with the headings visible on the screen.

TASK 10: FREEZE WORKSHEET PANES TO ASSIST VIEWING:

1 Place the insertion point in cell A11.

2 Select Freeze Panes from the Window menu.

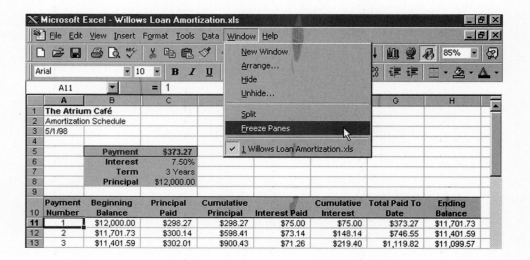

3 Select Go To from the Edit menu.

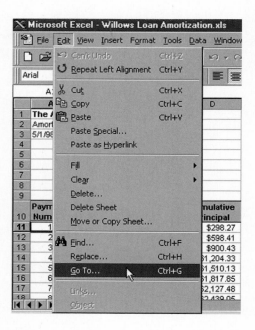

4 Type **A46** in the Reference text box of the Go To dialog box.

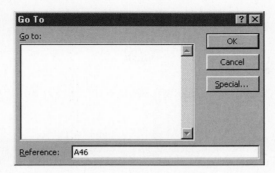

5   Click OK. Cell A46 becomes the active cell, and rows 1 through 10 and additional rows up to row 46 become visible.

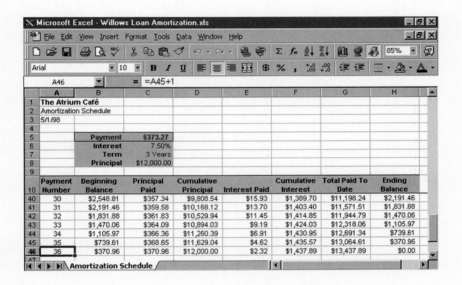

As you scroll through the worksheet, rows 1 through 10 always remain visible.

> **Tip** To unfreeze the panes, select Unfreeze Panes from the Window menu.

Changing the Loan Scenario

Using this workbook, Mr. Gilmore can easily compare alternative loan scenarios. To see how easy it is to view another loan scenario, simply change the principal and term values, and then add additional rows to the worksheet.

TASK 11: TO CHANGE THE LOAN SCENARIO:

1 Enter **4** in cell C7 and press (ENTER).

2 Type **10000** in cell C8 and press (ENTER). Notice that the monthly payment changes to $241.79.

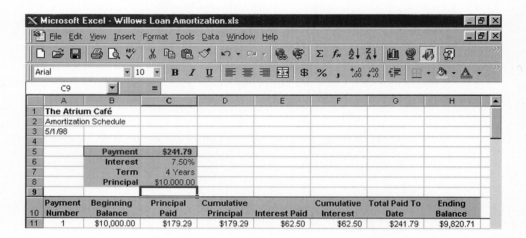

3 Scroll to the bottom of the worksheet, and highlight the range A46:H46.

4 Using the Fill Handle, drag the selection through row 58 and release the left mouse button. Your amortization schedule should now resemble the one shown in the figure below.

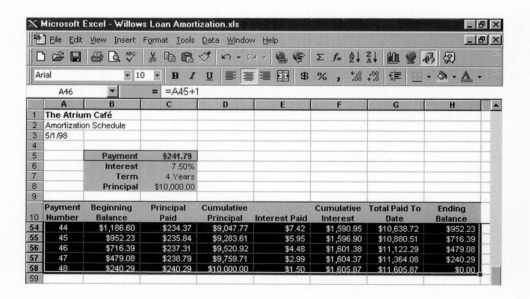

5 Using the vertical scroll bar, move to the top of the worksheet, and make cell A1 the active cell.

6 Save your workbook.

Creating Excel Macros

When using Excel you often may need to complete a series of tasks more than once. By recording a macro, you can easily apply these procedures again by simply playing the macro. A *macro* is a series of commands and functions stored in a Visual Basic module that can be run whenever you need to perform the task again. (*Visual Basic* is the programming language used throughout the Office environment for recording macros. If you know Visual Basic, you can easily edit a macro you have created.)

It would be nice if your amortization worksheet could easily be returned to a predictable state after the loan's term is changed, because the worksheet will either display errors or not display the entire repayment schedule. You can create a macro to set the default values and create the appropriate number of loan repayment formulas.

TASK 12: TO RECORD A MACRO:

1   Select Macros from the Tools menu, and choose Record New Macro.

2   Type **SetDefaults** as the name of the macro, and make sure the macro is stored in the current workbook, as shown in the figure below. Click OK.

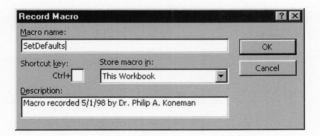

> **Tip**   Every procedure you now apply will become a part of the macro. You will also notice that the Stop Recording toolbar is now visible on the screen.

3   Click cell A13 to make it the active cell.

4   While simultaneously holding down the (SHIFT) and (CTRL) keys, press the (END) key. The range A13:H56 is now selected.

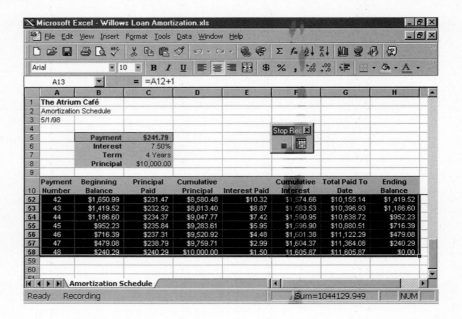

5 Press the (DELETE) key to delete the selected portion of the amortization schedule.

6 Type **3** in cell C7 as the term, and type **12000** in cell C8 as the principal.

7 Select the range A12:H12 and use the Fill Handle to copy the formulas through row 46.

8 Scroll to the top of the worksheet and make cell A1 the active cell.

9 Click the Stop Recording button.

10 You have now successfully recorded a macro. Save your workbook.

Running a Macro

After you have recorded a macro, it can be run. When you ***run*** a macro, each step included in the macro is applied to the workbook. Before running the macro, you will change the loan scenario to see the results of applying the macro.

TASK 13: TO RUN A MACRO:

1 Type **10** in cell C7 and **50000** in cell C8.

2 Scroll to the bottom of the worksheet and select the range A46:H46.

3 Using the Fill Handle, copy the selection through row 130, as shown on the next page.

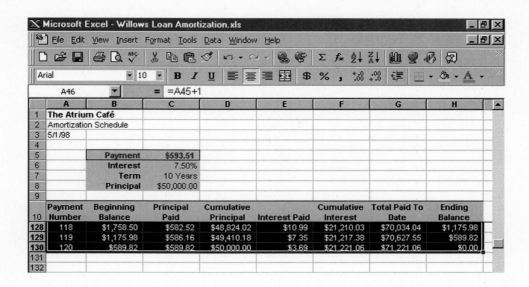

4 Select Macro from the Tools menu, and then choose Macros.

5 Select the SetDefaults macro and click the Run command button.

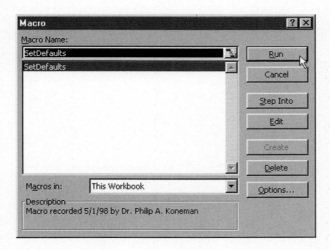

The macro will change the term and principal of the loan, and modify the amortization schedule accordingly. You can easily change the loan scenario to a predictable state at any time by simply running the SetDefaults macro.

The Conclusion

The worksheet you have created in this project serves as a powerful tool for analyzing different loan scenarios. The numeric constants in the upper portion of the Amortization Schedule worksheet can easily be changed to compare alternate loan scenarios.

Summary and Exercises

Summary

- Text constants are used to define a workbook's structure.
- Excel contains many financial functions.
- In an amortization schedule workbook, numeric constants for the principal, rate, and term are used to calculate the loan payment.
- The PMT function is used to calculate a loan payment.
- The PV function is used to calculate the present value of an annuity.
- The PPMT function is used to calculate the portion of a loan payment that applies toward the loan principal.
- The IPMT is used to calculate the portion of a loan payment that applies toward the accrued interest.
- A complex workbook such as an amortization schedule will often contain hundreds of formulas.
- Once created, formulas are easily copied using the Fill Handle.
- Worksheet panes can be frozen to assist in viewing large worksheets.
- A macro is used to record redundant tasks that can be applied again and again.

Key Terms and Operations

Key Terms

amortization	present value
amortization schedule	principal
annuity functions	rate
argument	run
loan scenario	syntax
macro	term
mixed reference	text constants
numeric constants	Visual Basic

Operations

construct a formula using the IPMT (interest payment) function
construct a formula using the PMT (payment) function
construct a formula using the PPMT (periodic payment) function
construct a formula using the PV (present value of an annuity) function
create an amortization schedule
create formulas to calculate the cumulative interest and cumulative principal
determine the ending balance
freeze worksheet panes
record a macro
run a macro
use AutoFill to copy formulas

Study Questions

Multiple Choice

1. A worksheet is being constructed to determine the monthly payment required to return $250,000 in the year 2025. Which financial function should be used to perform this calculation?
   a. PMT
   b. IPMT
   c. PV
   d. FV
   e. PPMT

2. A worksheet includes a formula for calculating the payment on a loan. To see the amount of the monthly payment that applies to the interest payment, you will use which function?
   a. PMT
   b. PV
   c. NOW()
   d. PPMT
   e. IPMT

3. Which statement concerning the use of the PV annuity function is false?
   a. An annuity payment should be entered as a negative value.
   b. The present value of the investment is required.
   c. The total number of payment periods in the annuity is required.
   d. Parentheses are not used when constructing this function.
   e. The interest rate cannot change over the life of the annuity.

4. Which of the following most likely refers to the principal of a loan in a financial function?
   a. H6/12
   b. I7*12
   c. –J7
   d. g3/12
   e. –a1*24

5. Which of the following formulas includes an absolute reference to an annuity payment?
   a. =PMT(a1/12,c7*12,d7)
   b. =PPMT(a1/12,c7*12,e7)
   c. =PMT(h6/12,I$7*12,–j7)
   d. =IPMT(a1/12,c7*12,–e7)
   e. =PMT(a1/12,$b7*12,–$r$5)

6. Which of the following is true about macros?
   a. After a macro is created, it cannot be edited.
   b. Macros aren't very useful in worksheets containing financial functions.
   c. Macros are used to record a series of redundant tasks.
   d. Macros cannot perform copy and paste operations.
   e. Macros are rarely used in Excel workbooks.

7. The Principal Payment (PPMT) function is similar to which function?
   a. PMT
   b. PV
   c. IPMT
   d. PPMT
   e. NOW()

8. Which function calculates the portion of a loan payment applied toward the principal?
   a. PMT
   b. PV
   c. IPMT
   d. PPMT
   e. FV

9. You can freeze worksheet panes using which menu?
   a. Format
   b. Edit
   c. Data
   d. View
   e. Window

10. The =NOW() function is in which category of functions?
   a. Financial
   b. Statistical
   c. Date/Time
   d. Logical
   e. String

Short Answer
1. Examine the function =PMT(H6/12,I7*12,–J7). Which element refers to the present value of the loan? How is it identified?

2. Explain how the term of a loan impacts the total amount paid.

3. What does the PMT function calculate?

4. What is a mixed cell reference?

5. Why should the formulas in an amortization schedule contain absolute references?

6. What is the maximum number of arguments that can be included with the PMT function?

7. What value does the PPMT function return?

8. If you are having difficulty viewing the headings in a large worksheet, what should you do?

9. What happens when you record a macro?

10. How should annuity payments be entered in a formula?

For Discussion

1. What is the FV function? How does the data it returns differ from the PV function?

2. What is a macro? How is a macro recorded and applied?

3. How can worksheets, such as the amortization schedule you created in this project, be protected from changes?

4. What arguments are required by the PMT function? Is the order in which these appear in a formula significant?

Review Exercises

1. Protecting cells in a workbook

In many settings, portions of a worksheet should be protected to prohibit users from inadvertently making destructive changes to the workbook. By unlocking the cells to which users need access and protecting the worksheet, this objective can easily be achieved. Open the *Willows Loan Amortization* workbook and do the following:

1. Select the following nonadjacent ranges: C6:C8 and A13:H370.

2. Select Cells from the Format menu.

3. Click the Protection tab.

4. Deselect the Locked check box in the Format Cells dialog box.

5. Click the OK button.

6. Select Protection from the Tools menu.

7. Select Protect Sheet from the cascading menu.

8. Do not enter a protection password in the Protect Sheet dialog box.

9. Click OK.

10. Save the updated workbook as *Protected Loan Analysis.xls*.

2. Creating a worksheet to predict the future value of an investment

The FV function is similar to the PV function, except that it returns the future value of an investment, assuming a constant interest rate. Create the workbook shown below as follows:

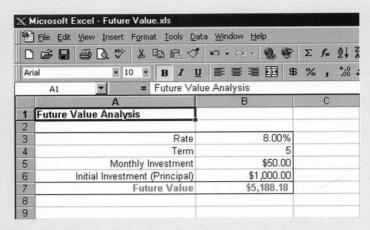

1. Launch Excel if isn't already running.

2. Create a new workbook.

3. Save the workbook as *Future value.xls*.

4. Enter the text and numeric constants shown in the figure on the previous page into the worksheet.

5. Type **=FV(B3/12,B4*12,–B5,–B6,1)** as the formula in cell B7. Look up FV in the Excel Help System for information about the arguments.

3. Using Goal Seek to determine a loan interest rate

Goal Seek is useful when you know the desired result but not the input value that a formula requires to return that result. It works on only one cell at a time. Say you want to purchase a house that costs $175,000 and you can only afford a monthly mortgage payment that does not exceed $1,200. These amounts are the desired result.

One mortgage company is offering a 9.5% rate on home mortgage loans. At that rate, the monthly payment for principal of $175,000 to be paid back over a 30-year term is $1,471.49, which is more than your budget will allow. Use Goal Seek to figure out what interest rate a loan of this amount and term would have to offer to result in a $1,200 monthly payment.

1. Open the Excel Worksheet entitled *Regional Sales Loan Analysis.xls*.

2. Type **.095** in cell C6, **30** in cell C7, and **175000** in cell C8.

3. Select Goal Seek from the Tools menu.

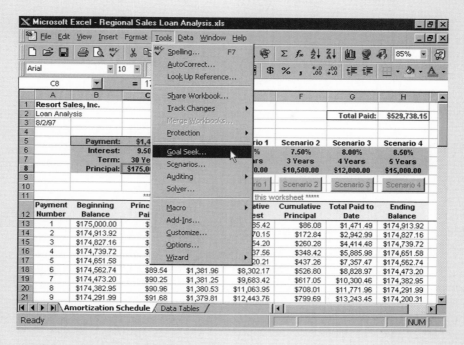

4. In the Goal Seek dialog box, enter the values shown.

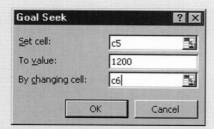

5. Click OK. Goal Seek finds the solution. If you, the potential home buyer, can secure a loan at 7.3%, the monthly payment will not exceed $1,200.

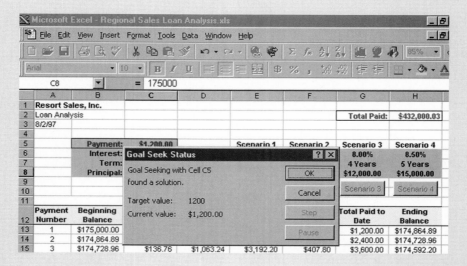

6. Click OK if you want to accept this solution. Click Cancel to retain the current values in the worksheet.

7. Close the worksheet.

Assignments

1. Creating macros to enable and disable protection for a worksheet

Open the *Protected loan analysis.xls* workbook. Create two macros: one that sets the protection for the worksheet, and one that removes the worksheet protection. Save the workbook as *Protected Loan Y-N.xls*.

2. Repaying a loan early

Visit Microsoft's New Spreadsheet Solutions site, which contains spreadsheet solutions created by Village Software. (http://www.microsoft.com/excel/ freestuff/templates/villagesoftware/). Download the Loan Manager file self-extracting file(*Loan.exe*), and install the *Loan.xlt* template to your floppy diskette. Open the *Loan.xlt* file, and enter the loan data from this project. Make three additional payments of $100.00 each. Save the workbook as *Prepaid.xls*.

Beyond the Basics: Exploring the Power of Microsoft Excel

In Projects 1 through 5 you have learned the basics of electronic spreadsheet technology. You are able to use Microsoft Excel to create a simple workbook by entering values and formulas and can then modify the values within the workbook and add formats to specific cells. In addition, you have learned how to represent data graphically using Excel's charting tools.

In the projects that follow, you will be challenged to apply what you have learned to more complex tasks. You will notice some differences in the level of detail and complexity. Excel is a powerful tool offering many features for accomplishing a wide variety of tasks and procedures. You will try out several useful features in Projects 6 through 12, and you are encouraged to explore further after completing Project 12.

We assume that you are able to navigate within an Excel workbook by using the tab feature. We also assume that you are familiar with the structure of Excel formulas and can create formulas using a variety of methods. Here is a summary of what you will learn in the next seven projects.

In Project 6 you are introduced to financial functions. By building an amortization workbook you will learn how to use the PMT, PV, and PPT functions. You will also learn three strategies for comparing multiple loan scenarios.

Project 7 shows you how to develop more complex workbooks for solving specific problems. A key issue in workbooks with several worksheets is data redundancy—the same data in more than one place. What is tricky is keeping the data accurate if you change it or update it. You will learn how to minimize redundant data by linking information among worksheets.

In Project 8 you will continue to build a complex workbook that minimizes redundant data. You will learn to use logical and lookup functions to summarize sales data.

Project 9 will introduce you to some of the tools Excel includes for analyzing data. In addition to using AutoFilter to summarize sales data, you will learn how to reduce the time required to complete repetitive tasks by creating and applying macros.

Excel includes functions and procedures for statistical analysis. In Project 10 you will learn how to look at your data from multiple perspectives by creating Pivot Tables. In addition, you will use the Forecast and Trends functions to predict future performance.

Excel contains the Analysis Toolpak add-on for running complex statistical procedures. In Project 11 you will create a data set similar to one you might use to conduct a research study. You will then use Excel to complete an analysis of variance.

In Project 12 you will learn how to consolidate data using 3-D references. Once you create one consolidation formula, it can easily be copied to other cells. To assist users with data entry and interpretation, you will add validation criteria and conditional formats to the workbook. You will also learn to use Excel's auditing features and how to publish worksheet data to the World Wide Web.

These projects will help you to extend your basic knowledge of Microsoft Excel. By the end of Project 12 you will have used Excel to model, analyze, and represent data in some sophisticated ways. We encourage you to develop additional workbooks for exploring Excel in more detail.

Creating a Three-Dimensional Workbook

Modern electronic worksheet applications such as Microsoft Excel enable you to enter the same data under various classifications in worksheets you keep in a *three-dimensional electronic workbook*.

Data linking formulas minimize redundant data by keeping data in one place where it can be referenced from various worksheets. The purpose is not just to save effort but to avoid inaccuracies that might result if you had to find and update each instance of the data separately.

Objectives

After completing this project, you will be able to:

➤ **Review seven steps for designing electronic workbooks**

➤ **Create a list of products**

➤ **Name a worksheet range**

➤ **Create an Excel template**

➤ **Insert worksheets based on an Excel template into an existing workbook**

➤ **Rename worksheets in a workbook**

➤ **Create a Sales Summary worksheet**

➤ **Enter linking formulas to display the list of products in the Sales Summary worksheet**

Introduction

In a business solution using an electronic spreadsheet like Microsoft Excel or a relational database management system like Microsoft Access, accuracy of information is jeopardized when the same data is entered in several different electronic worksheets or several places in the database. Such multiple instances of the same data are referred to as **redundant data** and can be difficult to keep track of, difficult to update, and therefore difficult to keep accurate.

Microsoft Excel supports two methods for minimizing redundant data. 3-D formulas link information among worksheets within or between workbooks. Using linking formulas to display information offers the advantage of reducing file size, simplifying the workbook over all, and avoiding redundancy of data and therefore redundant effort in updating. Excel also uses a *lookup table* of constant values so that data in one location can be referenced by formulas in other worksheets or workbooks. This also reduces the overall complexity of a workbook, and by keeping like information in one place, minimizes the potential for inaccuracies and errors when data are updated.

Both of these methods maintain the integrity of the data. *Data integrity* refers to the overall consistency and accuracy of the data you present in a workbook. As you may have guessed, it is easy to introduce errors into the design of a worksheet, and some errors are difficult to detect. Auditing tools in Excel help you to isolate and correct errors. Of course it's better to try to avoid errors in the first place. One good way is to run a sample set of data to test each worksheet you design and then carefully analyze the results. Consistently following the simple design process outlined below also minimizes errors. Work through the following Challenge case to learn how to design an Excel workbook without redundant data.

The Challenge

World Sales, Inc., owns a string of resort facilities throughout the country. The company has been so successful in franchising the Resort Sales, Inc. gift shops that top management is considering starting a catalog company to market products directly. In order to make a decision the executives need to review sales figures by region. They have requested a report listing the top ten best-selling items in each region. These regional data have been provided to you, and you have been asked to create a report by the end of the day.

The Solution

To make your workbook as efficient as possible, you decide to make use of two features supported by Microsoft Excel, table lookup and linking formulas. First, you will list the product information in the last worksheet of your workbook. A sheet for each Regional Sales, Inc. sales region will "look up" the data from that worksheet. Second, you will use Excel linking formulas to display the sales figures for each region to a summary report for World Sales, Inc., which in turn will be linked to a sales report in Microsoft Word. Since the regional worksheets have a similar structure, you will create a template for constructing identical worksheets. This approach, which minimizes data redundancy by creating a *three-dimensional workbook*, is graphically depicted in Figure 7.1.

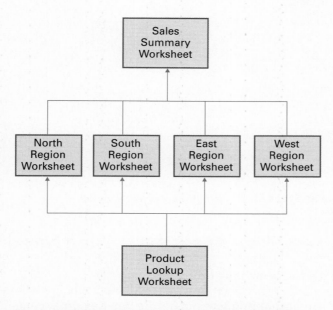

Figure 7.1 Solution for Minimizing Redundant Data

The Setup

To begin your three-dimensional sales summary workbook, start Microsoft Excel and select the settings shown in Table 7.1.

Table 7.1   Excel Settings

Element	Settings
Office Assistant	Close the Office Assistant
View, Toolbar	Display Standard toolbar Display Formatting toolbar
View, Formula toolbar	Display Formula toolbar
View, Status bar	Display Status bar
Maximize	Maximize the Application and Workbook windows

Seven Steps for Designing Workbooks

Errors are easy to introduce into workbooks and hard to eradicate. If you follow the simple seven-step design process for constructing worksheets outlined in Figure 7.2, you can minimize the potential for error.

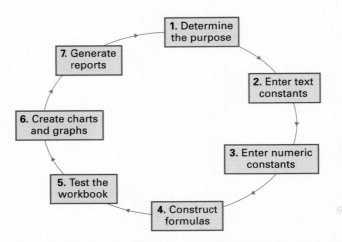

Figure 7.2 Seven Steps for Developing Excel Workbooks

TASK 1: FOLLOW SEVEN STEPS FOR DEVELOPING WORKBOOKS

1. **Determine the Worksheet's Purpose**
   Electronic worksheets consist of a matrix of cells that can contain text, numbers, formulas, and functions. Before you design a worksheet, you must have an idea of what will go into those cells. Thus it is essential to determine the worksheet's scope and purpose. You will need to decide whether the worksheet is to perform simple or complex calculations or to sort and filter data or do some other task.

2. **Enter Text Constants**
   Text constants provide the basic structure of an electronic worksheet and give meaning to the numbers residing the cells of the worksheet's matrix. You can format text constants to give the worksheet a particular look.

3.   **Enter Numeric Constants**
     The **numeric constants** in a worksheet are the data upon which calculations are performed. You can format numeric constants as currency (using leading characters such as the dollar sign), as dates, as percentages, or with units of measure.

4.   **Construct Formulas**
     Formulas give an electronic worksheet its power. Formulas, which always begin with an equals sign (=), can include one or more of Excel's functions. Formulas can also include conditional statements (IF-THEN) and Boolean logic (GREATER THAN OR EQUAL TO, etc.).

5.   **Test the Worksheet**
     Since worksheets can use any of three data types as well as formulas that contain complex functions and expressions, it is important to test a worksheet thoroughly before using it. Excel contains a number of auditing tools for isolating potential problems in a worksheet.

6.   **Create Charts and Graphs**
     Often, it is easier to understand the relationships that exist among numeric data when they are represented graphically. Excel's powerful charting features allow you to create the most common types of graphs and dynamically link them to your data. If the underlying data changes, this feature automatically updates charts and graphs to reflect the changes.

7.   **Generate Reports**
     The data represented in an Excel worksheet can be shared with other Microsoft Office applications. For instance, you can easily transfer to a Microsoft Word report or a Microsoft PowerPoint slide or other graphic. By using the tools together, you can make sure last minute changes are reflected in all documents where the data appears.

Creating a List of Products

Since each Resort Sales, Inc. regional sales worksheet will list the same products in the World Sales, Inc. summary worksheet, an efficient design for the workbook is a lookup table. A *lookup table* in Microsoft Excel is an array of data consisting of two or more columns. You can use a lookup formula to search for a value in one column and return a corresponding value in another column. The lookup table for the resort gift shops will consist of the product numbers and descriptions of the most popular items each gift shop sells. The completed lookup table will look like Figure 7.3.

	A	B
1	Product Number	Product Description
2	RA100201	World Resorts sunglasses
3	RA361001	World Resorts commemorative mug and coaster
4	RM279087	"Fun in the Sun" instant camera
5	RA451894	World Resorts monogrammed beach towel
6	RS354671	Smoked Salmon and Hearty Wheat Cracker gift set
7	RM389562	Photo Album
8	RS652908	"Sounds of Nature" CD collection
9	RA343127	World Resorts sweatshirt
10	RA398289	World Resorts postcard collection
11	RM398056	Traveler's 25 factor sunscreen
12	RS896231	Stationery and thank-you note set
13	RA592846	World Resorts 100% cotton long-sleeve T-shirt
14	RM501835	Traveler's umbrella
15	RA398121	World Resorts 8-ounce glass set (4 pack)
16	RM400582	Canvas tote bag
17		

Figure 7.3

TASK 2: CREATE A LIST OF PRODUCTS

1. Rename the Sheet1 worksheet tab **Products**.

2. Type **Product Number** in cell A1.

3. Type **Product Description** in cell B1.

4. Change the width of column A to 16.00 and column B to 50.00.

5. Save your workbook using the file name *Regional Sales.*

6. Enter the data shown in Figure 7.3 into the range A2:B16.

Naming a Worksheet Range

To make the product data easier to look up, you can give the range of cells containing the data a name. Naming the range will enable you to select the entire range or reference it in a formula.

> **Tip** You can create as many range names as needed. Once a range has been named, the name and range can be edited by selecting Name from the Insert Menu.

TASK 3: NAME A WORKSHEET RANGE

1. Select the range A2:B16.

2. Type **Products** in the Name box, as shown in Figure 7.4.

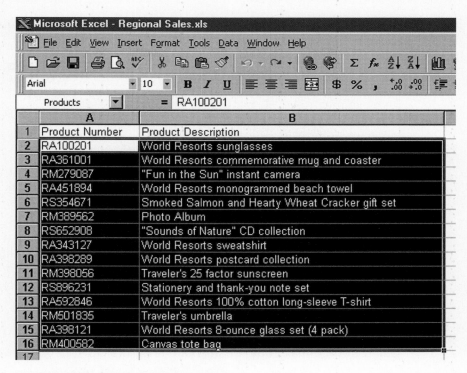

Figure 7.4 Naming the selected range

3   Press (ENTER).

Designing a Worksheet Template

Since all four regional sales worksheets in your workbook will have the same structure, you can create a template for constructing the worksheets. An Excel *template* is a pattern you create for use in formatting similar worksheets or workbooks. It contains text constants and formulas.

TASK 4: DESIGN THE REGIONAL SALES WORKBOOK TEMPLATE

1   Select New from the File menu.

2   Reduce the magnification of the worksheet by clicking the down arrow next to 100% in the Zoom Control box at right on the Standard toolbar. Select 75%.

3   Change the width of column A to 16.00, column B to 45.00, and columns C through G to 12.00.

4   In cell A1, type **Resort Sales, Inc.**, and change the format to bold.

5   In cell A4, type **Product Number**.

6   Type **Product Description** in cell B4.

7 Type **1st Quarter** in Cell C4.8. Select cell C4. Use the AutoFill feature to copy the contents of cell C4 through column F, as shown in Figure 7.5.

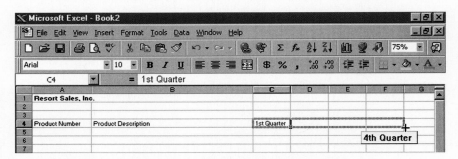

Figure 7.5 Extending the selection using AutoFill

8 Type **Total** in cell G4, and change the cell alignment to right aligned by selecting the button for right alignment in the Formatting toolbar.

9 Highlight the range A4:G4, set the character style to bold, and add a lower border.

10 Type **=sum(C5:F5)** in cell G5.

11 Using the AutoFill, copy the formula down the worksheet to row 19.

TASK 5: SAVE THE TEMPLATE

Before saving the worksheet as an Excel template, you will need to remove the two remaining worksheets from the workbook.

1 Select Sheet2, the second worksheet tab, and while pressing (SHIFT), click Sheet3, the third worksheet tab, as shown in Figure 7.6.

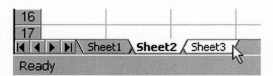

Figure 7.6

> **Tip** Depending upon how Microsoft Office is configured on your computer, you may have more than three default worksheets in a workbook. Delete all additional worksheets in the workbook by selecting Delete Sheet from the Edit menu. 2. Select Delete Sheet from the Edit menu, as shown in Figure 7.7.

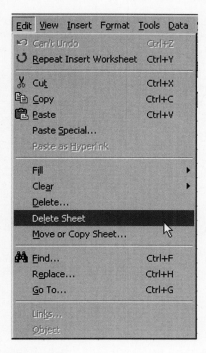

Figure 7.7

2 When the dialog box shown in Figure 7.8 appears, click OK to confirm that you wish to delete the selected sheets.

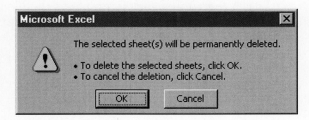

Figure 7.8

Note Once you have deleted a worksheet, you cannot restore it using Undo!

3 Click the Save button 💾 on the Standard toolbar. The Save As dialog box will appear, since the workbook has not yet been saved.

4 Select Template from the Save As Type drop-down list, and save the workbook as *Regional Sales,* as shown in Figure 7.9. Close the workbook after you have saved it.

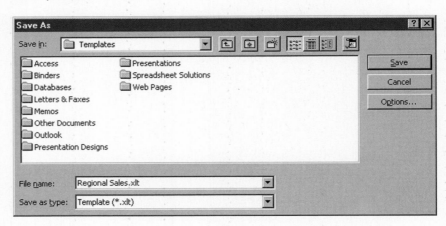

Figure 7.9

> **Tip** Once you create a template, you can edit the *.xlt* template file as you would a workbook file in Excel.

> **Troubleshooting** When you select Template as the file type, Excel will automatically save the workbook template in a folder on the local hard drive or network server and add the appropriate file extension. If you have problems saving your template, your write permissions may be restricted, and you will need to contact your instructor.

Inserting Worksheets Based on a Template into an Existing Workbook

Once you have created a template, you can easily add to any workbook a worksheet based on it. Earlier, after creating the *Regional Sales* template, you were shown how to delete additional worksheets in the *Regional Sales.xlt* file. The reason for deleting the additional worksheets is to make sure Excel will insert only one worksheet based upon the template.

TASK 6: INSERT A WORKSHEET BASED ON A TEMPLATE INTO AN EXISTING WORKBOOK

1 Place the insertion point over the **Products** worksheet tab, and click the right mouse button.

2   Select Insert from the right click menu, as shown in Figure 7.10.

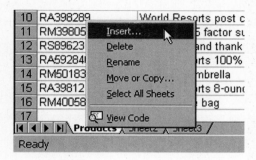

Figure 7.10

The Insert dialog box shown in Figure 7.11 will appear.

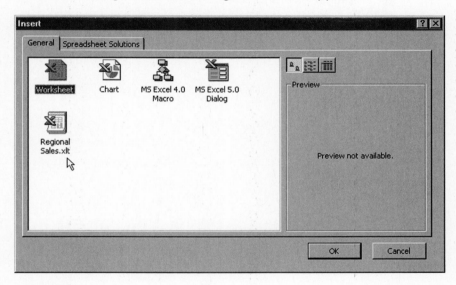

Figure 7.11

3   Highlight the *Regional Sales.xlt* template, and click OK.
Excel will insert an additional worksheet into the workbook, as shown in Figure 7.12.

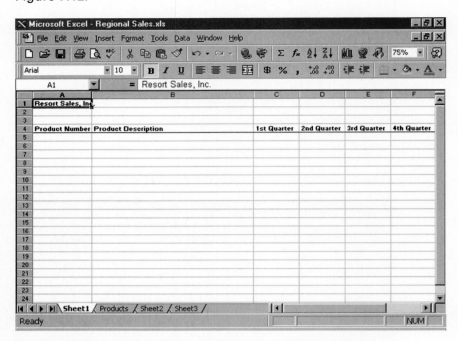

Figure 7.12 New worksheet inserted into the existing workbook

TASK 7: INSERT THREE MORE WORKSHEETS BASED ON THE TEMPLATE AND RENAME ALL FOUR WORKSHEETS BY REGION

1   Place the insertion point over the **Products** worksheet tab and click the right mouse button.

2   Repeat the steps of Task 6 three times to add three additional worksheets based upon the *Regional Sales.xlt* template into the *Regional Sales* workbook. At the bottom of the new worksheets Sheet1 will be the highlighted worksheet tab, as shown in Figure 7.13.

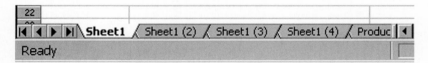

Figure 7.13

3   Double-click the Sheet1 tab with the left mouse button to select it, as shown in Figure 7.14.

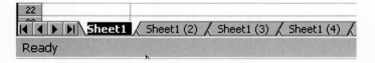

Figure 7.14

4   Type **North** as the name of the sheet. The tab will now look like Figure 7.15.

Figure 7.15 Worksheet tab displaying new name

5   Repeat the procedure outlined in Steps 1 to 4 to name the next three sheets **South**, **East**, and **West**, respectively.

6   Delete the worksheets named Sheet2 and Sheet3. Your workbook should now look like Figure 7.16.

7   Save the changes to your workbook.

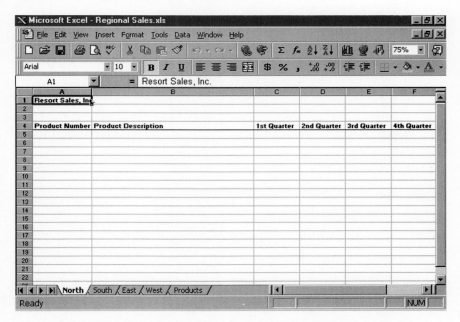

Figure 7.16 The Regional Sales workbook with five named worksheets

Creating the Sales Summary Worksheet

The structure for the *Regional Sales* workbook is almost complete. You still need to construct a fifth and final worksheet—the **Sales Summary** worksheet. You will now add that fifth worksheet to the workbook, name it, and enter the appropriate text constants. After you construct the summary worksheet, you can link the product data from the lookup sheet to it.

TASK 8: CREATE A SALES SUMMARY WORKSHEET

1   Click the **North** worksheet tab to make it the active sheet.

2   Select Worksheet from the Insert menu, as shown in Figure 7.17.

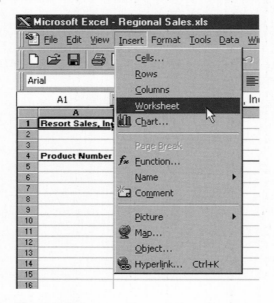

Figure 7.17

3   Name the worksheet **Sales Summary.**

4   Type **World Sales, Inc.** in cell A1.

5   Type **Sales Summary (By Region)** in cell A2.

6   Type **Product Number** in cell A4, and change the column width of column A to 16.00.

7   Type **Product Description** in cell B4, and change the column width to 45.00.

8   Type **North**, **South**, **East**, **West** in cells C4, D4, E4, and F4, respectively.

9   Type **Total Sales** in cell G4.

10   Select columns C through G and change the column width to 12.00, as shown in Figure 7.18.

Figure 7.18

11 Highlight row 4 by clicking the row number. When the row is selected, your worksheet will look like Figure 7.19. Change the font style to bold.

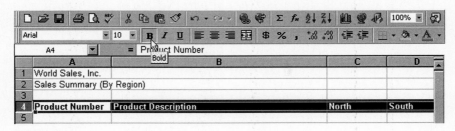

Figure 7.19

12 Change the alignment of the range C4:F4 to center aligned by selecting the center align button, as demonstrated in Figure 7.20.

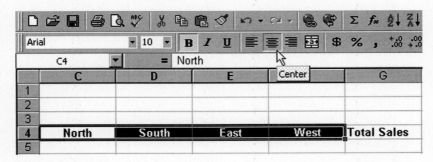

Figure 7.20

13 Select the range A4:G4, and add a border to the bottom of the selection using the Borders drop-down list. The button for adding a border below the cell is shown in Figure 7.21.

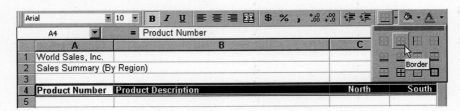

Figure 7.21

14 Change the font style of the range A1:A2 to bold.

15 Save the changes to your workbook.

Adding Linking Formulas to Display the Product Information in the Sales Summary Worksheet

To complete your **Sales Summary** worksheet, you need to insert in it the product numbers and descriptions from the **Products** worksheet. Excel enables you to do this very easily by using linking formulas. A *linking formula* is a formula that references information in another worksheet or workbook. Recall that linking formulas eliminate redundant effort and make updating information in Excel easy and accurate. Each location containing a link to the original data, which is kept in one place, is automatically updated when the original data is changed.

TASK 9: ENTER LINKING FORMULAS TO DISPLAY THE LIST OF PRODUCTS IN THE SALES SUMMARY WORKSHEET

1   Click the **Products** worksheet tab to select it as the active worksheet.

2   Select the range A2:B16 and select Copy from the Edit menu, as shown in Figure 7.22.

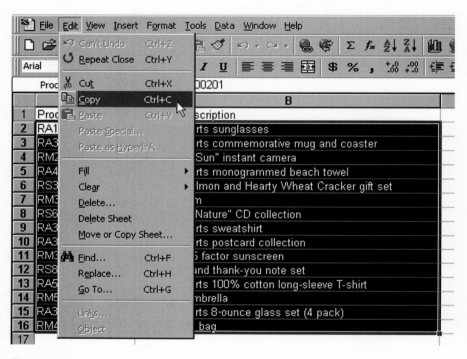

Figure 7.22

3   Select the **Sales Summary** worksheet tab.

4   Place the insertion point in cell A5 and select Paste Special from the Edit menu.

Tip To establish a dynamic link, select Paste Special, as shown in Figure 7.23.

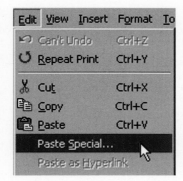

Figure 7.23

5   Select the Paste Link button in the lower right corner of the Paste Special dialog box, as shown in Figure 7.24.

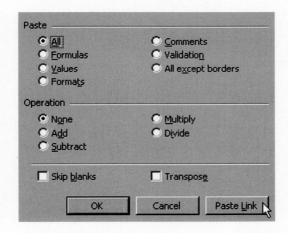

Figure 7.24 Establishing a link by selecting Paste Link

6 The information will appear in the range A5:B19 of the **Sales Summary** worksheet, as shown in Figure 7.25.

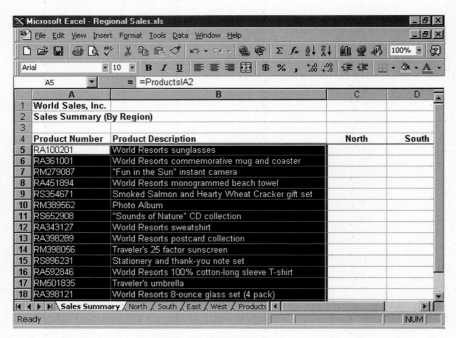

Figure 7.25 Worksheet containing linking formulas

7 Notice the formula, =Products!A2, displayed in the Formula bar. It references cell A2 of the **Products** worksheet, as indicated by the name of the worksheet and exclamation character before the cell address.

> **Troubleshooting** If your formula does not look like the one shown in Figure 7.25, click the Undo button, and select Paste Special again from the Edit menu. Be sure to select the Paste Link button in the Paste Special dialog box to establish a dynamic link.

The Conclusion

You have now created the structure of a three-dimensional workbook that is ready to accept numeric data. You will be able to create the nationwide resort gift shop sales report the management of World Sales, Inc. needs in order to decide whether to launch a resort gift catalog sales business. Save all changes to your workbook and exit Microsoft Excel if you have finished working.

Summary and Exercises

Summary

- You can design an efficient "three-dimensional" electronic workbook by using the seven-step process outlined in this project.
- Excel worksheets can easily reference data, such as a list of products, maintained in a lookup table.
- Once you name a range of data, you can select it or reference it by means of a linking formula in Excel.
- You can save a worksheet that you format with specific settings as a template, which is a pattern for producing similar worksheets without further formatting.
- An Excel template can be used to add identically formatted worksheets to an existing workbook.
- The worksheet tabs in a workbook (Sheet1, Sheet2, etc.) can be renamed for easy reference.
- A summary worksheet, such as a Sales Summary worksheet, can include linking formulas to link dynamically to data in other worksheets.

Key Terms and Operations

Key Terms	Operations
Data integrity	List data in a lookup table
Linking formula	Construct a template
Lookup table	Establish linking formulas
Numeric constant	Delete worksheets
Redundant data	Insert worksheets based on a template
Template	Rename worksheet tabs
Text constants	
Three-dimensional workbook	

Study Questions

Multiple Choice

1. Which step in constructing an electronic worksheet defines the worksheet structure?
   a. Creating formulas
   b. Typing numeric constants
   c. Typing text constants
   d. Creating graphs and charts
   e. Checking formulas

2. Which step in constructing an electronic worksheet is essential for maintaining data integrity?
   a. Typing formulas
   b. Typing numeric constants
   c. Typing text constants
   d. Creating graphs and charts
   e. Checking formulas

3. Which of the following will minimize data redundancy?
   a. Creating a document template
   b. Using linking formulas
   c. Applying a document template
   d. Using Paste Special/Paste link
   e. b and d.

4. Which statement is false?
   a. An Excel workbook contains multiple worksheets.
   b. Multiple workbooks can be open at the same time.
   c. Multiple worksheets can be selected simultaneously.
   d. An Excel workbook is the same thing as an Excel worksheet.
   e. An Excel workbook must contain at least one worksheet.

5. Which of the following does not minimize data redundancy?
   a. Naming a range of data.
   b. Using Copy and Paste Special to copy data from one worksheet to another.
   c. Using OLE.
   d. Using a lookup table.
   e. Using linking formulas.

6. Which of the following statements is true?
   a. Once a worksheet has been named, it cannot be renamed.
   b. Worksheets cannot be added to a workbook.
   c. Once a worksheet has been deleted, it cannot be restored using Undo.
   d. Workbooks cannot be deleted.
   e. Once a template is created, it cannot be deleted.

7. Which statement is true concerning the formula =Sheet2!A7?
   a. The cell reference will not be changed when the formula is copied.
   b. The cell reference is absolute.
   c. The cell reference refers to a named range.
   d. The formula contains a mixed reference.
   e. The formula contains a link to another worksheet.

8. How does an Excel template differ from Excel workbooks?
   a. A template is named differently.
   b. A template is usually stored in the Templates folder.
   c. A template file will be visible in the New dialog box when New is selected from the File menu.
   d. None of the above is true.
   e. All are true.

9. Which of the following statements concerning data integrity is true?
   a. Data integrity is not an issue when developing electronic workbooks.
   b. Excel's auditing features are necessary and sufficient for ensuring data integrity.
   c. Data integrity is generally increased when linking formulas are used.
   d. Data integrity is generally decreased when linking formulas are used.
   e. Using lookup tables generally decreases data integrity.

10. To rename a worksheet tab, you:
    a. Double-click the tab and enter a new name.
    b. Highlight a tab and select Save As from the File menu.
    c. Place the insertion point over the tab, click the right mouse button, and select Rename.
    d. Highlight the tab and select Name from the Insert menu.
    e. a and c.

Short Answer

1. What is a text constant? What role do text constants play in the design of workbooks?

2. How do you add a new worksheet based on a template to an Excel workbook?

3. How do you create a linking formula?

4. How might using a lookup table reduce redundant data in a workbook?

5. How are worksheet tabs renamed?

6. What is a named range? How do range names simplify the construction of formulas?

7. How does data redundancy jeopardize data integrity?

8. A formula appears as =Products!B17. What kind of formula is this?

9. Can a linking formula on two different worksheets reference the same cell on one worksheet? Explain your answer.

10. What are the seven steps for creating a workbook?

For Discussion

1. What is data integrity? How can it be maintained in three-dimensional workbooks?

2. What is data redundancy? What are some of the problems redundant data creates in three-dimensional workbooks?

3. What is a template? How might applying a template assist in building workbooks containing multiple worksheets?

4. What is a linking formula? How do linking formulas minimize redundant data?

Review Exercises

1. Creating a Product Summary Report

Figure 7.26 displays a worksheet that is a product summary report listing the product numbers and descriptions for three hardware and three software products.

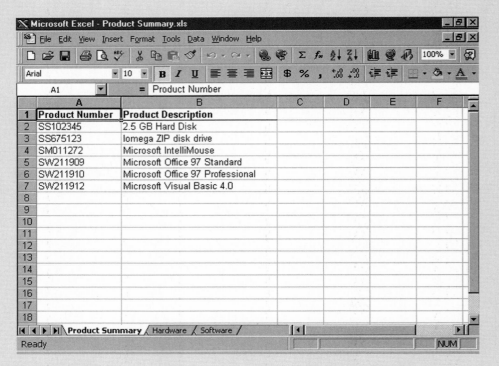

Figure 7.26

Create an Excel workbook named Product Summary that displays the information shown. Do the following to create the workbook:

1. Name the three worksheet tabs in a new Excel workbook **Product Summary**, **Hardware**, and **Software**.

2. For all three worksheets, set the width of column A to 16.00 and the width of column B to 30.00.

3. Type the column heading **Product Number** in cell A1 of all three worksheets, and the column heading **Product Description** in cell B1 of the worksheets.

4. In the **Hardware** worksheet, type the data displayed in the range A2:B4 in the range A2:B4.

5. In the **Software** worksheet, type the data displayed in the range A5:B7 of the **Product Summary** worksheet in the range A2:B4.

6. Create linking formulas to display the hardware and software data in the **Product Summary** worksheet.

2. Creating a Profit and Loss Worksheet

Create the template shown in Figure 7.27.

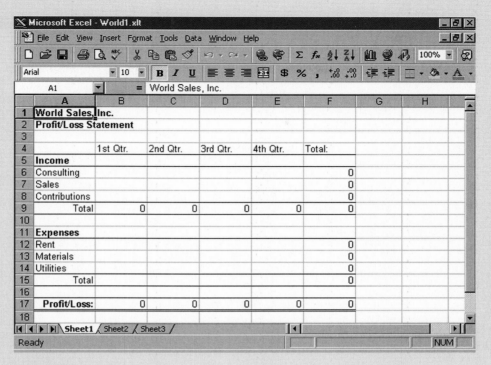

Figure 7.27

Enter text constants and formulas as follows:

1. Type the text constants shown in the figure.

2. Type **=sum(B6:E6)** as the formula in cell F6.

3. Copy the formula to the range F7:F9 and F12:F15.

4. Type **=sum(B6:B8)** as the formula in cell B9.

5. Copy the formula to range C9:E9 and B15:E15.

6. Type **=bB9-B15** as the formula in cell B17.

7. Copy the formula to the range C17:E17.

8. Save the template as *World1*.

Assignments

1. Adding Numeric Constants to a Profit and Loss Statement
Open a new Excel workbook. Insert a worksheet based upon the *World1* template. Type the numeric constants shown in Figure 7.28 in the worksheet. Apply a currency format to all values. Save the workbook as *World2*.

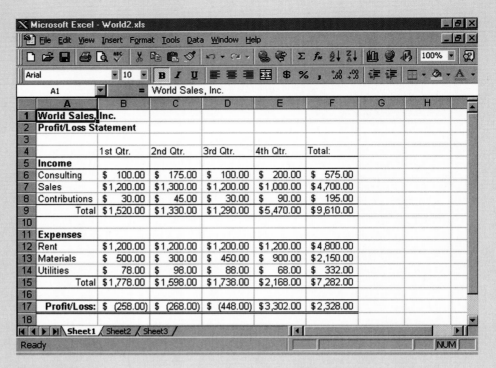

Figure 7.28

2. Visiting Microsoft's Web Site

Visit Microsoft's Web site (http://www.microsoft.com). Search for information on workbook templates. Download the *Business Planner* template, which can be found at (http://www.microsoft.com/excel/freestuff/templates/villagesoftware/ default.htm). Create a folder named Templates on your floppy diskette, and install the template files in this folder. Open the template and enter data in the **Data** worksheet. Save the file as *Planner.xls*.

Completing a Three-Dimensional Workbook Using Logical and Lookup Functions

In this project you will enter data in the *Regional Sales* workbook whose skeleton you constructed in Project 7. After typing in sales data for each region, you will use Excel's logical and lookup functions to display the data where it is needed. Finally, you will use Excel's sorting and summing functions to produce a **Sales Summary** worksheet for useful analysis.

Objectives

After completing this project, you will be able to:

➤ **Establish a link between the Products worksheet and each of the four regional sales worksheets**

➤ **Enter numeric constants into the four regional sales worksheets**

➤ **Construct formulas in the regional worksheets containing Excel's lookup function**

➤ **Insert names for three additional data ranges**

➤ **Sort the named ranges to display data in a specified order**

➤ **Construct formulas in the Sales Summary worksheet using the VLOOKUP function**

➤ **Use the SUM function to total the sales figures returned by the VLOOKUP function**

➤ **Specify conditions and returning values using a Nested IF function**

Introduction

Each Resort Sales, Inc. gift shop owned by World Sales, Inc., sells the same products. The sixth worksheet of the *Regional Sales* workbook you designed in Project 6 is a list of the product numbers and descriptions. It serves as a lookup table (Figure 8.1) from which formulas in the other worksheets replicate and update information by means of Excel's ***VLOOKUP function***.

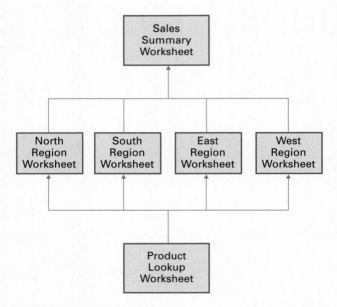

Figure 8.1 A Lookup Table

To use the lookup feature, you will need to construct simple formulas containing Excel's VLOOKUP function in the regional sales worksheets. The formulas instruct Excel to look up a specified value in a data array and return a corresponding value. In your Regional Sales workbook, the lookup function will search the product list for a specific product number and return the corresponding product description. Excel will sort the sales figures in each regional sheet in descending order by units sold.

The **Sales Summary** worksheet will also use the VLOOKUP function. This sheet shows not only which regions were most profitable but also which products were the biggest sellers in each region. To do the latter, the VLOOKUP function searches for each specific product, and returns the sales figure for that product.

The lookup feature is a convenient and efficient tool for completing your Excel workbook accurately without redundant data or effort.

The Challenge

The regional sales data requested by the executives of the World Sales corporation must be designed to produce four specific outputs:

1. A list, for each region, of sales data sorted in descending order by quantity of each item sold

2. A list, in the Sales Summary worksheet, of each region's top ten best-selling products

3. Formulas that total the sales data by item in the Sales Summary worksheet

4. A list showing the region with the highest sales amount for each product

The Solution

To minimize redundant data, you will use the VLOOKUP function to fill in product descriptions for each item in each regional sales worksheet. Then, you will use Excel's sorting feature to present the annual regional sales data in descending order by quantity. The next task is to create formulas in the **Sales Summary** worksheet to list the top ten best-selling items for each region. You will also need to create formulas containing both an IF function and the VLOOKUP function to return the total units sold for each region. Finally, you will use a Nested IF function in column H to determine which sales regions sold the most of each product. Your completed Sales Summary Worksheet will look like Figure 8.2.

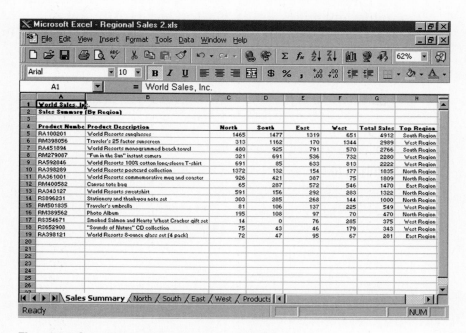

Figure 8.2 Completed Sales Summary Worksheet

The Setup

To complete the three-dimensional workbook, start Microsoft Excel, open the *Regional Sales* workbook, and select the settings shown in Table 8.1.

Table 8.1   Excel Settings

Element	Settings
Office Assistant	Close the Office Assistant
View, Toolbars	Display the Standard and Formatting toolbars
View, Formula bar	Display the Formula bar
View, Status bar	Display the Status bar
Maximize	Maximize the Application and Workbook windows
Zoom	Use the Zoom control to set the zoom of the first five worksheets to 75%
File, Save As	Save the workbook as *Regional Sales 2*

Recording Regional Sales Data

The workbook you constructed in Project 6 contains only text constants and formulas. To specify the sales data for each sales region you will type two kinds of information into each worksheet: the product numbers and product quantities for each sales quarter. The formulas you created in Project 6 will automatically display the total sales of each item for each region.

TASK 1: ESTABLISH A LINK BETWEEN THE PRODUCTS WORKSHEET AND EACH OF THE FOUR REGIONAL SALES WORKSHEETS

1. Select the **Products** worksheet tab.

2. Highlight the range A2:A16, and choose Copy.

3. Select the **North** worksheet tab, place the insertion point in cell A5, and select Paste Special from the Edit menu.

4 Select the Paste Link button in the Paste Special dialog box, as shown in Figure 8.3.

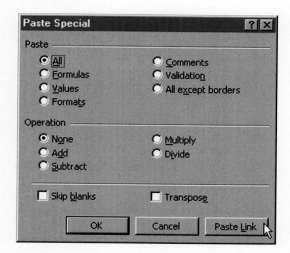

Figure 8.3

> **Hint** Notice the exclamation point that follows the reference to the source worksheet in the linking formula that is used to display the product number in the North worksheet. The exclamation point tells you that a linking formula has been created in Excel.

5 Select the **South** worksheet tab.

6 Place the insertion point in cell A5, choose Paste Special from the Edit menu, and select the Paste Link button.

7 Repeat this procedure for the **East** and **West** region worksheets. When you are finished, the product numbers from the **Products** worksheet will be displayed in the four regional sales worksheets.

TASK 2: TYPE NUMERIC CONSTANTS IN THE FOUR REGIONAL SALES WORKSHEETS

1 Select the **North** worksheet.

2 Type the data shown in Figure 8.4 in columns C through F of the **North** worksheet on your screen.

	Product Number	Product Description	1st Quarter	2nd Quarter	3rd Quarter	4th Quarter
5	RA100201		147	376	654	288
6	RA361001		392	123	121	290
7	RM279087		82	34	107	98
8	RA451894		0	45	423	12
9	RS354671		0	0	0	14
10	RM389562		45	67	34	49
11	RS652908		14	18	22	21
12	RA343127		136	145	89	221
13	RA398289		278	344	403	347
14	RM398056		6	76	169	62
15	RS896231		74	76	72	81
16	RA592846		46	132	311	202
17	RM501835		11	33	32	5
18	RA398121		7	17	34	14
19	RM400582		13	12	36	4
20						
21						
22						

North / South / East / West / Products /

Figure 8.4 North Sales Region Numeric Constants

3 Select the **South** worksheet.

4 Type the data shown in Figure 8.5 into columns C through F of the **South** worksheet.

	Product Number	Product Description	1st Quarter	2nd Quarter	3rd Quarter	4th Quarter
5	RA100201		188	421	567	301
6	RA361001		87	89	103	142
7	RM279087		184	179	162	166
8	RA451894		324	207	196	198
9	RS354671		0	0	0	0
10	RM389562		21	18	37	32
11	RS652908		7	6	18	12
12	RA343127		54	31	23	48
13	RA398289		33	41	28	30
14	RM398056		277	256	328	301
15	RS896231		78	56	87	64
16	RA592846		21	18	17	29
17	RM501835		31	13	25	37
18	RA398121		6	12	18	11
19	RM400582		64	77	79	67
20						
21						
22						

North \ **South** / East / West / Products /

Figure 8.5 South Sales Region Numeric Constants

5 Select the **East** worksheet.

6 Type the data shown in Figure 8.6 in columns C through F of the **East** worksheet.

	Product Number	Product Description	1st Quarter	2nd Quarter	3rd Quarter	4th Quarter	
3							
4	Product Number	Product Description	1st Quarter	2nd Quarter	3rd Quarter	4th Quarter	
5	RA100201		178	412	453	276	
6	RA361001		78	76	98	135	
7	RM279087		143	121	160	112	
8	RA451894		307	155	186	143	
9	RS354671		12	14	16	34	
10	RM389562		18	27	31	21	
11	RS652908		12	11	14	9	
12	RA343127		67	45	102	78	
13	RA398289		34	47	31	42	
14	RM398056		18	21	79	52	
15	RS896231		77	54	79	58	
16	RA592846		193	121	118	201	
17	RM501835		34	46	45	12	
18	RA398121		18	17	23	37	
19	RM400582		98	121	200	153	
20							
21							
22							

◄ ◄ ► ►◄ / North / South / **East** / West / Products /

Figure 8.6 East Sales Region Numeric Constants

7 Select the **West** worksheet.

8 Enter the data shown in Figure 8.7 into columns C through F of the **West** worksheet.

	Product Number	Product Description	1st Quarter	2nd Quarter	3rd Quarter	4th Quarter	
3							
4	Product Number	Product Description	1st Quarter	2nd Quarter	3rd Quarter	4th Quarter	
5	RA100201		119	121	234	177	
6	RA361001		28	17	12	18	
7	RM279087		118	207	298	109	
8	RA451894		211	134	118	107	
9	RS354671		67	66	34	118	
10	RM389562		13	12	32	13	
11	RS652908		34	42	44	59	
12	RA343127		33	67	56	127	
13	RA398289		32	41	48	56	
14	RM398056		311	354	467	212	
15	RS896231		43	34	29	38	
16	RA592846		207	201	188	217	
17	RM501835		67	78	35	45	
18	RA398121		12	15	19	21	
19	RM400582		107	118	167	154	
20							
21							
22							

◄ ◄ ► ►◄ / North / South / East / **West** / Products /

Figure 8.7 West Sales Region Numeric Constants

Constructing Formulas in the Regional Worksheets Using the Lookup Function

To complete the regional sales worksheets, you will need to display a description of each item beside the product numbers and units sold. When you need to find values in a list, you can use one of Excel's lookup functions. A *lookup function* checks for a specified value in one cell of a data array, and returns a corresponding value in a related cell. A *data array* is simply a range of cells.

Since the data in each region's worksheet will be sorted, a lookup function is the best method for returning each item's description.

Excel's VLOOKUP function searches for a value in a source—in the leftmost column of a lookup table—and then returns a value to a destination—the same row in a column you have specified in the table. The place in a formula where you specify the source and destination and other *parameters* is called the *argument* of the function. The argument for the VLOOKUP function has four parameters: the value to be looked up, the range in which to look up the value, the column in the data table from which to return a corresponding row value, and a logical value specifying whether an exact or approximate match should be returned. A logical value of FALSE returns an exact match; a logical value of TRUE returns the closest match.

TASK 3: CONSTRUCT FORMULAS USING THE LOOKUP FUNCTION

1 Select the **North** worksheet, and place the insertion point in cell B5.

2 Type **=VLOOKUP(5,Products,2,FALSE)** as a formula. This formula tells Excel to search for the value found in cell A5 of the current sheet in the Products data range, and if an exact match is found, return the corresponding value in the second column of the Products data range.

[handwritten note: Should be = Vlookup (A5, same, 2, same)]

> **Tip** Naming the range A2:B16 in the **Products** worksheet allows you to refer to the range by name when constructing a formula. Had the range not been named, the VLOOKUP function would require an absolute reference to the range $A$2:$B$16 in the **Products** worksheet.

Your screen should now look like Figure 8.8.

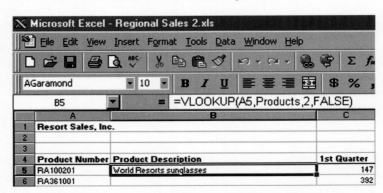

Figure 8.8 Formula Containing the VLOOKUP Function

Reminder Formulas are not case specific when entered using the keyboard.

3   Using AutoFill, copy the formula through cell B19. The values shown in Figure 8.9 should be returned from the Products Lookup table.

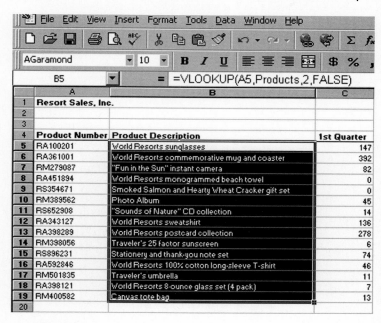

	File Edit View Insert Format Tools Data Window Help	
AGaramond	10	B I U $ %
B5	= =VLOOKUP(A5,Products,2,FALSE)	

	A	B	C
1	Resort Sales, Inc.		
2			
3			
4	Product Number	Product Description	1st Quarter
5	RA100201	World Resorts sunglasses	147
6	RA361001	World Resorts commemorative mug and coaster	392
7	RM279087	"Fun in the Sun" instant camera	82
8	RA451894	World Resorts monogrammed beach towel	0
9	RS354671	Smoked Salmon and Hearty Wheat Cracker gift set	0
10	RM389562	Photo Album	45
11	RS652908	"Sounds of Nature" CD collection	14
12	RA343127	World Resorts sweatshirt	136
13	RA398289	World Resorts postcard collection	278
14	RM398056	Traveler's 25 factor sunscreen	6
15	RS896231	Stationery and thank-you note set	74
16	RA592846	World Resorts 100% cotton long-sleeve T-shirt	46
17	RM501835	Traveler's umbrella	11
18	RA398121	World Resorts 8-ounce glass set (4 pack)	7
19	RM400582	Canvas tote bag	13
20			

Figure 8.9

4   Select cell B5 again, and choose Copy .

5   Select the **South** worksheet tab. Place the insertion point in cell B5 and choose Paste .

6   Use AutoFill to copy the formula through row 19.

7   Repeat the procedure to paste the formula in cell B5 of the **East** and **West** worksheets, using AutoFill to copy the formula through row 19 on both sheets.

8   Save your workbook.

Inserting Names for Three Additional Data Ranges

The **Sales Summary** worksheet will contain lookup formulas to display the annual sales data from each regional worksheet. These formulas will refer to a product number in column A of the **Sales Summary** worksheet, then look up the same product number in column A of each regional worksheet, and return the value in row G, if the lookup condition is met. These formulas will be easier to construct if you give the range A5:G19 of each regional worksheet a name. The purpose of a range name is twofold: it allows you to select the range easily using the Name box and to use the range name in a formula instead of a range reference.

TASK 4: INSERT NAMES FOR THREE ADDITIONAL DATA RANGES

1 Select the **North** worksheet.

2 Highlight the A5:G19, and type **NorthSales** in the Name box, as shown in Figure 8.10.

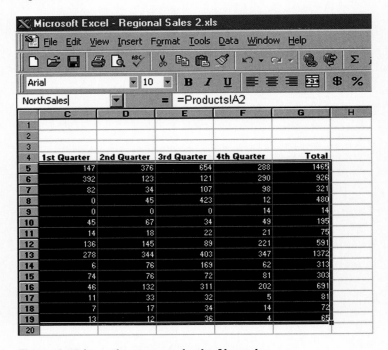

Figure 8.10 Inserting a name in the Name box

3 Press ⒺⓃⓉⒺⓇ.

4 Repeat the procedure to name the range A5:G19 in the **South**, **East**, and **West** worksheets, naming the ranges SouthSales, EastSales, and WestSales, respectively.

5   Choose Name from the Insert menu, and choose Define, as shown in Figure 8.11.

Figure 8.11

6   Select the EastSales name in the Define Name dialog, as shown in Figure 8.12. Note the reference in the Refers to: textbox. Using this dialog box, you can check the range of cells each name references.

> **Tip** If you need to edit or delete a named range, choose Name from the Insert menu.

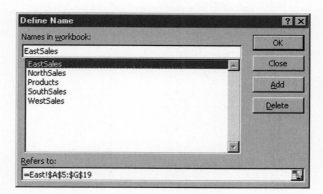

Figure 8.12

7   Save your workbook.

Sorting Data Ranges

The data listed in the **Regional Sales** workbook needs to be sorted by units sold. The sorted data will be easier for the World Sales, Inc. executives analyzing your Sales Summary to interpret than unsorted data would be. When using a sorting function, you must specify whether you want the data rearranged in ascending or descending order.

TASK 5: SORT THE NAMED RANGES TO DISPLAY DATA IN A SPECIFIED ORDER

1 Select the **North** worksheet.

2 Select the NorthSales data range in the Name box, as shown in Figure 8.13.

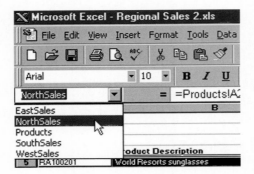

Figure 8.13 Using the Name Box to Select a Data Range

3 Choose Sort from the Data menu.

4 In the Sort by list of the Sort dialog box, select Total, and click the option button to sort the range in descending order, as shown in Figure 8.14.

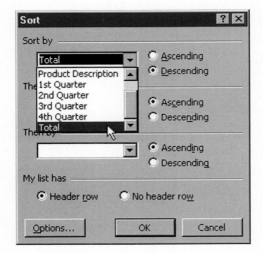

Figure 8.14

5 Select OK.

6 Repeat the procedure above to sort the sales data ranges in the remaining regional worksheets in descending order by the values in the Total column.

7 Save the changes to your workbook.

Constructing Formulas in the Sales Summary Worksheet Using the VLOOKUP Function

The **Sales Summary** worksheet is structured so as to display annual sales figures for each sales region. Rather than typing the annual sales figures in the columns, you can construct formulas that refer to the existing data. Since the data is ordered differently on each regional worksheet, you will need to use Excel's VLOOKUP function rather than a dynamic link. The function searches a data array and returns a corresponding value, regardless of where it appears in lookup range.

TASK 6: CONSTRUCT FORMULAS IN THE SALES SUMMARY WORKSHEET USING THE VLOOKUP FUNCTION

1 Select the **Sales Summary** worksheet.

2 Place the insertion point in cell C5.

3 Type **=VLOOKUP(A5,NorthSales,7,FALSE)** as the formula in this cell, and press (ENTER).
The function will return in cell C5 of the **Sales Summary** worksheet the results of the SUM function in cell G5 of the **North** worksheet, as shown in Figure 8.15.

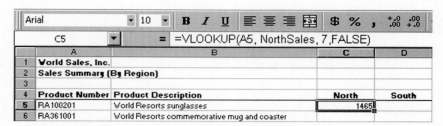

Figure 8.15

4 Place the insertion point in cell D5.

5 Type **=VLOOKUP(A5,SouthSales,7,FALSE)** and press (ENTER).

6 Place the insertion point in cell E5.

7 Type **=VLOOKUP(A5,EastSales,7,FALSE)** and press (ENTER).

8 Place the insertion point in cell F5.

9 Type **=VLOOKUP(A5,WestSales,7,FALSE)** and press (ENTER). Your worksheet will now look like Figure 8.16.

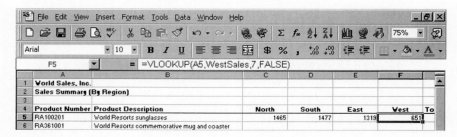

Figure 8.16

10 Highlight the range C5:F5 and use AutoFill to copy the formulas through row 19, as shown in Figure 8.17.

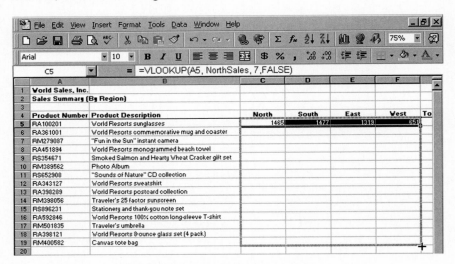

Figure 8.17 Copying Formulas Using AutoFill

Using the SUM Function to Total the Sales Figures Returned by the VLOOKUP Function

To determine your corporation's top ten best-selling items, you will need to create a formula containing the SUM function in rows 5 to 19 of column G of the **Sales Summary** worksheet to find the total for each product.

TASK 7: ENTER FORMULAS TO TOTAL THE SALES DATA AND SORT THE SALES FIGURES BY TOTAL

1 Place the insertion point in cell G5 of the **Sales Summary** worksheet.

2 Select the AutoSum tool on the Standard toolbar.

3 Select the Enter button on the Formula bar, as shown in Figure 8.18.

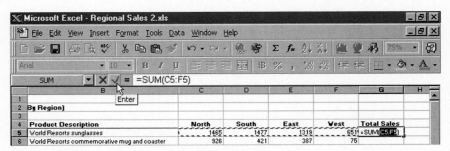

Figure 8.18 Creating a Formula Using the AutoSum Tool

4 Using AutoFill, copy the formula through cell **G19**.

5 Select the range A5:G19.

6 Select Sort from the Data menu, and sort by Total Sales in descending order.

7 Save your worksheet.

Using the IF Function to Determine the Sales Region with the Greatest Number of Sales for Each Product

To complete the *Regional Sales* workbook, you will enter formulas in cells H5:H19 to return a text string listing the sales region with the greatest number of sales for each product. Excel's **IF function** is used to test for a condition, where one value is returned if the logical test is true, and an alternate value is returned if the test is false. The general syntax of the function is:

IF(logical_test,value_if_true,value_if_false)

> **Tip** The IF function can return numeric constants or text strings.

You will need to include three logical tests in the IF function. This is so because for any given product, any one of the sales regions—North, South, East, or West—could have the highest number of sales.

To demonstrate the use of the IF function, consider the following formula:

=IF(C5>100,"Greater","Less")

The logical test is C5>100. The value to be returned if the test evaluates to true is the text string "Greater". If the test evaluates to false, the text string "Less" is returned. The test will evaluate to true or false depending upon the value found in cell C5.

To include more than one test in an IF function, you "nest" one test within another within the IF function. A **Nested IF function** is a function containing more than one logical test. The value returned if the first test is false depends upon the results of the second test, and so on.

TASK 8: SPECIFY CONDITIONS AND RETURNING VALUES USING A NESTED IF FUNCTION

1 Select the **Sales Summary** worksheet, if it is not currently the active sheet.

2 Place the insertion point in cell H5.

3 Type the following formula:

=IF(C5=MAX(C5:F5),"North Region",IF(D5=MAX(C5:F5),"South Region",IF(E5=MAX(C5:F5),"East Region","West Region")))

Press (ENTER).

Troubleshooting If you receive an error message while entering this formula, make sure to retype the formula exactly as shown here.

The condition tested by this function is whether the value in a specific cell is the greatest value in a range of values. The MAX function returns the greatest value in the range of cells. If the test condition for cell C5 returns the greatest value, a text string for the North is returned. If not, the next logical test is performed, returning the appropriate text string. If none of the three nested conditions evaluate to true, the greatest value must be for the West region. The results of the formula for cell H5 are displayed in Figure 8.19.

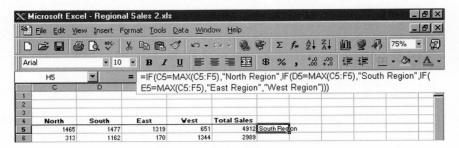

Figure 8.19 The results returned by a Nested IF function

4   Using AutoFill, copy the formula in cell H5 down the worksheet through cell H19. The results returned by each formula are displayed in Figure 8.20.

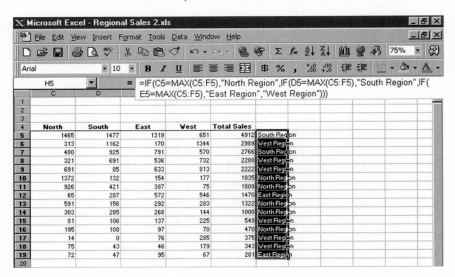

Figure 8.20

5   Type **Top Region** in cell H4.

6   Use the format painter to copy the format from cell G4 to cell H4.

7   Change the width of column H to 14.00 and the alignment of the entire column to right aligned.

8   Save your workbook.

The Conclusion

Your *Regional Sales* workbook is now complete! The workbook contains a minimal amount of redundant data, and by naming data ranges, sorting these ranges, and using the VLOOKUP function, you were able to display regional sales data in the **Sales Summary** worksheet. By using a nested IF function, you were able to create a list of sales regions selling the greatest amount of each product.

Summary and Exercises

Summary

- Data can be shared among worksheets by establishing links.
- Numeric constants are the data upon which calculations are performed.
- A Lookup table contains an array of data.
- Excel's Lookup functions are used to return data from a lookup table anywhere within a workbook.
- The VLOOKUP function returns data matching a specified value from a column corresponding to the data that is looked up.
- A Name can be given to a range of cells.
- Range names can be used in formulas instead of a reference to the range.
- Data appearing in a range can be sorted by multiple criteria.
- The SUM function can be used to perform calculations upon data returned by a Lookup function.
- An IF function returns one value if a specified condition is true and an alternate value if the condition is false.
- A Nested IF function can be used to test for more than two conditions.

Key Terms and Operations

Key Terms	Operations
Argument	Create linking formulas
Data array	Enter numeric constants
IF function	Construct formulas containing the VLOOKUP function
Lookup function	Name three data ranges
Nested IF function	Check the names and references of the named ranges in a
Parameter	worksheet
VLOOKUP function	Sort a range of data by a specified column
	Construct formulas with the VLOOKUP function and named worksheet ranges
	Construct formulas using a nested IF function

Study Questions

Multiple Choice

1. Which type of function returns a value associated with a particular cell?
   a. Logical
   b. Statistical
   c. Financial
   d. String
   e. Lookup

2. Which of the following functions tests a logical condition?
   a. VLOOKUP
   b. IF
   c. SUM
   d. MIN
   e. MAX

3. Which Excel feature reorders a data range according to a specified criterion?
- **a.** Range
- **b.** Name
- **c.** IF
- **d.** VLOOKUP
- **e.** Sort

4. The formula =VLOOKUP(A5,Sales,3,TRUE)will return data from which column of a named range?
- **a.** The first
- **b.** The second
- **c.** The third
- **d.** The fourth
- **e.** The fifth

5. The formula =VLOOKUP(A5,Sales,3,TRUE)searches for data from which column of a worksheet?
- **a.** The first
- **b.** The second
- **c.** The third
- **d.** The fourth
- **e.** The fifth

6. If the function =(IF B7>0,"True","False") evaluates to true, which of the following is known to be true?
- **a.** The value in cell A5 is greater than zero.
- **b.** The value in cell B7 is less than zero.
- **c.** The value in cell A5 is less than zero.
- **d.** The value in cell A5 is equal to zero.
- **e.** The value in cell B7 is greater than zero.

7. A worksheet contains sales data as follows: Column A contains product descriptions, column B unit price, column C units sold, column D the extended price, and column E the percent markup. To sort the data range A2:D16 by unit price, you would sort by column:
- **a.** A
- **b.** B
- **c.** C
- **d.** D
- **e.** E

8. A worksheet contains a lookup table with product descriptions starting in column A and product numbers in column B. A VLOOKUP function on a different sheet searches for "CD-ROM drive" in column A of the lookup table. What data is most likely returned?
- **a.** The product's price.
- **b.** The product's markup.
- **c.** The product's description.
- **d.** The current quantity in stock.
- **e.** The product's number.

9. Which function returns the greatest value in a data range?
   a. MIN
   b. IF
   c. VLOOKUP
   d. SUM
   e. MAX

10. What will the function =IF(B5=1.2,4,"False") return if the test evaluates to true?
    a. A numeric value.
    b. A text string.
    c. The value 5.
    d. The word "False"
    e. The value 1.2.

Short Answer

1. What will the function =IF(B7>20000,"Profit","Loss") return if the test evaluates to False?

2. What does the function =VLOOKUP(A7,"Sales",3,"True") search for?

3. What will the function =IF(B7>20000,"Profit","Loss") return if cell B7 contains the value 15000?

4. Where will the function =VLOOKUP(A7,"Sales",3,"True") search for the specified value?

5. What test does the function =IF(B7>20000,"Profit","Loss") conduct?

6. Does the function =VLOOKUP(A7,"Sales",3,"True") return an exact match or does it return an approximate match? Explain.

7. Cell E5 contains the following function:
   =IF(D5>.90,"A",IF(D5>.80,"B",IF(D5>.70,"C",IF(D5>.60,"D","F")))).
   If cell D5 contains .75, what will be displayed in cell E5?

8. What does the function in Question 7 return if all logical tests evaluate to False?

9. How can an IF function be written to return a Null value if the logical test is true?

10. Write a formula for an IF function that returns the value 5 if the test A1=200 evaluates to true, and a null string if the test evaluates to false.

For Discussion

1. How is data integrity maintained by using a Lookup function?

2. Why are named ranges useful when constructing formulas?

3. What is a Nested IF function, and why is it useful?

4. How do the HLOOKUP and VLOOKUP functions differ?

Review Exercises

1. Creating a VLOOKUP function to Display Product Summaries

Open the worksheet named **Product Summary** that you created in Project 6. Make the following changes:

1. Delete the data in the range B2:B7.

2. Construct a formula containing the VLOOKUP function in cell B2 that returns the description from the **Hardware** worksheet matching the product number specified in cell A2.

3. Copy the formula in cell B2 down the worksheet through cell B4.

4. Construct a formula containing the VLOOKUP function in cell B5 that returns the description from the **Software** worksheet matching the product number specified in cell A4.

5. Copy the formula in cell B4 down the worksheet through cell B7.

6. Save the worksheet as **Product Summary 2**. The workbook should look like the one shown in Figure 8.21.

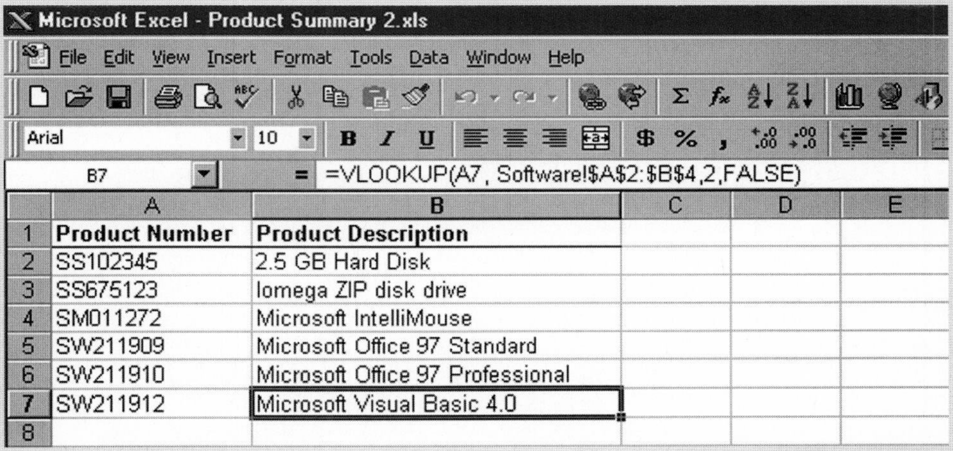

Figure 8.21

2. Entering Numeric Constants and an IF Function into a Worksheet

Create a new workbook based upon the *World1* template you created in Project 6. Complete the worksheet as follows:

1. Enter the numeric constants shown in Figure 8.22 into the range B6:E8. And B12:E14.

2. Type **=if(B17<0,"Loss","Profit")** in cell B18.

3. Using AutoFill, copy the formula across row 18 through column E.

4. Save the workbook as *World2b*.

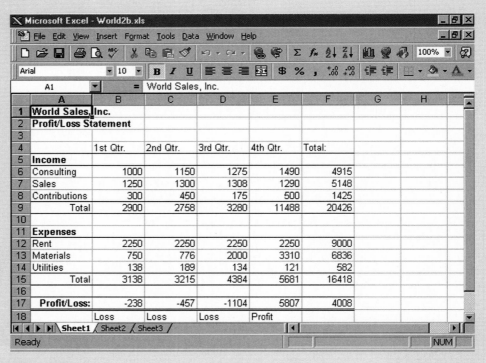

Figure 8.22

Assignments

1. Adding Numeric Constants to a Profit and Loss Statement
Open the *World2* workbook you created in Project 6. Add a formula in cell B18 with an IF function that returns the text string "Loss" if the value in cell B17 is less than zero, returns "No Gain" if the value equals zero, and returns "Profit" if the value exceeds zero. Copy the formula across row 18 through column E. Save the workbook as *World2c*.

2. Online Technical Support for Microsoft Excel
Visit Microsoft's World Wide Web site, and locate the Help area for Microsoft Excel. Search for information about the VLOOKUP function. Construct a simple workbook using the VLOOKUP function that returns an approximate, not an exact value.

Analyzing the Sales Data

Sometimes sales results need to be presented not just in summary but sorted, filtered, or subtotaled from different perspectives. Project 9 shows you two shortcuts for performing such data transformations without repeated effort. They are macros and custom views. If you need to perform data transformations frequently or apply them to additional worksheets, you can store the steps required in a macro, which can be applied at any time. Another way to store repeated actions is called a custom view.

Objectives

After completing this project, you will be able to:

➤ **Create a macro for automating tasks that are repeated often**

➤ **Hide worksheet columns**

➤ **Filter sales data using AutoFilter**

➤ **View the contents of a macro**

➤ **Apply a macro to additional worksheets**

➤ **Add Product Categories to the Sales Summary worksheet**

➤ **Sort the Sales Summary data using multiple criteria**

➤ **Add subtotals to the Sales Summary worksheet**

➤ **Create custom views**

➤ **Show custom views**

The Challenge

The management of World Sales, Inc. appreciates greatly the work you have put into designing an electronic workbook containing the sales figures that they need for making strategic decisions. The **Sales Summary** worksheet gives a good overview of the sales by region, but it does not provide enough detail. To decide whether to start a gift catalog business, the corporation's marketing management also needs a report listing the top sales items by category and subtotals for each category. This report should display only annual totals.

The Solution

To create the regional reports needed by management, you will record a macro—a series of steps that are often repeated to accomplish similar tasks. The macro will contain all the steps you need to transform each regional worksheet, just as the **North** worksheet has been transformed, so it looks like Figure 9.1.

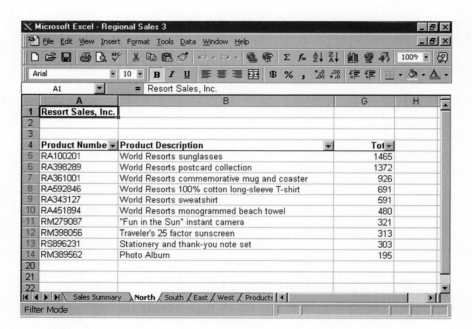

Figure 9.1

Since the format for all the transformed regional worksheets will be the same, the macro you record for the **North** worksheet can be applied to the remaining sheets. Next you will insert a column of data describing each item's general category. You will then sort the **Sales Summary** worksheet using multiple criteria, and add subtotals by item category, as shown in Figure 9.2. You will complete your reports by creating custom views to change the way the data in the entire workbook is displayed.

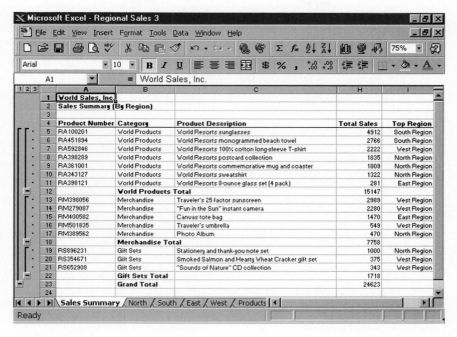

Figure 9.2

The Setup

To compile the necessary reports, start Microsoft Excel, open the *Regional Sales 2* workbook, and select the settings shown in Table 9.1.

Table 9.1 Excel Settings

Element	Settings
Office Assistant	Close the Office Assistant
View, toolbars	Display the Standard and Formatting toolbars
View, Formula bar	Display the Formula bar
View, Status bar	Display the Status bar
Maximize	Maximize the Application and Workbook windows
Zoom	Use the Zoom control to set the zoom of the first five worksheets to 100%
File, Save As	Save the workbook as *Regional Sales 3*

Creating a Macro for Automating Redundant Tasks

When using Excel there are often times when you must complete a series of procedures in several worksheets or workbooks. By recording a macro, you can easily apply this series of procedures again simply by playing the macro. A *macro* is a series of commands and functions for performing a task that are stored in a Visual Basic module and can be run whenever you need to perform the task again. You will create a macro to transform the appearance of the North region worksheet, and then apply this macro to the remaining regional worksheets.

> **Note** This task will include other tasks that are a part of formatting the North region worksheet. An example of the Visual Basic code for the procedures you need to accomplish is shown in Figure 9.14.

TASK 1: RECORDING A MACRO

1. Select the **North** worksheet.

2. Place the cell pointer in the home cell (cell A1).

3. Select Macro from the Tools menu, and select Record New macro, as shown in Figure 9.3.

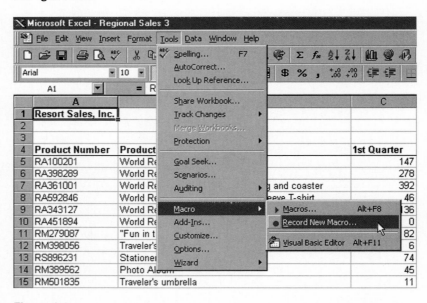

Figure 9.3

4   Type **Format_Regional_Worksheets** as the macro name, and select OK, as shown in Figure 9.4.

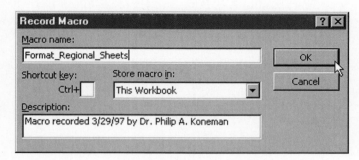

Figure 9.4

> **Tip** Macro names should be descriptive of the tasks they accomplish. Macro names cannot contain spaces, so underscore characters are often used to separate words in a name.

The Stop Recording toolbar will appear on the screen. Each function or procedure you complete will be recorded as a part of the macro. Complete the following tasks, and stop recording the macro as specified below.

Hiding Worksheet Columns

Since you need to display only the annual sales figures on each regional worksheet in the new report, you can use the **_hidden column format_** to hide the contents of certain columns. Task 2 shows how to use this method to prevent the data in columns C through F from being displayed.

TASK 2: TO HIDE WORKSHEET COLUMNS

1   Select columns C through F, and select Column and Hide from the Format menu, as shown in Figure 9.5.

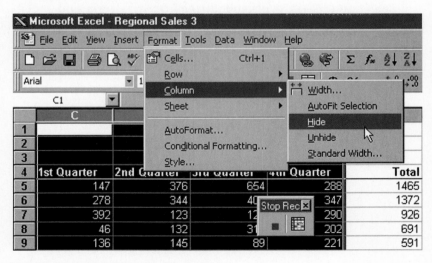

Figure 9.5 Hiding Worksheet Columns

2 Place the insertion point in cell A1.
Your worksheet will now look like Figure 9.6. Notice how the column headings appear; columns A, B, G, and H are visible. Also notice the word "Recording" in the Status bar. This indicates that the macro is still being recorded.

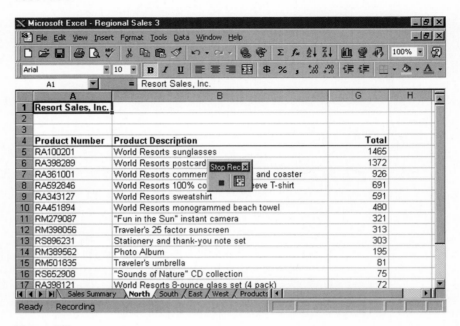

Figure 9.6

Filtering Sales Data Using AutoFilter

The transformed regional sales worksheets should list only the top ten best-selling products. You will reformat the North region worksheet and then record the steps as a macro so the same actions can be repeated automatically for each regional worksheet even though their data vary. To accomplish the task of recording a macro, you will use Microsoft Excel's AutoFilter function. The *AutoFilter* function allows you to automatically select data in the worksheet based upon criteria you specify.

TASK 3: FILTER SALES DATA USING AUTOFILTER

1   Select the range A4:G19, as shown in Figure 9.7.

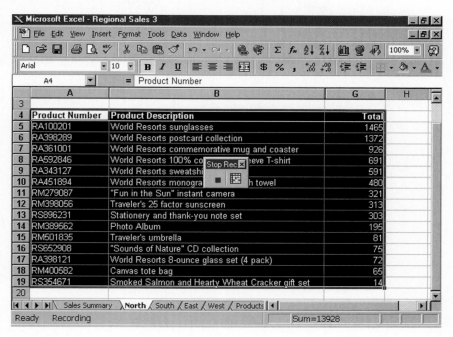

Figure 9.7

2   Select Filter, and then AutoFilter from the Data menu, as shown in Figure 9.8.

Figure 9.8

An AutoFilter will appear in the first row of each column of data in the selection. These arrows allow you to filter the selection by a data item appearing in the column. Excel also includes three preset selection options.

3   Click the AutoFilter arrow in column G.

4 Select the second option in the list (Top 10...), as shown in Figure 9.9

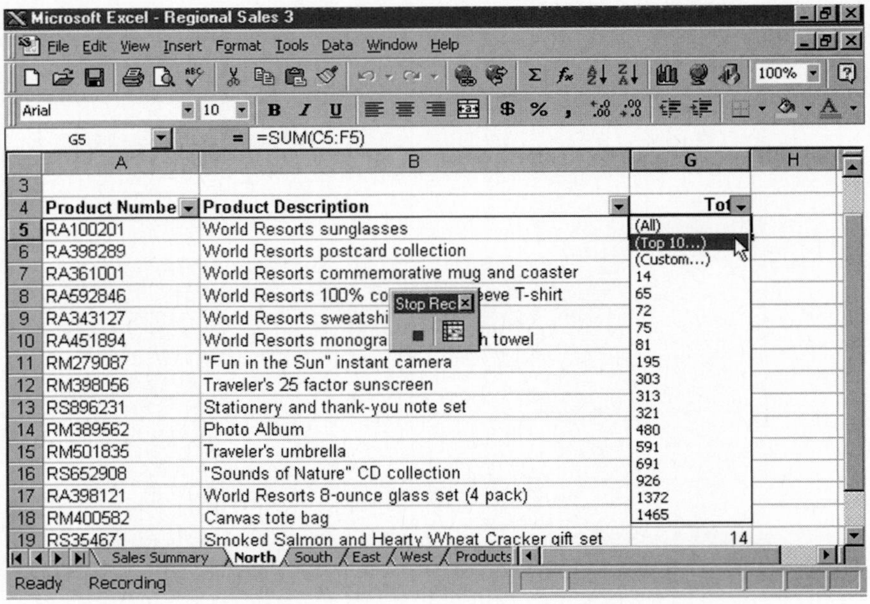

Figure 9.9

The Top 10 AutoFilter dialog box shown in Figure 9.10 will appear. You can use this dialog box to modify the set of data items you want to appear.

5 Click OK to accept the current selection.

Figure 9.10

Your worksheet will now display the top ten best-selling items, as shown in Figure 9.11.

	A	B	G	H
3				
4	Product Numbe ▾	Product Description ▾	Tot ▾	
5	RA100201	World Resorts sunglasses	1465	
6	RA398289	World Resorts postcard collection	1372	
7	RA361001	World Resorts commemorative mug and coaster	926	
8	RA592846	World Resorts 100% co[Stop Rec]eve T-shirt	691	
9	RA343127	World Resorts sweatshi	591	
10	RA451894	World Resorts monogra...h towel	480	
11	RM279087	"Fun in the Sun" instant camera	321	
12	RM398056	Traveler's 25 factor sunscreen	313	
13	RS896231	Stationery and thank-you note set	303	
14	RM389562	Photo Album	195	
20				

Figure 9.11

6 Select the Stop Recording button. This will conclude the macro recording that you started in Task 1.

7 Save your workbook.

The worksheet interface provides a number of visual cues indicating that the view is currently filtered. First, *Filter mode* appears in the Status bar at the bottom of the worksheet. This indicates that the current worksheet is filtered. Second, the drop-down list button in column G turns blue, indicating that the data is currently filtered by the data in this column. Third, the row labels for rows 5 through 14 also appear blue, indicating that this range includes the top ten data items listed in column G. They appear as a contiguous range because you sorted the range by column G in Project 7. Had this task not been completed, the range would contain a nonadjacent selection.

Viewing the Contents of a Macro

A Microsoft Excel macro is recorded in Visual Basic code as a subprocedure. In a *Visual Basic sub procedure,* each line is executed in order. You can view macro code by means of the *Visual Basic Editor.* This editor appears as a window that displays the actual Visual Basic code the macro comprises.

Tip If you have no interest in how Excel uses Visual Basic code to record macros, you may skip this task.

TASK 4: VIEWING THE CONTENTS OF A MACRO

1 Select Macro from the Tools menu, and Visual Basic Editor from the cascading menu that appears.

2 The Visual Basic Editor will appear. Select the Macros option from the Tools menu, as shown in Figure 9.12.

Figure 9.12 The Microsoft Visual Basic Editor Menus

3 Select the Step Into button in the Macros dialog box, as shown in Figure 9.13.

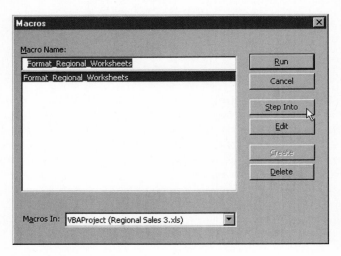

Figure 9.13

Caution The Format_Regional_Worksheets macro will appear highlighted as the default if it is the only macro that exists in your workbook. If you have created other macros, be sure to select this macro before you select the Step Into button.

4 Depending upon how your computer or network is configured, you may see up to three windows simultaneously on the screen. If the Properties or Project windows are visible, select the Close button in each window to make more room on the screen for the macro Module Code window. If the Module

Code window is not maximized, click the Maximize button so it fills the entire screen, as shown in Figure 9.14.

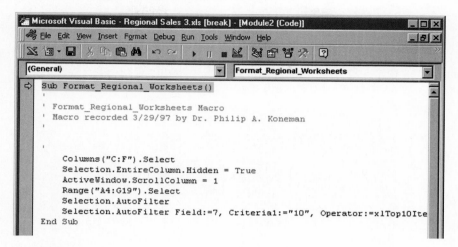

Figure 9.14

The name of the Visual Basic sub procedure is the same as the name you chose and typed for the macro. The macro includes six actions. Any changes to the Visual Basic code appearing in this window would change the macro, potentially resulting in an error message whenever the macro is run. **Do not** change the code of the macro!

5   Select the Close button for the Visual Basic Editor.

6   When the dialog box displayed in Figure 9.15 appears, select **OK**. The view will now return to the workbook.

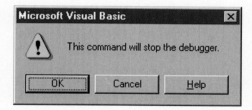

Figure 9.15

Apply the Macro to Additional Worksheets

The purpose of a macro is to automate repetitive tasks. Since the changes made to the North region worksheet also need to be applied to the remaining regional worksheets, you can now run the macro you recorded in each of these sheets. To **run** a macro means to execute the Visual Basic sub procedure, which applies each action included in the macro to the active worksheet.

TASK 5: APPLYING THE MACRO TO ADDITIONAL SHEETS

1 Select the **South** worksheet.

2 Place the cell pointer in cell A1.

3 Select Macro from the Tools menu, and Macros from the cascading menu that appears. Format_Regional_Worksheets macro will appear highlighted as the default, since it is the only macro in the workbook.

4 Select the Run button, as shown in Figure 9.16.

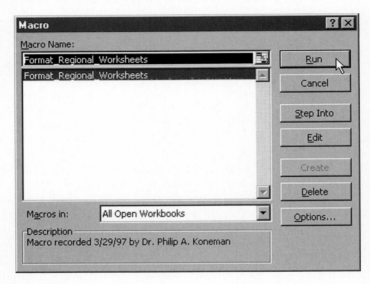

Figure 9.16

5 Using the same procedure, apply the macro to the **East** and **West** worksheets.

6 Save your workbook.

Sort the Sales Summary Data Using Multiple Criteria

Before adding subtotals to the **Sales Summary** worksheet, you will need to sort the data by multiple criteria. *Sort criteria* are the specifications you provide to tell the computer how to reorder the data. A *multilevel sort* in Excel is a sort based upon up to three sort criteria.

The management of World Sales, Inc. wants the sales figures to be sorted by product category. The worksheets you created and completed in Projects 6 and 7 had no categories specified. However, if you look closely at the product numbers, you will see three general groupings of categories.

TASK 6: ADDING PRODUCT CATEGORIES
TO THE SALES SUMMARY WORKSHEET

1 Select the **Sales Summary** worksheet.

2 Highlight the range A4:H19.

3 Select Sort from the Data menu.

4 Select Product Number in the Sort by list in the Sort dialog box, and select the descending option, as shown in Figure 9.17.

Figure 9.17

5 Click OK. The range you selected is now sorted by Product Number.

6 Place the cell pointer in cell B1.

7 Select Columns from the Insert menu to add a column to the worksheet. This column will contain the product descriptions.

8 Type **Category** in cell B4 and press (ENTER).

9 Type **Gift Sets** in cell B5 and press (ENTER).

10 Use AutoFill to copy the entry in cell B5 through cell B7.

11 Type **Merchandise** in cell B8 and press (ENTER).

12 Copy the entry in cell B8 through cell B12.

13 Type **World Products** in cell B13 and press (ENTER).

14 Copy cell B13 through cell B19.

15 Save these changes. Your worksheet will now look like Figure 9.18.

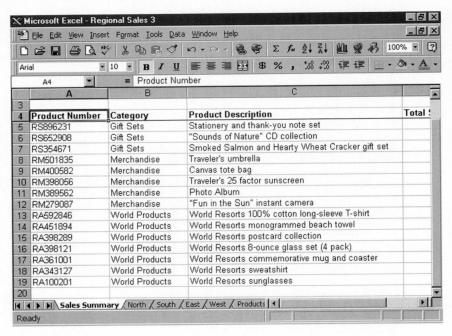

Figure 9.18

You are now ready to sort the worksheet by multiple criteria. To make the summary data easier to view, you will hide columns C through F of the worksheet.

TASK 7: SORTING THE SALES SUMMARY DATA BY MULTIPLE CRITERIA

1 Select columns D through G, and select Columns/Hide from the Format menu.

2 Select the range A4:I19.

3 Select Sort from the Data menu.

4 Select Category in the Sort by list, and Total Sales in the first Then by list. Select the descending option for both sort criteria.

5   Select OK, as shown in Figure 9.19.

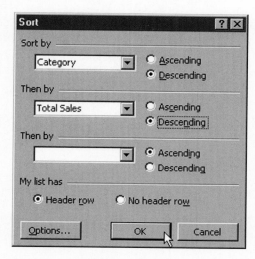

Figure 9.19 Specifying Multiple Sort Criteria

6   Change the zoom of the worksheet to 75%.

7   Your screen will now look like Figure 9.20.

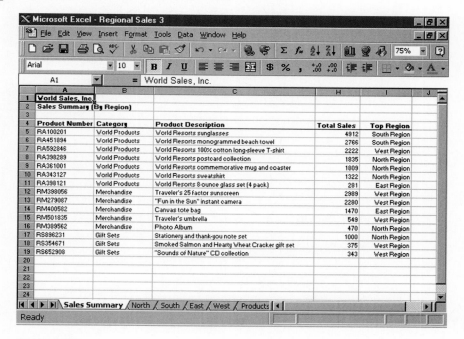

Figure 9.20

8   Save your workbook.

Add Subtotals to the Sales Summary Worksheet

A list of sales figures is often summed by subtotals. In this case, the total sales figures will be subtotaled by product category. A *subtotal* in Excel is the sum of a range of related cells. When subtotals are applied to a worksheet, buttons for expanding and collapsing the subtotal data appear on screen.

TASK 8: ADDING SUBTOTALS TO THE SALES SUMMARY WORKSHEET

1 Highlight the range A4:I19, if it is not currently selected.

2 Select Subtotals from the Data menu, as shown in Figure 9.21.

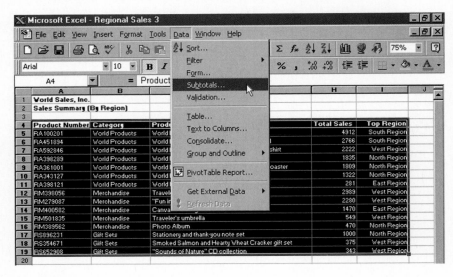

Figure 9.21

3 In the Subtotal dialog box, select Category in the At each change in: list, select Sum in the Use function: list, and select the Total Sales checkbox in the Add subtotal to: list, as shown in Figure 9.22.

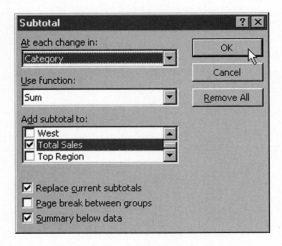

Figure 9.22 Subtotal Dialog Box Settings

4 Click OK.

5 Place the cell pointer in cell A1. Your screen should now look like Figure 9.23.

6 Save your workbook.

	A	B	C	H	I
1	World Sales, Inc.				
2	Sales Summary (By Region)				
3					
4	Product Number	Category	Product Description	Total Sales	Top Region
5	RA100201	World Products	World Resorts sunglasses	4912	South Region
6	RA451894	World Products	World Resorts monogrammed beach towel	2766	South Region
7	RA592846	World Products	World Resorts 100% cotton long-sleeve T-shirt	2222	West Region
8	RA398289	World Products	World Resorts postcard collection	1835	North Region
9	RA361001	World Products	World Resorts commemorative mug and coaster	1809	North Region
10	RA343127	World Products	World Resorts sweatshirt	1322	North Region
11	RA398121	World Products	World Resorts 8-ounce glass set (4 pack)	281	East Region
12		World Products Total		15147	
13	RM398056	Merchandise	Traveler's 25 factor sunscreen	2989	West Region
14	RM279087	Merchandise	"Fun in the Sun" instant camera	2280	West Region
15	RM400582	Merchandise	Canvas tote bag	1470	East Region
16	RM501835	Merchandise	Traveler's umbrella	549	West Region
17	RM389562	Merchandise	Photo Album	470	North Region
18		Merchandise Total		7758	
19	RS896231	Gift Sets	Stationery and thank-you note set	1000	North Region
20	RS354671	Gift Sets	Smoked Salmon and Hearty Wheat Cracker gift set	375	West Region
21	RS652908	Gift Sets	"Sounds of Nature" CD collection	343	West Region
22		Gift Sets Total		1718	
23		Grand Total		24623	
24					

Sales Summary / North / South / East / West / Products

Figure 9.23 Worksheet Displaying Subtotals

When subtotals are displayed in a worksheet, controls for collapsing and expanding the subtotal view appear on the screen. Immediately to the left of the Select All button are three buttons that you can use to collapse the subtotal view. Use the button numbered 1 to display only the grand total; use button 2 to display only the subtotals; and use button 3 to show the entire subtotal view. Alternatively, you can use the minus buttons shown in Figure 9.24 to collapse and expand the view. Since the current view displays the entire subtotal view, only the collapse option is available for all buttons.

Figure 9.24

Tip The numbered buttons behave in a similar manner to the collapse (minus) and expand (plus) buttons in Windows Explorer.

Creating Custom Views

Now that you have altered the worksheets in the Regional Sales 3 workbook, you need a shortcut to avoid the time-consuming task of reformatting the worksheets every time changes need to be made to the underlying data. The remedy to this problem is to create a custom view. A *custom view* is a named and saved list of the settings for the appearance of the current workbook.

TASK 9: CREATE CUSTOM VIEWS

1 Select Custom Views from the View Menu, as shown in Figure 9.25.

Figure 9.25

2 Select the Add button, as shown in Figure 9.26.

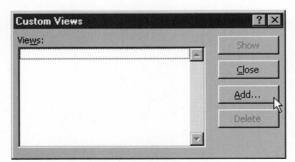

Figure 9.26

3   Type **Top Ten Items** as a name for the current view, as shown in Figure 9.27.

Figure 9.27

4   Select OK.

5   Select columns C through H.

6   Select Columns from the Format menu, and select Unhide. All columns in the worksheet will now be displayed.

7   Select the **North** worksheet tab.

8   Select Filter from the Data menu. The AutoFilter option is active, as shown in Figure 9.28.

Figure 9.28

9   Deselect the AutoFilter option to remove the Top Ten filter.

10   Highlight columns B through G, select Column from the Format menu, and then select Unhide.

11   Repeat the procedures described above to remove the AutoFilter setting from the **South**, **East**, and **West** worksheets, and to display all columns in these sheets.

12   Select the **North** worksheet, and place the cell pointer in cell A1.

13   Create a custom view named *Default Workbook*.

14   Save your workbook.

Showing Custom Views

Once you have created custom views for a workbook, you can show a specific view by selecting it by name in the Custom View dialog box. Keep in mind that views include applied filters and formats such as hidden columns, but not worksheet enhancements such as subtotals.

TASK 10: SHOW CUSTOM VIEWS

1 Select the **North** worksheet and place the cell pointer in cell A1.

2 Select Custom Views from the View menu.

3 Select Top Ten Items in the Custom Views dialog box and select the Show button, as shown in Figure 9.29.

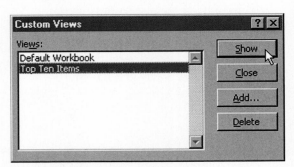

Figure 9.29

The view will change to the **Sales Summary** worksheet. When any of the regional worksheets are selected, the data will be displayed with the Top Ten filter, and columns C through F formatted as hidden.

The Conclusion

Your workbook is now complete and ready for printing. You have provided management with the information they need as they want to see it, without significantly increasing the complexity of the workbook. By using macros, multilevel sorts, and Excel's subtotals feature, you have increased the functionality of this model. You may now exit Excel, or continue by completing the Study Questions and Review Exercises.

Summary and Exercises

Summary

- Macros are often created because they automate redundant tasks.
- Once a macro is created, it can be run in other worksheets or workbooks.
- The contents of a macro can be viewed using the Visual Basic Editor.
- Data in worksheet columns can easily be hidden from view.
- The Excel AutoFilter is used to display data that meets specific criteria.
- Worksheet rows can be sorted by information that identifies each row of data.
- Worksheet data can be sorted by multiple criteria.
- Subtotals can be added to a worksheet.
- Once a custom view is created it can be applied to the worksheet repeatedly.

Key Terms and Operations

Key Terms	Operations
AutoFilter	Add a custom view
Custom view	Add subtotals
Filter mode	Apply an AutoFilter
Hidden column format	Create a macro
Macro	Create a multilevel sort
Multilevel sort	Enter item descriptions
Run	Evoke the Visual Basic Editor
Sort criteria	Hide worksheet columns
Subtotal	Run a macro
Visual Basic Editor	Show a custom view
Visual Basic sub procedure	Sort data using a single criterion

Study Questions

Multiple Choice

1. A macro is used to:
   a. Apply subtotals to a worksheet data range.
   b. Reorder data according to a specified criteria.
   c. Hide or unhide columns prior to printing.
   d. A macro can be used for none of the above.
   e. A macro can be used for all of the above.

2. A custom view applies to:
   a. The first worksheet in a workbook.
   b. The current worksheet in a workbook.
   c. The sheet that was active when the view was created.
   d. The last worksheet in a workbook.
   e. All worksheets in a workbook.

3. What is the greatest number of criteria by which a range of data can be sorted?

a. One

b. Two

c. Three

d. Four

e. Five

4. Which of the following does selecting AutoFilter add to a worksheet?

a. A macro.

b. Subtotals.

c. Acustom view.

d. An additional column.

e. Drop-down list buttons.

5. According to how many criteria does AutoFilter allow you to view the data?

a. One

b. Two

c. Three

d. Four

e. Five

6. To create a Macro, from which menu do you select Macros?

a. View

b. Insert

c. Format

d. Tools

e. Data

7. Which menu item is used to hide a selected column?

a. View/Custom Views

b. Insert/Columns

c. Format/Column

d. Tools/Macro

e. Data/Subtotals

8. Which menu do you use to apply filters?

a. View

b. Insert

c. Format

d. Tools

e. Data

9. Subtotals have been added to a worksheet. How many buttons appear adjacent to the Select All button for expanding and collapsing the Subtotals view?

a. One

b. Two

c. Three

d. Four

e. Five

10. Once a macro has been created, which option do you use to apply it to other worksheets?
    a. Custom Views
    b. Subtotals
    c. Run
    d. AutoFilter
    e. Sort

Short Answer

1. A workbook consists of five sheets, the first four of which have an identical structure. If you select columns C through F in the first worksheet and change the format of the selection hidden, how many columns in the workbook will be hidden?

2. A macro is created in a workbook consisting of four worksheets with an identical structure. The macro selects columns A through C, and changes the format to currency. Can this macro be applied successfully to the remaining three worksheets?

3. A worksheet contains product data as follows: column A contains product numbers, column B product descriptions, and column C the product's unit price. How many sort criteria can be specified when sorting the data?

4. The Visual Basic Editor is used to view the contents of a macro. You have accidentally deleted the opening Sub procedure statement and then updated the Visual Basic code for the macro. What will happen when the macro is run?

5. A worksheet contains product data as follows: column A contains product numbers, column B product descriptions, and column C the product's unit price. By which column should subtotals be grouped?

6. In the worksheet listed above, which column of data should be used to add the subtotals?

7. Columns F through J in a worksheet are hidden. What steps must you follow to unhide the columns?

8. What do you call a sort using three sort criteria?

9. A worksheet contains the following employee data: First Name in column A, Last Name in column B, Social Security Number in column C, Department in column D, and Annual Salary in column E. What will be the effect on data integrity if you compute subtotals in this worksheet?

10. In the worksheet listed above, what would be an effective way of sorting the data using three sort criteria?

For Discussion

1. What is a macro? How can a macro be used to automate repetitive tasks?

2. Why are subtotals useful? What are two methods for collapsing or expanding subtotal data?

3. What is a custom view? How are custom views created?

4. Why might you want to hide one or more columns in a worksheet? How are hidden columns displayed?

Review Exercises

1. Sorting a List of Product Summaries

Open the Worksheet **Product Summary 2** that you created at the end of Project 7. Change the worksheet as follows:

1. In the **Product Summary** worksheet, add a column after column A.

2. Type **Category** in cell B1.

3. Type **Storage** in cell B2.

4. Copy cell B2 to cell B3.

5. Type **Input Device** in cell B4.

6. Type **Software** in cell B5.

7. Copy the contents of cell B5 through cell B7.

8. Highlight the range A1:C7.

9. Select Sort from the Data menu.

10. Set the sort criteria to sort first by product category, and then by product name.

11. Save the workbook as *Product Summary 3*.
    Your updated workbook should look like Figure 9.30.

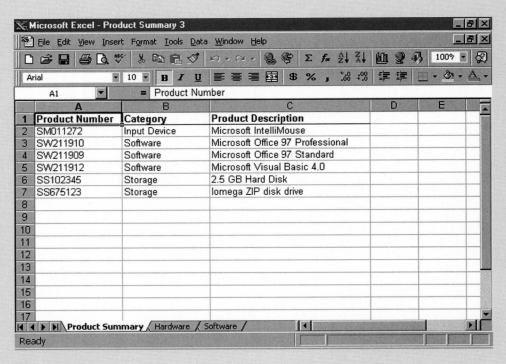

Figure 9.30

2. Sorting Data Ranges and Hiding Worksheet Columns

Open the Worksheet **World2b** that you created at the end of Project 7. Change the worksheet as follows:

1. Sort the data in cells A6:F8 and A12:F14 by column A in ascending order.

Tip You will need to sort these ranges in two steps, since Excel cannot sort data in a nonadjacent selection.

2. Change the format of columns B through G to hidden.

3. Save the workbook as *World2d*.
   Your completed workbook should look like Figure 9.31.

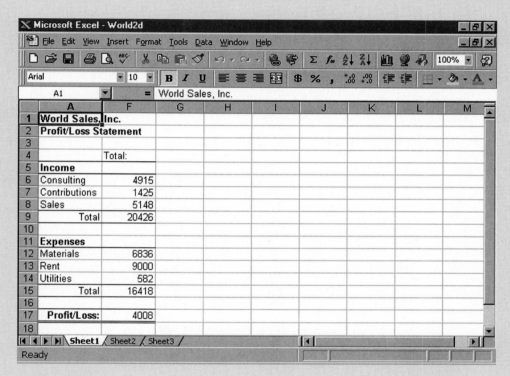

Figure 9.31

Assignments

1. Adding Subtotals to a Profit and Loss Statement
Open the *World2c* workbook you created in Project 7. Add a column between A and B to display the transaction type: Revenue or Expense. Delete rows 5, 10, 11, 16, 17, and 18. Add subtotals to calculate the total revenue and the total expenses. Modify the Grand Total formula so it displays the correct result. Save the updated workbook as *World2e*.

2. On-Line Technical Support for Microsoft Excel
Visit the Microsoft Web site (http://wwww.microsoft.com). Navigate to the help area for Microsoft Excel. Search for information on macro viruses. Create an Excel workbook containing a macro. Save the workbook as *Sample*. Close the workbook, and open it again in Excel. Should you enable or disable the macros in this workbook?

10 PROJECT

Using Statistical Functions

Microsoft Excel has convenient statistical functions and cross-tabulation tools for analyzing raw transaction data that has not been summarized, such as the record of individual sales in database. In this project you will learn how to use statistical functions for analyzing transaction data to determine sales by product category, to show minimum, maximum, and average sales by month, as well as to show trends and forecast future sales.

Objectives

After completing this project, you will be able to:

➤ **Import a delimited text file into Excel**

➤ **Set up data for PivotTables**

➤ **Create a Simple PivotTable**

➤ **Group data in the PivotTable**

➤ **Organize a PivotTable using a page field**

➤ **Add Statistical functions to the PivotTable**

➤ **Hide worksheet rows**

➤ **Create a sales forecast**

➤ **Determine sales trends**

Introduction

In many settings, summaries are created from individual transactions. A *transaction* is an event, such as the sale of a product to a customer. Companies often record the details of each transaction, such as the name of the customer and the items purchased, in computer databases. Sometimes it is necessary to analyze raw transaction data that has not yet been summarized. In this project you will learn how to do that.

Microsoft Excel supports a variety of statistical functions and procedures for analyzing data. You can import into Excel the transaction data from a database file and then use an Excel feature called a PivotTable to look at the data in different ways. Once you have constructed a PivotTable, you can add formulas to the worksheet to obtain specific information from the data, such as determining the minimum, maximum, and average sales. Excel also provides other statistical functions for analyzing data trends such as TREND and for predicting future sales, FORECAST.

The Challenge

World Sales Direct is the mail order company that Resort Sales, Inc. established after reviewing the Excel regional sales summaries and loan analysis you provided in Projects 6–9. The mail order company markets a line of products sold in the gift shops of the parent corporation's resort facilities throughout the United States. Your office recently received sales data that needs to be analyzed to determine sales trends. The data you received was exported from the company database and consists of raw transaction data. You have been asked to create a Microsoft Excel workbook that summarizes the sales data and projects sales for the next month.

The Solution

Your first task is to examine the raw transaction data. If it is stored in a consistent form, you can import it into Excel. You then can create a Pivot-Table to summarize the data. Once the PivotTable is created, you can use other statistical functions to further analyze the data and predict future trends. Your PivotTable will look like Figure 10.1.

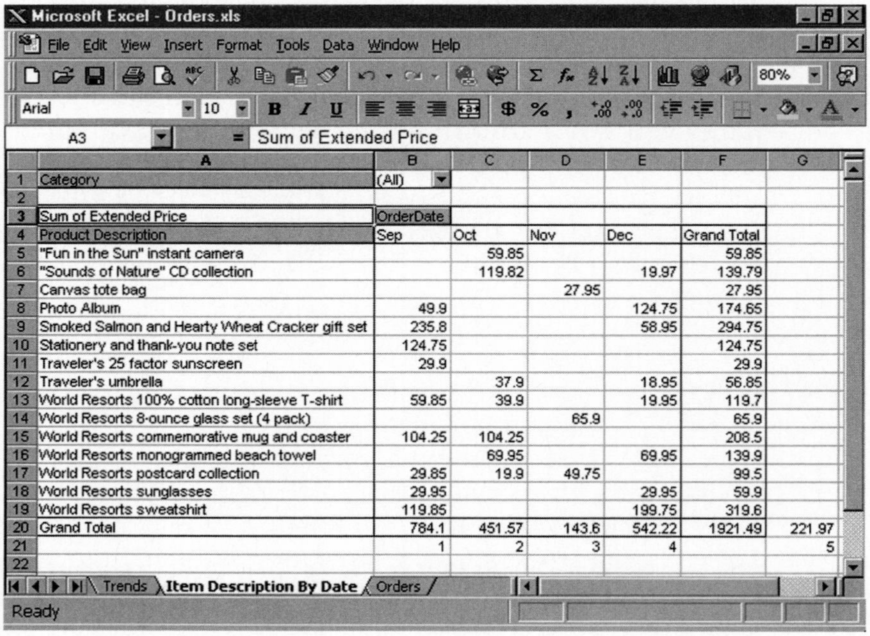

Microsoft Excel - Orders.xls

A3 = Sum of Extended Price

	A	B	C	D	E	F	G
1	Category	(All)					
2							
3	Sum of Extended Price	OrderDate					
4	Product Description	Sep	Oct	Nov	Dec	Grand Total	
5	"Fun in the Sun" instant camera		59.85			59.85	
6	"Sounds of Nature" CD collection		119.82		19.97	139.79	
7	Canvas tote bag			27.95		27.95	
8	Photo Album	49.9			124.75	174.65	
9	Smoked Salmon and Hearty Wheat Cracker gift set	235.8			58.95	294.75	
10	Stationery and thank-you note set	124.75				124.75	
11	Traveler's 25 factor sunscreen	29.9				29.9	
12	Traveler's umbrella		37.9		18.95	56.85	
13	World Resorts 100% cotton long-sleeve T-shirt	59.85	39.9		19.95	119.7	
14	World Resorts 8-ounce glass set (4 pack)			65.9		65.9	
15	World Resorts commemorative mug and coaster	104.25	104.25			208.5	
16	World Resorts monogrammed beach towel		69.95		69.95	139.9	
17	World Resorts postcard collection	29.85	19.9	49.75		99.5	
18	World Resorts sunglasses	29.95			29.95	59.9	
19	World Resorts sweatshirt	119.85			199.75	319.6	
20	Grand Total	784.1	451.57	143.6	542.22	1921.49	221.97
21		1	2	3	4		5
22							

Trends \ Item Description By Date \ Orders /

Ready

Figure 10.1

The Setup

To create the workbook, start Microsoft Excel and select the settings shown in Table 10.1.

Table 10.1   Excel Settings

Element	Settings
Office Assistant	Close the Office Assistant
View, Toolbars	Display the Standard and Formatting toolbars
View, Formula bar	Display the Formula bar
View, Status bar	Display the Status bar
Maximize	Maximize the Application and Workbook windows

Importing External Data into Microsoft Excel

Like most modern computer applications, Microsoft Excel can import data from a variety of sources. *Importing data* is the process of reading data stored in a file format other than Excel, and converting it to an Excel format. The data you will import is in a standardized text format, the ASCII format. Data stored as **ASCII text** contains only letters, numbers, and symbols and is not formatted in any way. Text that is stored in this standardized format can be used on different computers with different operating systems. In addition, ASCII data can be read by virtually all computer applications.

ASCII text files that have been exported from database applications often store data in a specific format. Each row of data in an ASCII file usually constitutes one database record. Recall that a record is all the information about an entity, such as a customer, that is kept in the database. Field data comprises the categories of information that define each entity. In a customer address database, last name, first name, and city are three examples of field data.

An ASCII file is called **delimited** because the field data in each row can be distinguished. To delimit means to fix the limits, or specify a boundary for something. ASCII delimited files delimit field data with one or more characters. The **delimiting character,** or **delimiter,** is the specific ASCII character used to separate field data. Figure 10.2 displays an ASCII-delimited text file opened with the Microsoft Windows 95 Notepad application.

Figure 10.2 ASCII-delimited Text File

This file uses the comma character as a delimiter. ASCII-delimited files can easily be imported into Microsoft Excel. The delimiter designates the columns the data is imported to. Each record becomes a row in the worksheet.

TASK 1: IMPORT AN ASCII-DELIMITED TEXT FILE INTO MICROSOFT EXCEL

1 Select Open from the File menu.

2 In the Open dialog, select Text Files in the Files of Type: listbox, as shown in Figure 10.3.

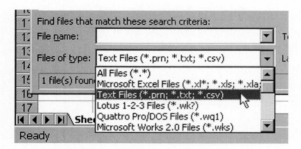

Figure 10.3

3 Select 3½ Floppy (A:) in the Look In: list (or the appropriate drive for the *Orders.txt* file).

> **Troubleshooting** If you do not have a floppy diskette containing this file, ask your instructor for the file. If you have access to the World Wide Web, download the file from the Addison-Wesley Web site. (www.awl.com/is/select).

4 Highlight the *Orders.txt* file and click the Open button, as shown in Figure 10.4. This is the text file containing transaction data. The Text Import Wizard dialog will appear.

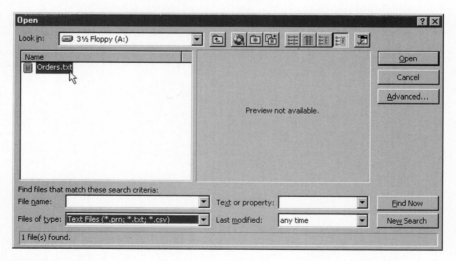

Figure 10.4

5 Make sure the Delimited option button under Original data type is selected and that the import will begin with row 1, as shown in Figure 10.5. Click the Next button.

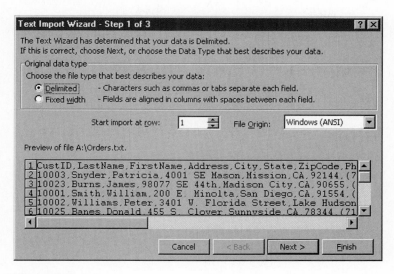

Figure 10.5

6 In Step 2 of the Text Import Wizard, select Comma as the delimiter, as shown in Figure 10.6. Click the Next button.

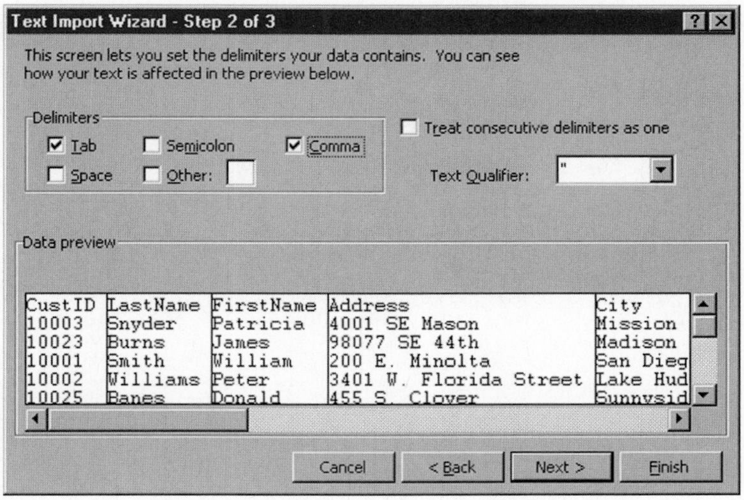

Figure 10.6

7 In Step 3 of the Wizard, use the horizontal scroll bar to display the OrderDate data. Select the Date option button in the Column data format box and select MDY as the date type, as shown in Figure 10.7.

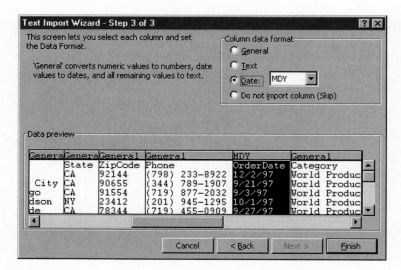

Figure 10.7

8 Click the Finish button. Your workbook with imported data will look like Figure 10.8.

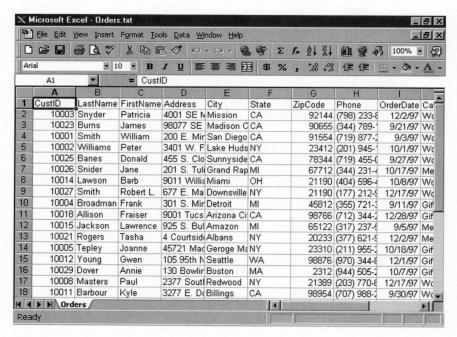

Figure 10.8

9 Select Save from the File Menu.

10 In the Save As dialog, select Microsoft Excel Workbook in the Save As type: listbox, and click Save.

Setting Up Data for a PivotTable

For Excel to construct a PivotTable for the transaction data in the *Orders.xls* workbook, all three conditions must be met. First, each row must contain a unique record, since PivotTables summarize data stored in rows. Second, each column must have a descriptive label identifying its contents. Third, any date values must be in date format.

If you look at the data, you will see that it already meets these conditions. To complete the workbook, you will format it to make it easier to read, using a bold font for the headings and a border at the bottom of each heading cell. Finally, you will need to add a series of formulas to each transaction in the worksheet which will multiply the unit item price by the order quantity to determine the total price for the order (called the Extended Price).

TASK 2: SET UP THE DATA FOR THE PIVOTTABLE

1 Type **Extended Price** in cell O1.

2 Type **=m2*n2** as the formula in cell O2 and press (ENTER).

3 Using the Fill Handle, copy the formula through row 31.

4 Select column M, hold down the (CONTROL) key, and select column O.

5 Change the format of the nonadjacent selection to Currency, and select 2 decimal places.

6 Highlight the range A1:O1 and change the font style of the selection to Bold.

7 Add a lower border to the selection.

8 Save the workbook.

Analyzing Data Using PivotTables

Now that you have set up the data consistently throughout the worksheet, you can create a PivotTable to analyze the transaction data. An Excel *PivotTable* is a tool for cross-tabulating data in a worksheet to explore the underlying relationships. A *cross-tabulation* is a representation of data in a row and column format. Market research departments, sales departments, economists, and statisticians often use cross-tabulation tables to compare data by multiple criteria. Each column of data in the worksheet can be thought of as a variable, since the contents in each cell vary. To create the cross-tabulation table, you will designate one or more row and column variables that contribute to a data variable. Since PivotTables contain no formulas, they are easy to create and easy to modify.

Two questions are of primary interest here. Marketing wants to know sales trends for particular items: which items are hot? Both Advertising and Marketing want to know how sales fluctuate seasonally and want to isolate sales patterns based upon the purchase date. A PivotTable will assist in finding information buried in the transaction data.

TASK 3: CREATE A PIVOT TABLE

1 Make cell A1 the active cell.

2 Select PivotTable Report from the Data Menu, as shown in Figure 10.9. The PivotTable Wizard will appear.

Figure 10.9

3 In Step 1, verify that the data to be analyzed is in an Excel list or database, as shown in Figure 10.10. Click the Next button.

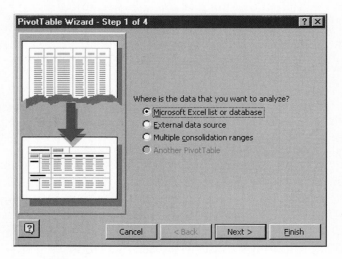

Figure 10.10

4   Step 2 of the PivotTable Wizard verifies the data range. The range should be $A$1:$O$31, as shown in Figure 10.11. Click Next.

Figure 10.11

Step 3 of the Wizard presents the design grid shown in Figure 10.12. It includes a field name for each data field in the worksheet. Using drag and drop, you can place the field names in the row, column, data, and page areas of the layout.

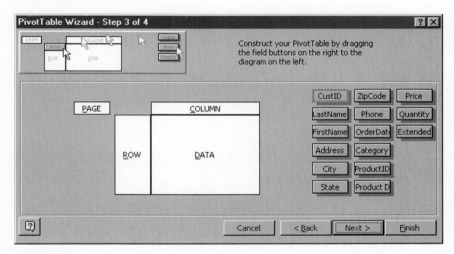

Figure 10.12

5   Drag the Order Date field name to the Column area of the layout.

6   Drag the Product Description field name to the Row area of the layout.

7 Drag the Extended field name and drag it to the Data area of the layout. The layout should now look like Figure 10.13.

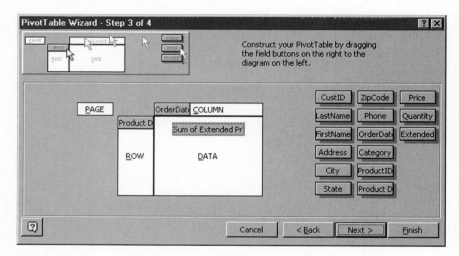

Figure 10.13

8 Click the Next button.

9 The last step of the PivotTable Wizard specifies where to insert the table. Accept the default, New Worksheet, by clicking the Finish button.
You have added the PivotTable shown in Figure 10.14 to the workbook. Note that the PivotTable occupies a new worksheet named Sheet1.

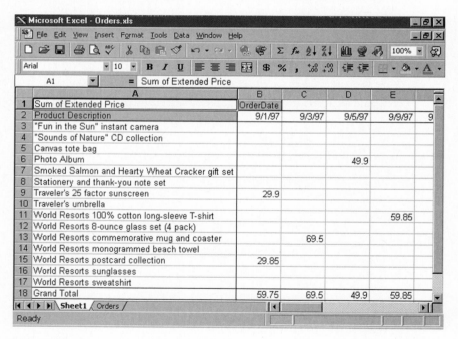

Figure 10.14

10 Save your workbook.

Grouping Data in the PivotTable

The PivotTable you created summarizes the sales transactions by item and date, but it is difficult to understand. To present the summary information in a form that is easier to read, you can group the data.

TASK 4: GROUP DATA IN THE PIVOTTABLE

1 Change the worksheet zoom to 85%.

2 Click the right mouse button twice over cell B1, the OrderDate field. The Right Click menu shown in Figure 10.15 will appear.

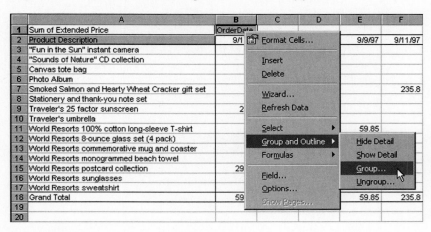

Figure 10.15

3 Select Group and Outline from the menu, and Group from the cascading menu.

4 Select Months in the Grouping dialog box, as shown in Figure 10.16.

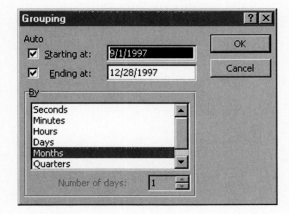

Figure 10.16

5 Click OK.

6 Rename the Sheet1 worksheet tab **Item Description By Date**. Your PivotTable should now look like Figure 10.17.

	A	B	C	D	E	F	G
1	Sum of Extended Price	OrderDate					
2	Product Description	Sep	Oct	Nov	Dec	Grand Total	
3	"Fun in the Sun" instant camera		59.85			59.85	
4	"Sounds of Nature" CD collection		119.82		19.97	139.79	
5	Canvas tote bag			27.95		27.95	
6	Photo Album	49.9			124.75	174.65	
7	Smoked Salmon and Hearty Wheat Cracker gift set	235.8			58.95	294.75	
8	Stationery and thank-you note set	124.75				124.75	
9	Traveler's 25 factor sunscreen	29.9				29.9	
10	Traveler's umbrella		37.9		18.95	56.85	
11	World Resorts 100% cotton long-sleeve T-shirt	59.85	39.9		19.95	119.7	
12	World Resorts 8-ounce glass set (4 pack)			65.9		65.9	
13	World Resorts commemorative mug and coaster	104.25	104.25			208.5	
14	World Resorts monogrammed beach towel		69.95		69.95	139.9	
15	World Resorts postcard collection	29.85	19.9	49.75		99.5	
16	World Resorts sunglasses	29.95			29.95	59.9	
17	World Resorts sweatshirt	119.85			199.75	319.6	
18	Grand Total	784.1	451.57	143.6	542.22	1921.49	
19							
20							
21							
22							

Figure 10.17 PivotTable with Date Grouped by Month

7 Save your workbook.

Organizing a PivotTable Using a Page Field

You can use PivotTable page fields to display data for one item independent of other items in a field. When you select an item in a page field, the data displayed in the PivotTable changes accordingly. You can easily view sales summary data independently by item category by making the Category field a page field in a PivotTable.

TASK 5: ORGANIZE A PIVOTTABLE USING A PAGE FIELD

1 Select PivotTable Report from the Data Menu.

2 Drag the Category field name to the Page area of the PivotTable layout, as shown in Figure 10.18.

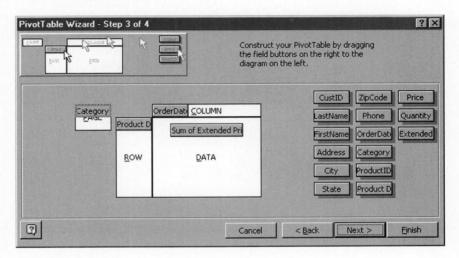

Figure 10.18

3 Click Next.

4 In Step 4 of the PivotTable Wizard, select Existing Worksheet as the location for the PivotTable, as shown in Figure 10.19.

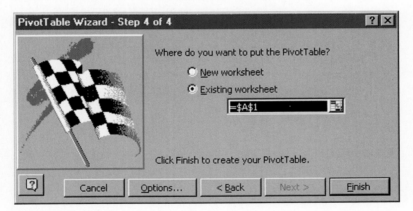

Figure 10.19

5 Click Finish.

You have now added a new row to the PivotTable. Figure 10.20 displays the Category field button in cell A1 of the PivotTable, and a drop-down list for product categories in cell B1.

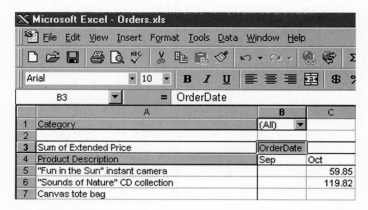

Figure 10.20

6 Select columns B through E of the PivotTable and change the width to 12.00.

7 Click the drop-down list button in cell B1 and select World Products, as shown in Figure 10.21.

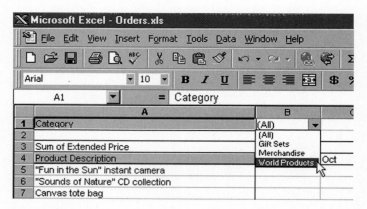

Figure 10.21

The PivotTable view will change. The view displays only the World Products items, as shown in Figure 10.22.

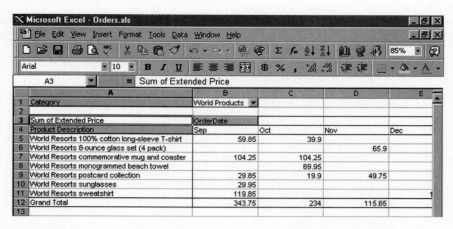

Figure 10.22

Adding Statistical Functions to the PivotTable

Besides showing total sales by product category, you may want to show the maximum, minimum, and average sales for each category by month. Once you have created the PivotTable, you can add Excel statistical formulas to do so. Formulas incorporating the MAX and MIN statistical functions find the smallest and largest values in the table. The function called AVERAGE calculates the average sales for each product category by month.

TASK 6: ADD STATISTICAL FUNCTIONS TO THE PIVOTTABLE

1 Click the drop-down list in cell B1 and select (All).

2 Type **Minimum Sale** in cell A22, **Maximum Sale** in cell A23, and **Average Sales** in cell A24.

3 Select the range A22:A24. Change the font style to Bold and the cell alignment to Right aligned.

4 Type **=MIN(B5:B19)** in cell B22.

5 Type **=MAX(B5:B19)** in cell B23.

6 Type **=AVERAGE(B5:B19)** in cell B24.

7 Select the range B22:B24.

8 Using the Fill Handle, copy these formulas through column E.

9 Select the range B22:E24 and change the format to Number, with 2 decimal places.

The summary statistics shown in Figure 10.23 will be added to the PivotTable, as shown in Figure 10.23.

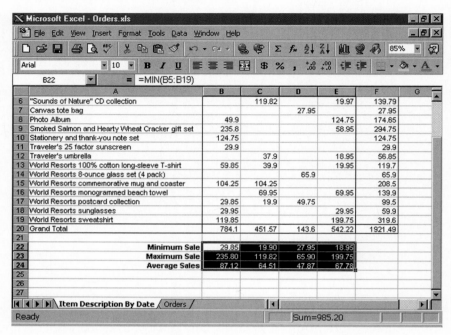

Figure 10.23 Summary Statistics Displayed in the PivotTable

10 Save your workbook.

Hiding Worksheet Rows

Since summary statistics formulas were added below the last row of data in the PivotTable, they will apply to any page in the PivotTable. However, as you select different page views using the drop-down list in cell B2, you may find the summary statistics figures not visible unless you scroll to the bottom of the worksheet. You can solve this problem and display the statistics immediately below any page view by hiding worksheet rows.

TASK 7: HIDE WORKSHEET ROWS

1 Select Gift Sets from the Category drop-down list in cell B1.

2 Highlight the range A10:A20 of the PivotTable.

3   Select Row from the Format menu, and Hide from the cascading menu, as shown in Figure 10.24.

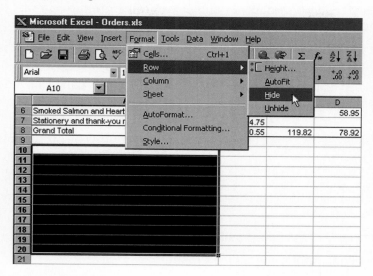

Figure 10.24

The PivotTable will now look like the one shown in Figure 10.25. Notice that the headings for rows 10 to 20 do not appear.

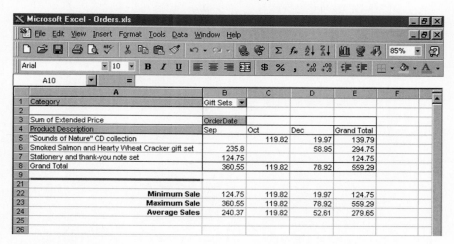

Figure 10.25

Tip To display the hidden rows, highlight the row headings for rows 9 to 21, select Row from the Format Menu, and Unhide from the cascading menu.

Creating a Sales Forecast

Now that you have summarized the data according to product categories by date, you can forecast next month's sales. The FORECAST statistical function uses existing data to project an unknown value.

TASK 8: CREATE A SALES FORECAST

1 Highlight rows 9 through 21 and select Row from the Format Menu and Unhide from the cascading menu.

2 Click the button in cell B1 and select (All) as the category to display all product data.

3 Type **1** in cell B21, **2** in cell C21, **3** in cell D21, and **4** in cell E21. These refer to each month of known sales.

> **Comment** The FORECAST function requires all arguments to be numeric data.

4 Type **5** in cell F21. This refers to the month for which an unknown value will be predicted.

5 Make cell G20 the active cell.

6 Select Function from the Insert menu.

7 In the Paste Function dialog box, select FORECAST from the list of available Statistical functions, as shown in Figure 10.26. Note that the FORECAST function requires three arguments.

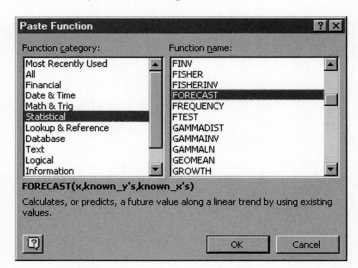

Figure 10.26

8 Click OK.

9 Enter the arguments shown in Figure 10.27 into the Function dialog.

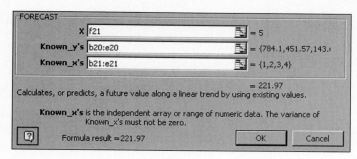

Figure 10.27

10 Click OK. The value 221.97 appears in cell G20. This is the projected sales figure for month 5, based upon the existing data in the PivotTable.

11 Save your workbook.

> **Tip** Notice that all values displayed in the PivotTable are numeric, even though the underlying data (in the Orders worksheet) appear in currency format. This is due to the fact that when you create a Pivot-Table, you paste the data values to a new worksheet. Since General is the default format for the new worksheet cells, all numeric data appear in the general format, which is numeric.

Determining Sales Trends

Most retail businesses want to know something about sales trends. Excel includes the TREND statistical function to determine trends based upon known values. The TREND function is used to create a *trendline,* which, when represented graphically will show the general direction of future sales. You will now determine the sales trends for the WorldSales Direct.

TASK 9: DETERMINE SALES TRENDS

1 Select Worksheet from the Insert menu to add a new worksheet to the workbook.

2 Rename the new worksheet **Trends**.

3 Type **September** in cell A1 of the **Trends** worksheet.

4 Use AutoFill to create labels for the months of October through April (A1 through H1).

5 Select the **Item Description By Date** worksheet.

6 Click the drop-down list in cell B1 and select World Products as the item category.

7 Highlight the range B12:E12 and select Copy from the Edit menu.

8 Select the **Trends** worksheet, place the insertion point in cell A2, and select Paste from the Edit menu. The **Trends** worksheet should now look like Figure 10.28.

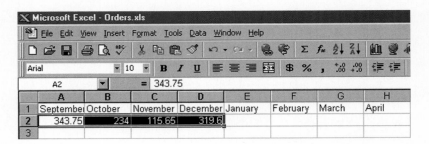

Figure 10.28

9 Highlight the range E2:H2 in the **Trends** worksheet.

10 Type **=TREND(A2:D2,,{5,6,7,8})** as a formula. Make sure you include brackets in the formula.

11 Press (CONTROL) (SHIFT) (ENTER) simultaneously on the keyboard to accept the formula.

> **Troubleshooting** The formula you entered includes a reference to the data array 5,6,7,8. This array specifies the trend values you desire to calculate. A formula containing an array requires the array-entry keystroke ((CONTROL) (SHIFT) (ENTER) combination) when entering a formula containing an array.

Excel displays the values shown in Figure 10.29. Notice that the TREND formula contains brackets as well as parentheses.

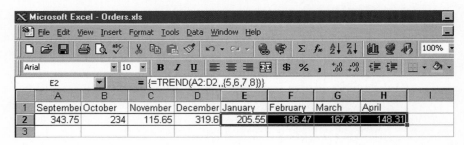

Figure 10.29

12 Save your workbook.

The Conclusion

Excel's PivotTable feature has provided an easy way to make sense of raw data that contains much detail. You have created an Excel PivotTable to summarize the data you received as ASCII text. Adding page fields made the comparison of product sales by category an easy task. By adding formulas containing the MIN, MAX, and AVERAGE statistical functions, you were able to see additional summary statistics for the products by category. Finally, you used the FORECAST and TREND functions to predict future sales.

Summary and Exercises

Summary

- Excel includes tools for performing statistical procedures and cross tabulations on numeric data.
- PivotTables are often used to cross tabulate data on one or more variables.
- Data in a PivotTable can be grouped to display data in summary form.
- A Page Field in a PivotTable displays data for one item independent of other items in a field.
- Statistical functions can be added to PivotTables.
- Worksheet rows can be hidden to assist in viewing summary data that appears after a series of worksheet rows.
- The FORECAST function uses existing data to project unknown values.
- The TRENDS statistical function is used to determine trends based upon known values.

Key Terms and Operations

Key Terms
ASCII text
Cross-tabulation
Delimited
Delimiting character (delimiter)
Importing data
PivotTable
Transaction
Trendline

Operations
Add page fields to a PivotTable
Create a PivotTable
Import ASCII delimited data
Set up data for a PivotTable
Use the FORECAST function
Use the MIN, MAX, and Average statistical functions
Use the TREND function

Study Questions

Multiple Choice

1. Which statistical feature available in Excel required no formulas?
   a. TREND
   b. PivotTable
   c. FORECAST
   d. AVERAGE
   e. MIN

2. What is the purpose of page fields in a PivotTable?
   a. To define the row variables
   b. To view all data simultaneously
   c. To define the Data variables
   d. To view data items independently
   e. To define the column variables

3. What will the formula =MAX(A5:G5) do?
   a. Return the greatest value in the range
   b. Return a projection for cell G5, based upon the values in cells A5:F5
   c. Return the mean value in the range
   d. Return a projection for cell A5 based upon the values in cells B5:G5
   e. Return the lowest value in the range

4. PivotTables are useful for quickly:
   a. Projecting future sales
   b. Calculating average sales
   c. Comparing data summaries
   d. Returning the lowest value in a range
   e. Testing logical conditions

5. Which of the following is not considered a statistical function?
   a. MIN
   b. AVERAGE
   c. SUM
   d. IF
   e. MAX

6. To which of the following does the formula =TREND(A2:D2,,{5,6,7,8}) contain a reference?
   a. An array
   b. An absolute reference
   c. A relative reference
   d. A Row variable
   e. A page field

7. In the ASCII text data Smith,Bill W.,123 Main,Aurora,IL,80110–1114, which character serves as a delimiter?
   a. The number "1"
   b. The space character
   c. The letter "S"
   d. The hyphen character
   e. The comma character

8. ASCII text contains all of the following except:
   a. Letters
   b. Numbers
   c. Characters
   d. Symbols
   e. Formats

9. Data used in a PivotTable must meet all but which of the following conditions?
   a. One data item per row
   b. No spaces in the data
   c. Dates formatted to date format
   d. Labels above the columns

10. Which of the following functions will forecast sales for one additional month?
    a. PivotTable
    b. TREND
    c. FORECAST
    d. AVERAGE
    e. MAX

Short Answer

1. What is the array entry keystroke?

2. What is a trendline?

3. What function calculates the mean value of an array?

4. Which statistical function returns the largest numeric value in a list or range?

5. In a PivotTable layout, where does the DATA field go?

6. What is a page field?

7. What is a delimiting character?

8. What is a PivotTable Row variable?

9. How are statistical functions inserted into a formula?

10. Upon what is a PivotTable based?

For Discussion

1. How can trends be predicted without using the TREND function?

2. How do the TREND and FORECAST functions differ?

3. What are Row and Column variables? How do they relate to Data variables?

4. Why are ASCII files often used to share data among applications?

Review Exercises

1. Project Sales Trends by Charting a Trendline

1. Open the *Orders.xls* workbook.

2. Make **Trends** the active worksheet.

3. Delete the range E2:H2.

4. Select Save As from the File Menu, and save the workbook as *Trends.xls*.

5. Highlight the range A1:H2 and create a column chart as a new sheet.

6. When the chart appears, select Add Trendline from the Chart Menu.

7. Select the option to add a linear trendline. The chart should now look like Figure 10.30.

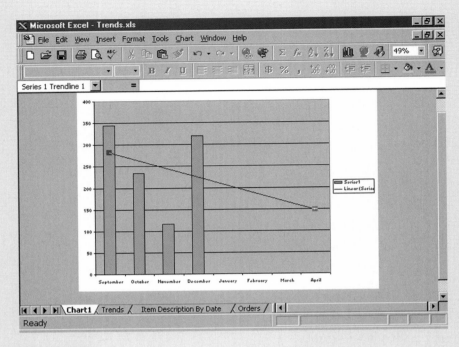

Figure 10.30

8. Save the workbook.

2. Adding Statistical Functions to a Grade Ledger

Ask your instructor how to obtain the file *Ledger.xls*. If you have access to the World Wide Web, it can be downloaded from the Addison-Wesley Website at www.awl.com/is/select.

1. Open the workbook.

2. Add formulas to calculate the minimum, maximum, and average scores for each assignment and examination.

3. Save your worksheet as **Ledger2.xls**.

3. Using Solver

Solver is a tool for conducting a what-if analysis when you need to adjust the values in more than one cell and have multiple constraints for those values. Assume that you are reviewing a profit and loss worksheet listing the revenues and expenses for four quarters of operation for a small manufacturing firm, displayed below.

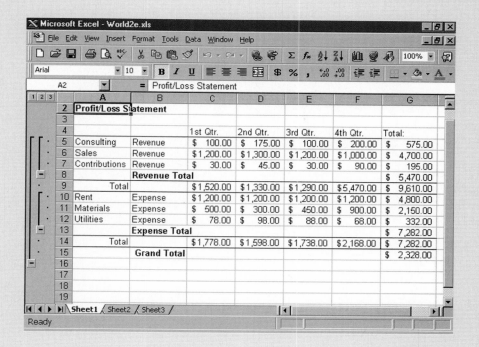

You want to know how to increase profit to $4,000 by reducing the cost of materials and utilities. You estimate that utilities cannot be reduced below $50 per quarter, and the cost of materials will not fall below $275 per quarter.

1. Open the worksheet named *World 2e.xls* that you created for Assignment 1 in Project 9.

2. Select Solver from the Tools menu.

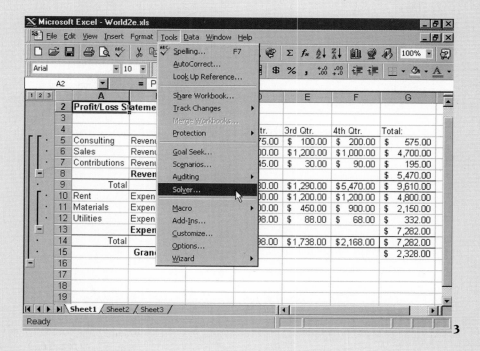

The Solver Parameters dialog will appear.

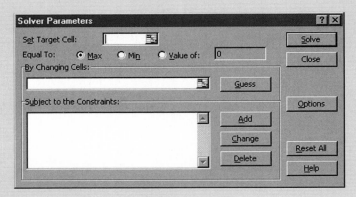

3. Type **g15** as the Set Target Cell: parameter.

Tip When you tab out of this control, Excel will automatically make the cell reference absolute.

4. To the right of Equal To:, select the Value of option button, and in the text box next to the button, type 4000 as the value. This sets the target cell equal to a value of 4000. The parameters should now appear.

5. Type the range **c10:f12** in the By Changing Cells: text box.

6. Click the Add button to add minimum utilities and materials value constraints.

7. The Add Constraint dialog box will appear. Type the values shown here.

Troubleshooting Select the greater than or equal to parameter using the drop-down list.

8. Click the Add button to add another constraint.

9. Enter the values shown here.

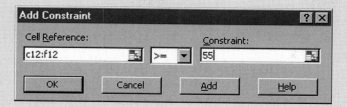

10. Click OK. The Solver Parameters should now appear.

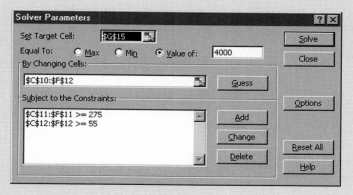

11. Click the Solve button. The Solver Results dialog box will appear. Notice that the rent, materials, and utilities values have all been adjusted to arrive at the solution.

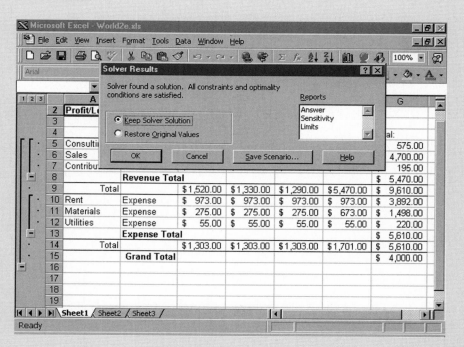

You now have a number of options. You may save the Solver Parameters as a scenario, accept the values and update the worksheet, or retain the original worksheet values.

12. Select the Restore Original Values option button and click OK.

Assignments

1. Creating a PivotTable

Open the *Regional Sales 2.xls* workbook. Save this copy as *Regional Sales 4.xls*. Delete all worksheets except the **North** and **Products** sheets. Add a column after column A and enter a product category description based upon the product number. Create a PivotTable summarizing Total Sales with Product Category as a page field. Update the workbook.

2. The PivotTable Tutorial

Visit the Microsoft Tutorial Website (http://www.microsoft.com/excel/work_tutorials.htm). Download the PivotTables lesson (*Pivottbl.xls*). Work through the lesson, experimenting with page fields.

11

Using the Excel Analysis ToolPak to Analyze Sales Data

Microsoft Excel provides a set of data analysis tools called the **Analysis ToolPak** for complex statistical analyses. The tool includes statistical tests such as the analysis of variance (ANOVA) and displays results in an output table. With Excel you can also display statistical results geographically with **Microsoft Map**.

Objectives

After completing this project, you will be able to:

➤ **Import ASCII data into Microsoft Excel**

➤ **Add additional formulas to the worksheet**

➤ **Use the IF logical function to recode the Gender variable**

➤ **Create two data sets containing the values to be tested**

➤ **Calculate descriptive statistics using the Data Analysis tools**

➤ **Conduct an analysis of variance comparing means for two groups**

➤ **Conduct an analysis of variance comparing the mean for each of three groups**

➤ **Display data on a map using Microsoft Map**

Introduction

Most businesses want to learn as much as they can about their customers' purchasing habits. Very sophisticated statistical computer application packages are available for the purpose of gleaning this information, but they are very expensive. Another solution is the Analysis ToolPak that is built into Excel, which you will learn to use in this project.

A word of caution: With Excel you can analyze *data,* defined as raw, uninterpreted facts, to produce *information,* defined as data interpreted in a specific context to make decisions. But the results of a statistical analysis are only as good as the care taken to interpret them. To use the Analysis ToolPak, you need to be familiar with the specific area of statistics for which you want to develop an analysis.

In this project you will use two related statistical procedures to analyze the sales data for World Sales, Inc. Researchers often use a T-Test to determine whether the differences in purchasing habits between men and women are statistically significant. The one-factor *analysis of variance (ANOVA)* procedure assists in determining the impact that location has on product sales.

The Challenge

You want to know if there are any statistically significant differences in purchasing trends between women and men. If there are, the company you work for will need to launch a new advertising campaign that reflects those differences. You also want to know if purchasing decisions vary depending upon where customers live. If there are differences, then Marketing will need to determine which products to sell in the various sales regions.

The Solution

Your analysis compares differences among a small number of customers, but you can extrapolate, or make inferences from that sample of customers to the general population. To do so you will need to use an inferential, parametric test. To compare the mean, or average purchases made by men versus women, and to compare purchasing habits in different regions of the United States, you can use the analysis of variance (ANOVA) procedure and then show the differences on Microsoft Map.

The Setup

To create the workbook, start Microsoft Excel and select the settings shown in Table 11.1.

Table 11.1   Excel Settings

Element	Settings
Tools, Add Ins	Install the Analysis ToolPak
Office Assistant	Close the Office Assistant
View, Toolbars	Display the Standard and Formatting toolbars
View, Formula bar	Display the Formula bar
View, Status bar	Display the Status bar
Maximize	Maximize the Application and Workbook windows

The data you will analyze is a small number of sales transactions exported from the corporate database as ASCII text.

Importing ASCII Data into Excel

The data for statistical tests you may want to conduct using Excel's Analysis ToolPak often originates from external sources. Either you or your firm deliberately collects data that is of interest, or, as is often the case with survey research, you acquire data as a by-product of activities such as business transactions. In this project, you will import into Excel for subsequent analysis sales transaction data similar in form to the data you used in Project 10. You must import data into Excel using the Import Wizard before analyzing it. The ASCII delimited text file is shown in Figure 11.1.

Figure 11.1

TASK 1: IMPORT ASCII DATA INTO MICROSOFT EXCEL

1 Select Open 📂 from the File menu, and select Text Files in the Files of type: list box.

2 In the Open dialog box, select the file *Salesdata.txt* from your floppy diskette and click Open.

> **Troubleshooting** If you do not have a floppy diskette containing this file, ask your instructor for the file. If you have access to the World Wide Web, download the file from the Addison-Wesley Web site (www.awl.com/is/select).

3 In Step 1 of the Text Import Wizard, specify the file as delimited, as shown in Figure 11.2. Click the Next button.

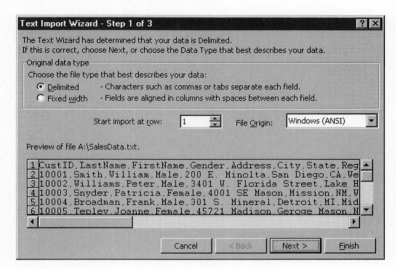

Figure 11.2

4 In Step 2 of the Wizard, specify the file as comma delimited by selecting the option shown in Figure 11.3. Click the Next button.

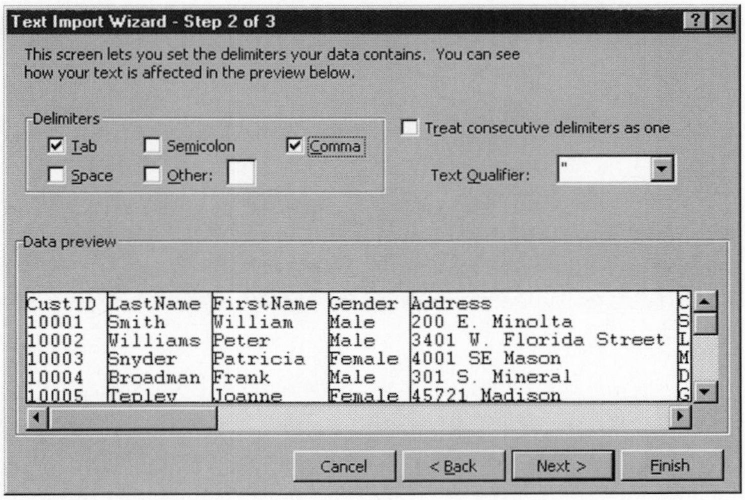

Figure 11.3

5   Select the defaults in Step 3 of the Wizard by clicking the Finish button, as shown in Figure 11.4.

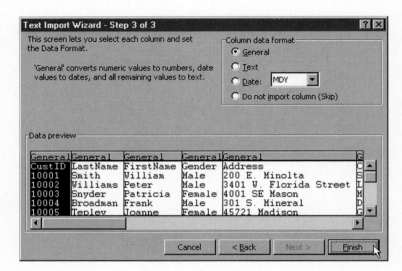

Figure 11.4

6   Save the worksheet as a Microsoft Excel workbook with the name *Analysis.xls*.
Your worksheet contains records for 30 sales transactions. In statistical terms, each row of data is a ***case***. Each column is a ***variable***, since the cell data differs from case to case. All the data in the workbook is a ***data set***. Statistical procedures analyze one or more variables for the cases specified. You must define additional variables before running the ANOVA procedure.

> **Comment** Notice that the workbook contains only one worksheet, named **SalesData**. When you open a text file in Excel and import data using the Text Import Wizard, a single worksheet is created. The name of this file is the same as the text file from which it originated.

Adding Formulas to the Worksheet

The raw transaction data does not contain totals for each order transaction. You will need to create formulas to calculate the extended price for each order. You will name this new variable *Extended Price*.

TASK 2: ADD FORMULAS TO CALCULATE THE EXTENDED PRICE

1   Type **Extended Price** in cell Q1 and press (ENTER).

2   Type **=O2*P2** in cell Q2.

3   Using the Fill Handle, copy the formula in cell Q2 through cell Q31.

4   Select the range O2:O31, hold down the (CONTROL) key, and select the range Q2:Q31.

5   Select Cells from the Format menu, and click the Number tab.

6   Format the nonadjacent selection as Currency, with 2 decimal places.

7   Highlight the range A1:Q1, and change the font style of the selection to Bold. Your worksheet should now look like Figure 11.5.

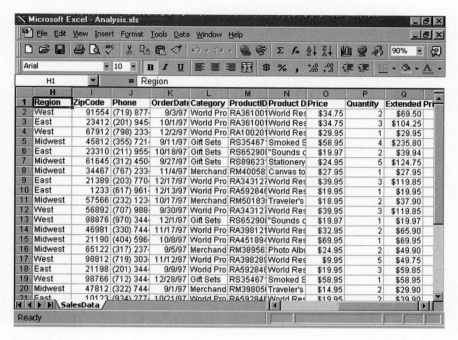

Figure 11.5

8   Save your workbook.

Converting Text Constants to Numeric Constants

In order to use the ANOVA procedure to compare purchases by men and women, which requires numeric data as input, you will need to change the text constants in column D to numeric constants. You can accomplish this by *coding* the variable, which means assigning a numeric value to each value the variable can assume. The text constant appearing as the

Gender variable is called a ***dichotomous variable*** because it can assume either one of two values: Female or Male, as shown in Figure 11.6.

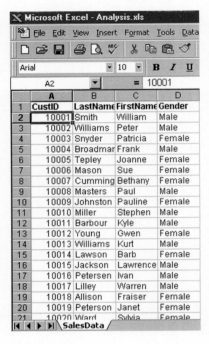

Figure 11.6

These text string values Female and Male must be converted to numeric values 0 and 1. To do so you will add to the data set a new variable containing the ***recoded values.*** You can use an IF function to recode each text entry in column D to a numeric value in column E.

TASK 3: USE THE IF LOGICAL FUNCTION TO RECODE THE GENDER VARIABLE

1 Place the cell pointer in cell E1.

2 Select Columns from the Insert menu to add a new column to the worksheet.

3 Type **Gender(Recoded)** in cell E1 as the variable name and press (ENTER). Cell E2 should now be the active cell.

4 Type the following formula in cell E2:

=IF(D2="Female",0,1)

This formula checks the values in column D of each case, and enters either a 0 or a 1 in column E of the same case. Thus, Female is recoded as 0, and Male as 1.

5 Using the Fill Handle, copy the formula in cell E2 through cell E31. When you scroll to the top of the worksheet, the data in column E should appear as shown in Figure 11.7.

	A	B	C	D	E	F	G	H	I	J	Pl—
1	CustID	LastName	FirstName	Gender	Gender (R	Address	City	State	Region	ZipCode	
2	10001	Smith	William	Male	1	200 E. Mir	San Diego	CA	West	91554	(7
3	10002	Williams	Peter	Male	1	3401 W. F	Lake Hud:	NY	East	23412	(2
4	10003	Snyder	Patricia	Female	0	4001 SE N	Mission	NM	West	67912	(7
5	10004	Broadmar	Frank	Male	1	301 S. Mir	Detroit	MI	Midwest	45812	(3
6	10005	Tepley	Joanne	Female	0	45721 Ma	Geroge M	NY	East	23310	(2
7	10006	Mason	Sue	Female	0	33975 E. I	Aurora	IL	Midwest	61645	(3
8	10007	Cumming	Bethany	Female	0	101 E. Re	Ft. Winche	IN	Midwest	34467	(7
9	10008	Masters	Paul	Male	1	2377 Sout	Redwood	NY	East	21389	(2
10	10009	Johnston	Pauline	Female	0	3 Paul Re	Boston	MA	East	1233	(6
11	10010	Miller	Stephen	Male	1	P.O. Box 3	Youngstov	MI	Midwest	57566	(2
12	10011	Barbour	Kyle	Male	1	3277 E. D	Billings	MT	West	56892	(7
13	10012	Young	Gwen	Female	0	105 95th N	Seattle	WA	West	98876	(9
14	10013	Williams	Kurt	Male	1	121 RR 5:	Alden	MI	Midwest	46981	(3
15	10014	Lawson	Barb	Female	0	9011 Willi	Miami	OH	Midwest	21190	(4
16	10015	Jackson	Lawrence	Male	1	925 S. Bul	Amazon	MI	Midwest	65122	(3
17	10016	Petersen	Ivan	Male	1	1211 Mos	Duane	CA	West	98812	(7
18	10017	Lilley	Warren	Male	1	P.O. Box 1	Jackson	NY	East	21198	(2
19	10018	Allison	Fraiser	Female	0	9001 Tucs	Arizona Ci	CA	West	98766	(7
20	10019	Peterson	Janet	Female	0	12122 S. I	Georgian	MI	Midwest	47812	(3
21	10020	Ward	Sylvia	Female	0	307 N. Hir	Bridge	MA	East	10123	(9

Cell reference: E2 = =IF(D2="Female",0,1)

Sheet tab: SalesData

Figure 11.7

6 Save your workbook.

Creating Two Data Sets Containing the Variables to Be Tested

Data to be analyzed via the ANOVA procedure in Excel must appear as an adjacent range of the values to be compared. Currently the data set contains all transaction data in the database for 30 individuals. The data you are interested in comparing includes the following variables: *Gender (Recoded)*, in column E; *Category*, in column M; and *Extended Price*, in column R. Since you will run two separate ANOVA tests, it will be easiest to create two new data sets, one for each analysis.

You can use what you learned in Project 6 about minimizing data redundancy to create two new data sets. First, you will name the current data set so it can be easily sorted. Then you can insert a worksheet into the workbook, and add links to the required variable data in the **SalesData** worksheet to each new worksheet.

TASK 4: CREATE THE BY GENDER DATA SET

1 Select Worksheet from the Insert menu to add a worksheet to the workbook.

2 Rename the inserted worksheet **By Gender**.

3 Highlight the range A2:R31 in the **SalesData** worksheet.

4 Type **SalesData** as a name for the range, as shown in Figure 11.8.

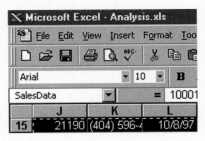

Figure 11.8

5 Press (ENTER) to name the range.

6 Select the SalesData name in the name box.

7 Select Sort from the Data menu.

8 Use the Sort dialog box to specify that you want to sort the data by the Gender (Recoded) variable, as shown in Figure 11.9. Click OK.

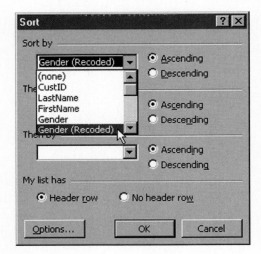

Figure 11.9

9 Type **Female** in cell A1 and **Male** in cell A2 of the **By Gender** worksheet.

10 Type **=SalesData!P2*SalesData!Q2** in cell A2 of the **By Gender** worksheet. This linking formula returns in cell A2 the product of the data values in cells P2 and Q2 of the **SalesData** worksheet.

11 Use the Fill Handle to copy this formula through cell A16 of the **By Gender** worksheet.

12 Format the selection to Currency, with 2 decimal places. The **By Gender** worksheet should look like Figure 11.10.

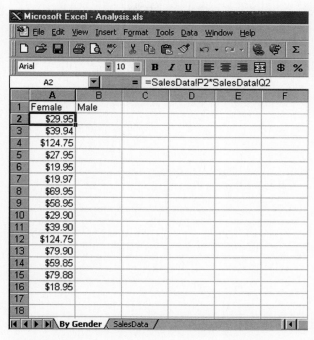

Figure 11.10

13 Type **=SalesData!P17*SalesData!Q17** in cell B2 of the **By Gender** worksheet. This references the first purchase by a male customer in the **SalesData** worksheet.

14 Use the Fill Handle to copy this formula through cell B16 of the **By Gender** worksheet. Format the selection to Currency, with 2 decimal places. The **By Gender** worksheet should look like Figure 11.11.

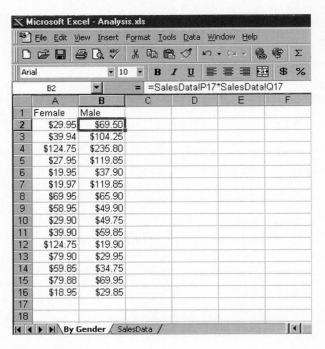

Figure 11.11

15 Save the workbook.

TASK 5: CREATE THE BY REGION DATA SET

1 Select Worksheet from the Insert menu to add a worksheet to the workbook.

2 Rename the inserted worksheet **By Region**.

3 Select the SalesData name in the name box of the **SalesData** worksheet.

4 Select Sort from the Data Menu.

5 In the Sort dialog box, specify that the data is to be sorted by the Region variable, as shown in Figure 11.12. Click OK.

Figure 11.12

6 Type **East** in cell A1 and **Midwest** in cell B1, and **West** in cell C1 of the By Region worksheet.

7 Type **=SalesData!P2*SalesData!Q2** in cell A2 of the **By Region** worksheet, and press (ENTER).

8 Type **=SalesData!P12*SalesData!Q12** in cell B2 of the **By Region** worksheet, and press (ENTER).

9 Type **=SalesData!P22*SalesData!Q22** in cell C2 of the **By Region** worksheet, and press (ENTER).

10 Select the range A2:C2.

11 Using the Fill Handle, copy the range of formulas down the worksheet through row 11.

12 Format the selection to Currency, with 2 decimal places. The **By Gender** worksheet should look like Figure 11.13.

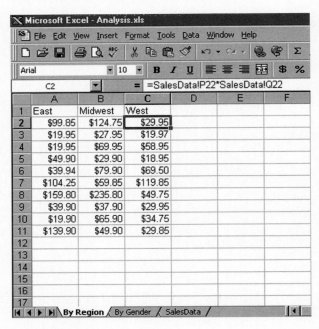

Figure 11.13

13 Save the workbook.

Calculating Descriptive Statistics Using the Data Analysis Tool

In statistical research, a common starting point is to calculate the descriptive statistics for a data set. *Descriptive statistics* express some characteristic of the data set, such as the mean or the standard deviation, and thus provide a quick overview of the data.

TASK 6: CALCULATE DESCRIPTIVE
STATISTICS FOR THE BY GENDER DATA SET

1   Click the **By Gender** worksheet tab to make it the active sheet.

2   Select Data Analysis from the Tools Menu, as shown in Figure 11.14.

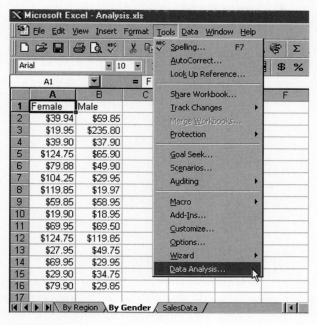

Figure 11.14

The Data Analysis dialog box shown in Figure 11.15 will appear.

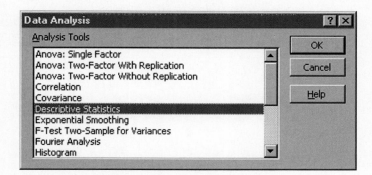

Figure 11.15

3   Select Descriptive Statistics, and click OK.

4   In the Descriptive Statistics dialog box, type **A1:B16** as the Input range, **D1** as the Output range, and select the Labels in First Row and Summary statistics check boxes, as shown in Figure 11.16. Click OK.

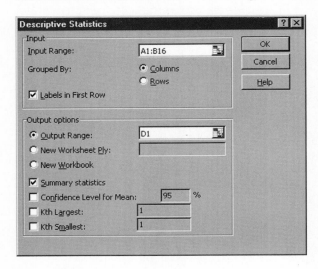

Figure 11.16

Excel adds descriptive statistics to the By Gender worksheet.

5   Format columns E and G to Number, with 2 decimal places. Change the width of columns D and F to 16.00. The **By Gender** worksheet with descriptive statistics added should now look like Figure 11.17.

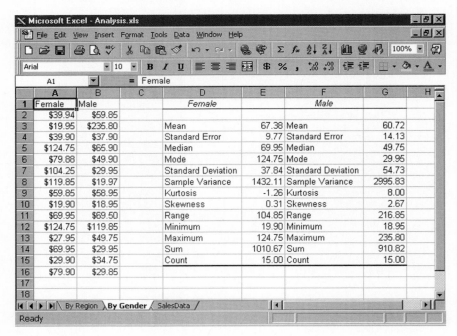

Figure 11.17

6 Save the workbook.
The descriptive statistics reveal certain characteristics about the data. The average sales by men and women are almost equal, although a male customer made the largest purchase. Soon you will determine if these differences are statistically significant. *Statistical significance* means that a difference is not due to chance but to some actual difference, in this case the difference would be between men's and women's purchasing habits.

TASK 7: CALCULATE DESCRIPTIVE STATISTICS FOR THE BY REGION DATA SET

1 Click the **By Region** worksheet tab to make it the active sheet.

2 Select Data Analysis from the Tools menu.

3 Select Descriptive Statistics, and click OK.
Enter the values shown in Figure 11.18 in the Descriptive Statistics dialog box.

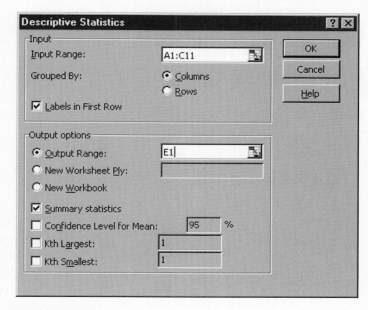

Figure 11.18

4 Change columns F, H, and J to Number format, with 2 decimal places.

5 Change the width of column D to 2.00.

6 Change the width of columns E, G, and I to 11.00. Your worksheet should now look like Figure 11.19.

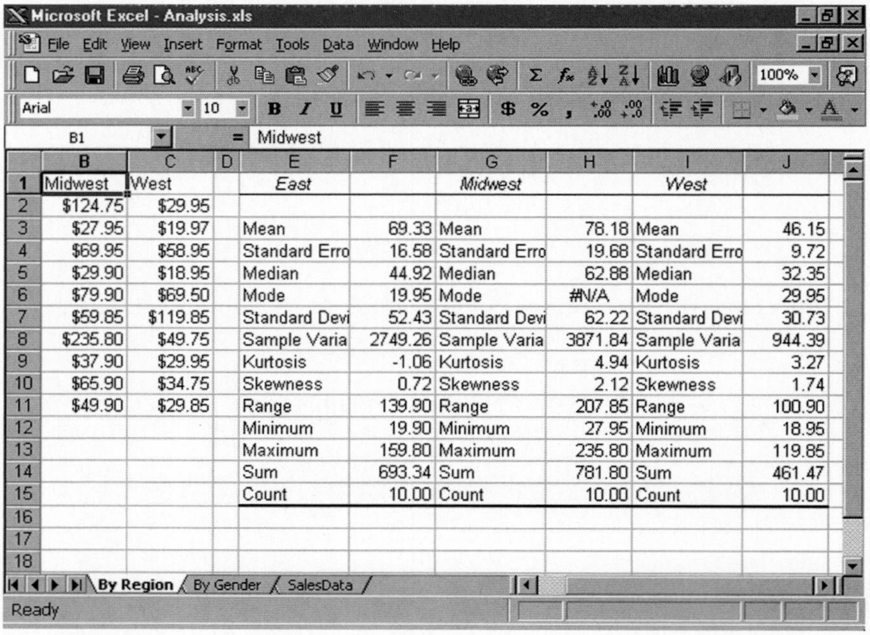

Figure 11.19

7 Save the workbook.

Conducting an Analysis of Variance
Comparing the Mean for Two Groups

Researchers often need to draw inferences about large groups based upon data from a few. They commonly use the analysis of variance, or ANOVA, procedure to compare data from two or more groups. The analysis of variance tests a specific hypothesis. In this case you want to know if shopping habits vary by gender. The **By Gender** worksheet contains data in two groups: column A contains data concerning the purchases made by women; column B purchases made by men. Researchers test to prove one of two hypotheses: the ***null hypothesis***, which claims there is no statistically significant difference between groups, or the ***alternate hypothesis,*** which claims there is indeed such a difference. A difference is considered statistically significant if it is too large to be due to chance and must instead be due to some underlying difference between the groups. The difference in question in this case is the difference in purchasing decisions between men and women.

ANOVA is a test used to measure the differences in the mean between groups. The descriptive statistics calculated for the **By Gender** worksheet reveal that on the average, men made larger purchases than women did. The analysis of variance attempts to rule out the possibility that this difference is merely due to chance.

All statistical tests return a value from the data, called the **test statistic** that is compared to an obtained statistic. The analysis of variance computes a value for F as a test statistic, and then compares the obtained value of F to a critical value from the **F distribution**. The **critical value** is the value that F must exceed for the difference to be considered statistically significant. The F distribution is a theoretical sampling of F values. If F is greater than the value specified by the F distribution for the conditions of the test, then it is probable that there is a true difference between the groups. The conclusion is considered "probable" rather than certain, because there are many sources of error that could potentially confound the results.

The ANOVA calculates F based upon the variance found within groups versus the variance between groups. Since the amount of purchase will vary in the general population, one expects variance within groups. If the variance for one group, such as women, however, is greater than that for the other group or groups in the analysis, the variance may be due to something besides the variance expected in the general population. The percentage of error a researcher is willing to take in making this decision is called **alpha**. When alpha is equal to .05, the researcher has 95% confidence that the results are true. Test results of analysis of variance are tabulated and summarized in an **ANOVA table**.

When using Excel to conduct an ANOVA test, you need to store the data in a consistent format in an adjacent area of the worksheet in columns or rows. In Task 7 you placed the sales data for women and men in two adjacent columns. You are now ready to conduct the analysis of variance.

TASK 8: CONDUCT THE ANOVA FOR THE BY GENDER DATA SET

1   Click the **By Gender** worksheet tab to make it the active sheet.

2   Select Data Analysis from the Tools menu.

3   In the Data Analysis dialog box, select ANOVA: Single Factor, as shown in Figure 11.20.

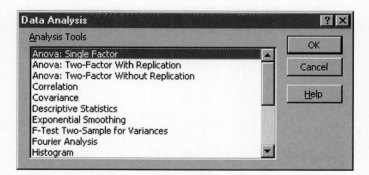

Figure 11.20

4 In the ANOVA: Single Factor dialog box, enter a1:b16 as the input range, check the box for labels in the first row, and the output range on a new worksheet ply, as shown in Figure 11.21.

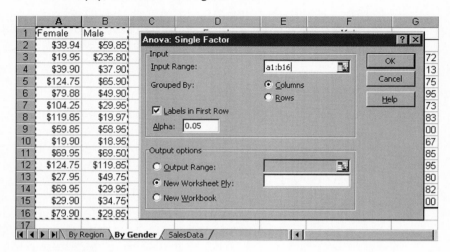

Figure 11.21

5 Click OK.

6 Change the width of column A of the new worksheet to 18.00.

7 Rename the new worksheet **By Gender ANOVA**.

8 Save the workbook.
Figure 11.22 shows the **By Gender ANOVA** table.

	A	B	C	D	E	F	G
1	Anova: Single Factor						
2							
3	SUMMARY						
4	Groups	Count	Sum	Average	Variance		
5	Female	15	1010.67	67.378	1432.113		
6	Male	15	910.82	60.72133	2995.83		
7							
8							
9	ANOVA						
10	Source of Variation	SS	df	MS	F	P-value	F crit
11	Between Groups	332.3341	1	332.3341	0.150108	0.701362	4.195982
12	Within Groups	61991.2	28	2213.971			
13							
14	Total	62323.53	29				
15							
16							
17							

Figure 11.22

The obtained F of 0.015 in cell E11 does not exceed the critical F value of 4.19 in cell G11. Therefore, you accept the null hypothesis that there is no statistically significant difference in purchasing decisions between women and men, based upon this sample.

Conducting an Analysis of Variance
Comparing the Mean for Three Groups

Using Excel, you can easily use the ANOVA procedure in situations when you want to compare means for two or more groups. Although another procedure, such as the T-Test, is appropriate when comparing means for only two groups, you must use the ANOVA procedure when comparing means for three or more groups.

TASK 9: CONDUCT THE ANOVA FOR THE BY REGION DATA SET

1   Click the **By Region** worksheet tab to make it the active sheet.

2   Select Data Analysis from the Tools menu.

3   In the Data Analysis dialog box, select ANOVA: Single Factor.

4   In the ANOVA: Single Factor dialog box, enter a1:c11 as the input range, check the box for Labels in the First Row, and the output range on a new worksheet ply, as shown in Figure 11.23.

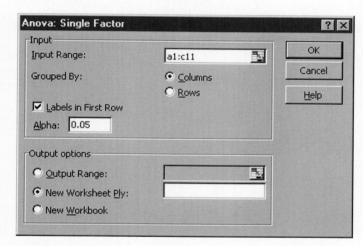

Figure 11.23

5   Click OK.

6   Change the width of column A of the new worksheet to 18.00.

7   Rename the new worksheet **By Region ANOVA**.

8 Save the workbook.
Figure 11.24 displays the By Region ANOVA table.

	A	B	C	D	E	F	G	H
1	Anova: Single Factor							
2								
3	SUMMARY							
4	*Groups*	*Count*	*Sum*	*Average*	*Variance*			
5	East	10	693.34	69.334	2749.26			
6	Midwest	10	781.8	78.18	3871.84			
7	West	10	461.47	46.147	944.3861			
8								
9								
10	ANOVA							
11	*Source of Variation*	*SS*	*df*	*MS*	*F*	*P-value*	*F crit*	
12	Between Groups	5473.339	2	2736.67	1.085193	0.352121	3.354131	
13	Within Groups	68089.37	27	2521.828				
14								
15	Total	73562.71	29					
16								
17								

By Region ANOVA / By Region / By Gender ANOVA / By

Figure 11.24

The obtained F value of 1.08 in cell E12 does not exceed the critical F of 3.35 in cell G12. Therefore, you accept the null hypothesis: there are no significant differences between the purchasing decisions of customers in the East, Midwest, and West.

Displaying Sales by State on a Map Using Microsoft Map

The analysis of variance you conducted comparing purchasing decisions by region used the Region variable to differentiate the groups. The value of this variable is determined by the state in which the customer lives. There may be times, particularly when conducting market research, when you need a good method for visually depicting sales by region. Excel includes a feature known as **Microsoft Map** for charting data associated with geographical regions. To see how Microsoft Map works, you will create a chart that lists sales by state.

> **Troubleshooting** To complete the following task, you will need to install Microsoft Map on your computer or network.

TASK 10: DISPLAY SALES DATA ON A MAP USING MICROSOFT MAP

1 Click the **SalesData** worksheet tab to make it the active sheet.

2 Highlight the range H1:H31.

3 Hold down the (CONTROL) key and select the range R1:R31.

4 Click the Map button on the Standard toolbar, as shown in Figure 11.25.

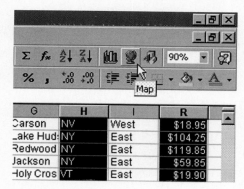

Figure 11.25

5 Drag an area on the worksheet indicating the size and location of the map you want to create. The exact size of the map is not important, as it can be resized later.

6 The Multiple Maps Available dialog box should appear. Select United States in North America, as shown in Figure 11.26.

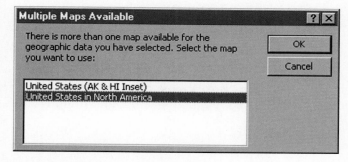

Figure 11.26

7 Click OK. Excel will create a map, and the Microsoft Map Control will appear.

8 Click the Close button on the Microsoft Map Control to close it.

9   Click an area outside the chart. Your screen should now look similar to Figure 11.27.

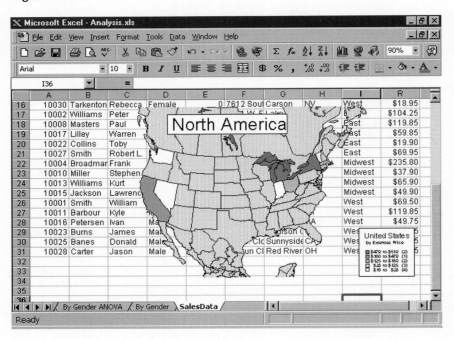

Figure 11.27

10   Save your workbook.
You can treat the map like any graphic object in your worksheet. That means you can resize it, copy it, and paste it into other Microsoft Office applications.

The Conclusion

Microsoft Excel contains powerful tools for analyzing data and displaying results. You can apply sophisticated statistical procedures to an Excel data set using the Analysis ToolPak. In addition, you may use features such as Microsoft Map to graphically depict worksheet information that includes geographical data.

Summary and Exercises

Summary

- Excel contains statistical functions for performing sophisticated statistical tests that are often used when conducting research.
- Data used for statistical analysis is often imported from simple ASCII text into Excel.
- The IF logical function can be used to recode text data into numeric variables.
- A data set contains the values that will be used in a statistical procedure.
- Data Analysis tools are used to calculate summary statistics.
- The Analysis of Variance (ANOVA) procedure is used when comparing means for two or more groups.

Key Terms and Operations

Key Terms

Alpha
Alternate hypothesis
Analysis of variance (ANOVA)
Analysis ToolPak
ANOVA table
Case
Coding
Critical value
Data
Data set
Descriptive statistics
Dichotomous variable
F distribution
Information

Microsoft Map
Null hypothesis
Recoded values
Statistical significance
Test statistic
Variable

Operations

Conduct an ANOVA comparing three groups
Conduct an ANOVA comparing two groups
Create a chart using Microsoft Map
Import ASCII data
Set up a data set
Use the IF function to recode values

Study Questions

Multiple Choice

1. An ANOVA is being used to determine whether people over 30 are more likely to purchase a product than are people under 30. People under 30 are in group 1; those over 30 are in group 2. What is the null hypothesis?
   a. There is a difference between group 2 and group 1.
   b. There is a difference between women in group 2 and women in group 1.
   c. There is no difference between women in group 2 and women in group 1.
   d. There is no difference between group 2 and group 1.

2. Which function should you use to read data in a cell and return recoded value in another cell?
   a. MIN
   b. MAX
   c. IF
   d. AVERAGE

3. What kind of data does Microsoft Map require?
   a. Numeric
   b. Currency
   c. Date
   d. Geographic

4. Which data from an ANOVA table displays the obtained value?
   a. F crit
   b. F
   c. SS
   d. P-value

5. Which analysis tool is appropriate for comparing means among two or more groups?
   a. Microsoft Map
   b. Descriptive statistics
   c. Analysis of variance
   d. IF function

6. A value in a worksheet must be changed for inclusion in a statistical procedure. What is the new value called?
   a. A recoded variable
   b. An absolute reference
   c. A linking reference
   d. A critical value

7. The formula =Data1!A1*!Data2!B4 contains
   a. A critical value
   b. A linking reference
   c. An absolute reference
   d. An obtained value

8. Which of the following is data?
   a. Sales transactions listed in an ASCII file
   b. An ANOVA summary table
   c. A list of descriptive statistics
   d. The obtained F statistic for a comparison

9. Which term communicates how data is differentiated from information?
   a. Critical
   b. Dichotomous
   c. Obtained
   d. Interpreted

10. The ANOVA procedure must be used when comparing means for how many groups?
    a. None
    b. One
    c. Two
    d. More than two

Short Answer

1. How do you arrange data when using the ANOVA procedure?

2. What is a variable?

3. What is a case?

4. How many values does a dichotomous variable assume?

5. How do you determine statistical significance when using a procedure such as ANOVA?

6. What is the null hypothesis?

7. What kind of data does Microsoft Map require?

8. What does the formula =Data1!A1*!Data2!B4 do?

9. What is a critical value?

10. How does *data* differ from *information*?

For Discussion

1. Why do you often calculate descriptive statistics before conducting procedures such as ANOVA?

2. An ANOVA returned an F of 23.07 and the critical value of F is 3.21. What is your conclusion?

3. Explain how to construct a formula containing an IF function that returns a value of 3 in column C of a worksheet for each item appearing as "Widowed" in column B of the same worksheet.

4. What statistical procedure is required to compare means for three or more groups?

Review Exercises

1. Comparing Data by Correlation

Another statistical procedure available in the Analysis ToolPak is *correlation,* a procedure for comparing values to determine the degree to which two data categories are related to one another. For example, the level of humidity and probability for rain are positively correlated, since the higher the humidity, the greater the likelihood it will rain. Create a workbook containing midterm and final examination scores. Use the correlation procedure to determine the degree to which scores on the two exams correlate.

1 Create a new workbook

2 Enter the data shown in Figure 11.28.

	A	B	C
1	Midterm	Final	
2	88	91	
3	89	88	
4	78	79	
5	74	82	
6	92	84	
7	98	92	
8	73	88	
9	67	72	
10	99	90	
11	86	88	
12			

Figure 11.28

3 Select Data Analysis from the Tool Menu.

4 Select Correlation in the Data Analysis dialog box and click OK.

5 Enter the data shown in Figure 11.29 into the Correlation dialog box.

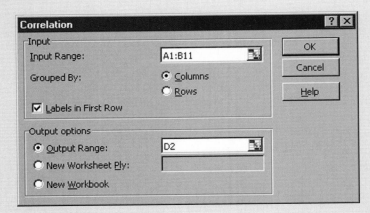

Figure 11.29

The correlation results should appear as shown in Figure 11.30.

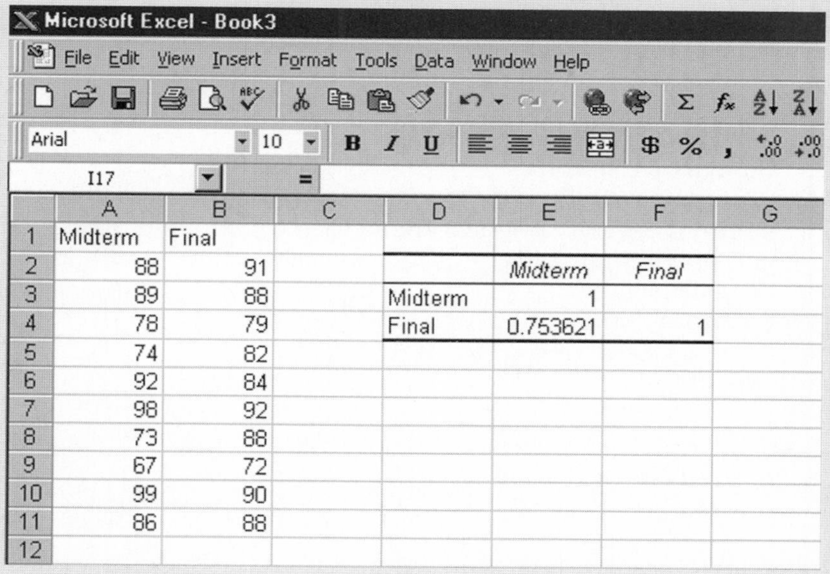

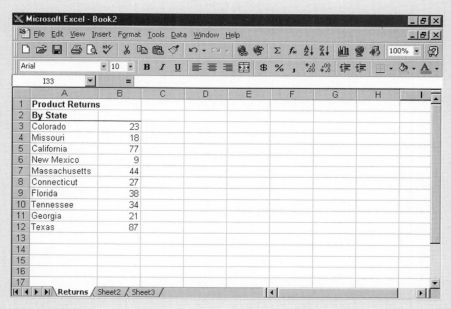

Figure 11.30

Save the workbook as *Correlate.xls*.

2. Creating a Map Containing Product Returns

Your manager has asked you to create a map showing how the number of returned products varies from state to state.

1 Create a new workbook.

2 Rename Sheet1 to **Returns**.

3 Enter the data shown in Figure 11.31.

Figure 11.31

4 Create a map displaying product returns using Microsoft Map.

5 Save the workbook as *Returns.xls*.

Assignment

Conduct an ANOVA

Create a workbook listing five people in cells A2:A6 and the amount of time each individual spends using a computer each week for four weeks. List the week data in columns B through E. Conduct an ANOVA. Save the workbook with an appropriate name.

12

Creating a Consolidated Workbook

In the preceding projects you learned how to build efficient three-dimensional workbooks using lookup and linking formulas. Another strategy you can employ for building efficient workbook solutions is to incorporate consolidated 3-D references. In this project you will learn how to create formulas that consolidate the values appearing in multiple worksheets. Then you will use Excel's auditing and data validation features to check and insure the accuracy of the workbook.

Objectives

After completing this project, you will be able to:

➤ **Create a formula with a 3-D reference to consolidate data**

➤ **Copy consolidation formulas to other cells in a worksheet**

➤ **Apply accounting formats to specific cells in a workbook**

➤ **Use Excel's auditing features**

➤ **Specify data validation criteria**

➤ **Apply conditional formats to a workbook**

➤ **Publish a worksheet as an HTML document**

The Challenge

You are responsible for developing an Excel workbook that summarizes the first quarter revenue and expenses for all Resort Sales Inc. sales regions. Your workbook must include revenue and expense data for each sales region, as well as the total revenue and expenses for the first quarter of 1997. It also must summarize how the actual expenses compare to the projected expenses. In addition, since your workbook will be used to track next year's revenue and expenses, you need to construct it so as to check the validity of the data as it is entered into the workbook. Finally, top management has requested that you prepare an HTML document that summarizes last year's revenue and expenses for the first quarter of 1997, which will be posted to the corporate intranet.

The Solution

Excel includes a number of features that will allow you to effectively and efficiently summarize quarterly sales data. In Project 6 you learned how to create three-dimensional workbooks as a way of minimizing the data entered into a workbook. Figure 12.1 graphically displays a three-dimensional workbook comprised of five worksheets that will consolidate sales data from four sales regions.

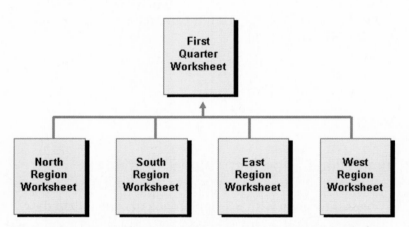

Figure 12.1: Solution for consolidating revenue and expenses data

This approach differs from what you created in Project 7 because it lists revenue data for sales categories and not the sales inventory for individual items. In addition, revenue is compared with expenses to show the profit or loss realized by each region and for the corporation as a whole. In this project you will enter consolidation formulas for summing revenue and expense data across the four sales regions.

Recall that as you develop more complex workbooks, it is very important to check the accuracy of both the workbook's structure and the data entered into it. By using Excel's auditing features, you can check the formulas a workbook contains for accuracy. By using data validation, you can check the accuracy of data as it is entered. To see how the actual expenses relate to projected expenses and the impact these have on the overall profit or loss, you can apply conditional formats to specific cells. Finally, you can easily create an HTML document of the revenue and expense data by publishing the worksheet to the Web. Figure 12.2 displays the First Quarter Worksheet in the consolidated workbook before saving it to the Web.

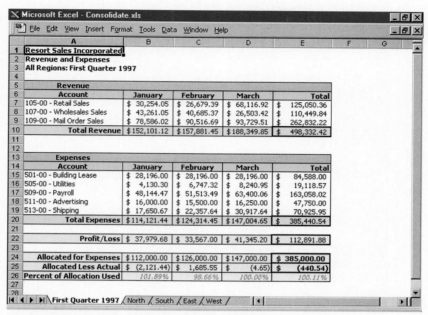

Figure 12.2: The First Quarter 1997 Worksheet

The Setup

To complete this workbook, start Microsoft Excel, select the settings shown in Table 12.1, and open the workbook named *Consolidated.xls*.

Table 12.1 Excel Settings

Element	Settings
Office Assistant	Close the Office Assistant
View, Toolbars	Display the Standard and Formatting toolbars
View, Formula bar	Display the Formula bar
View, Status bar	Display the Status bar
Maximize	Maximize the application and workbook windows
File, Open	Open the *Consolidated.xls* workbook

Troubleshooting If you do not have a floppy diskette containing the *Consolidated.xls* file, ask your instructor for this file.

Consolidating Data Using 3-D References

The *Consolidate.xls* workbook contains numeric sales data and SUM functions to calculate total revenue and expenses for each sales region. Click the North worksheet tab to review the structure of each regional worksheet. Your screen should look similar to Figure 12.3.

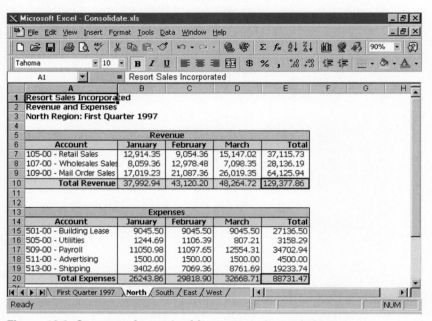

Figure 12.3 Structure for each of four quarterly worksheets

Troubleshooting Figure 12.3 displays at 90% to show all the worksheet rows.

As you review the remaining regional worksheets, you will see that each worksheet has the same data elements in the same cells. To calculate revenue and expense totals for the first quarter, you will need to be sure the cells for each revenue and expense line item by region are included in a SUM function. In Excel you can ***consolidate data***; that is, you can use 3-D references in formulas to perform a calculation on data in more than one worksheet. In this case a 3-D reference is a function that includes a range of worksheets and cell references as the argument for a SUM function.

TASK 1: TO ADD A 3-D CONSOLIDATION FORMULA TO THE FIRST QUARTER WORKSHEET

1 Click the *First Quarter 1997* worksheet tab to make it the active worksheet.

2   Place the insertion point in cell B7.

3   Choose Insert f_x, Function from the menu.

4   Select All as the Function category and SUM as the Function name.

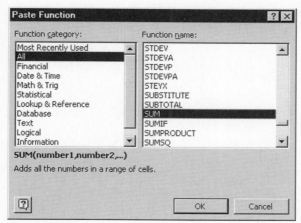

Figure 12.4

5   Click OK.

6   Click the button in the Formula Palette 🔢 to enter data for Number 1.

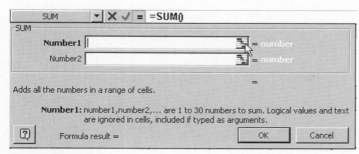

Figure 12.5

7   Click the North worksheet tab and select cell B7. Notice the formula in the Formula bar.

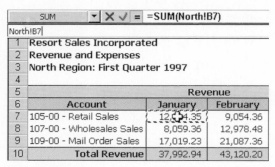

Figure 12.6

8 Press the (SHIFT) key and click the West worksheet tab. You will notice that the range of all regional worksheets is selected.

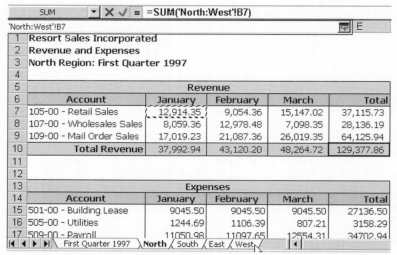

Figure 12.7

9 Click the button immediately below the Formula bar to return to the Formula Palette.

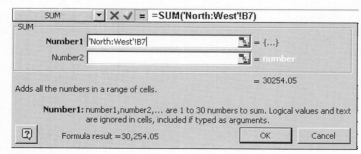

Figure 12.8

10 Click the OK button in the Formula Palette. The total for January retail sales is now displayed.

11 Save your workbook.

Copying 3-D References

Once you have created one consolidation formula, it can be copied to other cells in the worksheet. If you review the formula in cell B7 of the First Quarter 1997 worksheet, you will see that it contains relative references, which will automatically adjust the row and column references when the formula is copied.

TASK 2: TO COPY THE 3-D CONSOLIDATION FORMULA TO OTHER WORKSHEET CELLS

1 Select cell B7 of the First Quarter 1997 if it is not currently the active cell.

2 Use the Fill handle to copy this cell through cell D7.

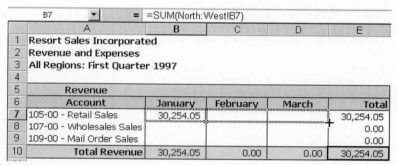

	B7 ▼		=	=SUM(North:West!B7)	
	A	B	C	D	E
1	Resort Sales Incorporated				
2	Revenue and Expenses				
3	All Regions: First Quarter 1997				
4					
5	Revenue				
6	Account	January	February	March	Total
7	105-00 - Retail Sales	30,254.05			30,254.05
8	107-00 - Wholesales Sales				0.00
9	109-00 - Mail Order Sales				0.00
10	Total Revenue	30,254.05	0.00	0.00	30,254.05

Figure 12.9

Troubleshooting   Make sure you click and drag the fill handle to copy this formula.

3 Click the Fill handle again and copy the formulas in rows 7 through 9.

5	Revenue				
6	Account	January	February	March	Total
7	105-00 - Retail Sales	30,254.05	26,679.39	68,116.92	125,050.36
8	107-00 - Wholesales Sales				0.00
9	109-00 - Mail Order Sales				0.00
10	Total Revenue	30,254.05	26,679.39	68,116.92	125,050.36

Figure 12.10

4 Your worksheet should now look like the one shown below.

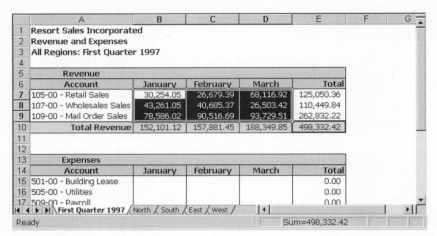

Figure 12.11

5   Highlight cell B7 and Copy ▤ the selection.

6   Select the range B15:D19.

	A	B	C	D	E
6	**Account**	**January**	**February**	**March**	**Total**
7	105-00 - Retail Sales	30,254.05	26,679.39	68,116.92	125,050.36
8	107-00 - Wholesales Sales	43,261.05	40,685.37	26,503.42	110,449.84
9	109-00 - Mail Order Sales	78,586.02	90,516.69	93,729.51	262,832.22
10	**Total Revenue**	152,101.12	157,881.45	188,349.85	498,332.42
11					
12					
13	**Expenses**				
14	**Account**	**January**	**February**	**March**	**Total**
15	501-00 - Building Lease				0.00
16	505-00 - Utilities				0.00
17	509-00 - Payroll				0.00
18	511-00 - Advertising				0.00
19	513-00 - Shipping				0.00
20	**Total Expenses**	0.00	0.00	0.00	0.00
21					
22	Profit /Loss	152101.12	157881.45	188349.85	498332.42

First Quarter 1997 / North / South / East / West /

Figure 12.12

7   Paste the contents of the clipboard ▤ into the selection. Your worksheet will now contain formulas that return the values listed below.

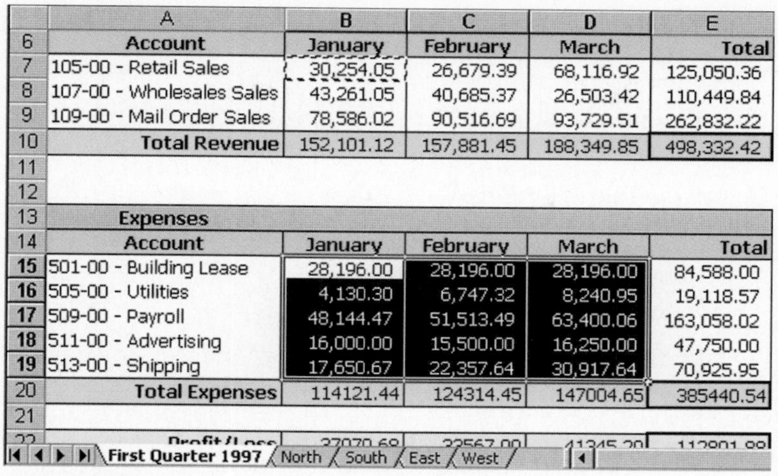

	A	B	C	D	E
6	**Account**	**January**	**February**	**March**	**Total**
7	105-00 - Retail Sales	30,254.05	26,679.39	68,116.92	125,050.36
8	107-00 - Wholesales Sales	43,261.05	40,685.37	26,503.42	110,449.84
9	109-00 - Mail Order Sales	78,586.02	90,516.69	93,729.51	262,832.22
10	**Total Revenue**	152,101.12	157,881.45	188,349.85	498,332.42
11					
12					
13	**Expenses**				
14	**Account**	**January**	**February**	**March**	**Total**
15	501-00 - Building Lease	28,196.00	28,196.00	28,196.00	84,588.00
16	505-00 - Utilities	4,130.30	6,747.32	8,240.95	19,118.57
17	509-00 - Payroll	48,144.47	51,513.49	63,400.06	163,058.02
18	511-00 - Advertising	16,000.00	15,500.00	16,250.00	47,750.00
19	513-00 - Shipping	17,650.67	22,357.64	30,917.64	70,925.95
20	**Total Expenses**	114121.44	124314.45	147004.65	385440.54
21					
22	Profit/Loss	37070.68	33567.00	41345.20	112901.88

First Quarter 1997 / North / South / East / West /

Figure 12.13

8   Save your workbook.

As you review each formula you added to the worksheet, you will see that the syntax of a 3-D reference for consolidating data is

= FUNCTION(Name of First Worksheet:Name of Last Worksheet!CellReference)

The argument contains a list of valid worksheet names, followed by an exclamation point and the cell reference.

When you consolidate data by using 3-D references, only cells in the worksheets that are named in the range of selected worksheets will be included in the calculation. For consolidation references to work properly, all worksheets in the calculation must appear as a continuous range.

Changing Cell Formats

As you review the data displayed in each workbook, you may notice that the display format for the numbers varies and that it is not in currency format. Since the values here represent large figures, there is no need to display two digits to the right of the decimal place.

Excel has a number of built-in formats you can apply to numeric values. By selecting Accounting format and rounding each value to the nearest dollar figure, the values will be easier to read. The *Accounting format* is one of Excel's built in number formats you can apply to one or more cells.

TASK 3: TO CHANGE THE FORMAT OF EACH WORKSHEET TO ACCOUNTING

1 Click the First Quarter 1997 worksheet tab to make it the active sheet, if necessary.

2 Select the range B7:E10.

3 While depressing the (CTRL) key, select the range B15:E20. A nonadjacent range should now be highlighted.

> **Tip** The (CTRL) key is used throughout the Windows environment to highlight a non-adjacent selection.

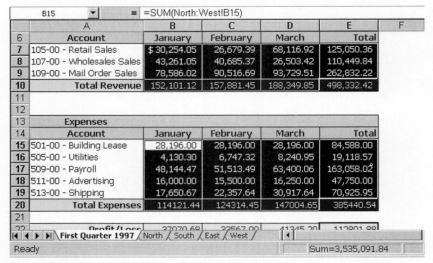

Figure 12.14

4 Depress the CTRL key again. Select the ranges B22:E22 and B24:E26 respectively.

5 Choose Format, Cells from the menu.

6 Click the Number tab if necessary. Select Accounting from the Category: list, and set the decimal places to 0. Make sure the Symbol: list displays a dollar sign.

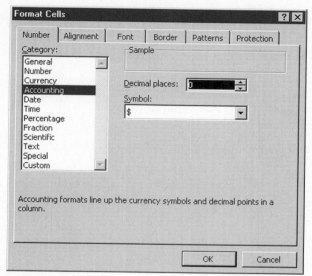

Figure 12.15

7   Click OK and click cell E10. Your worksheet should now display all numeric values in Accounting format with no decimal places.

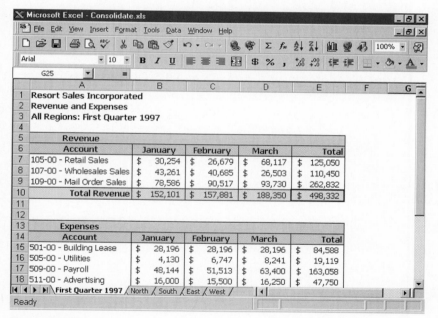

Figure 12.16

8   While depressing the (CTRL) key, select the following ranges in the North worksheet: B7:E10, B15:E20, B22:E22, B24:E26.

9   While depressing the (CTRL) key, click the South, East, and West worksheet tabs.

Figure 12.17

> **Troubleshooting** Make sure you continue to depress the (CTRL) key as you select each nonadjacent range and each worksheet tab.

10 Choose Format, Cells from the menu and apply the same Accounting format to the selected cells.

11 With the regional worksheets still selected, change the width of column E to 12.00.

12 Check each worksheet. All cells displaying values should now display Accounting format, with no decimal places and a dollar sign that appears left justified.

13 Save your workbook.

Using Excel's Auditing Feature

As you changed the format of the cells near the bottom of each worksheet, you may have noticed that #DIV/0! is displayed in some of the cells. This is an *error value*—a value that is displayed if there is an error in performing a calculation.

Excel contains auditing features that allow you to locate the source of errors. In addition, you can see which cells precede the values in formulas, and conversely, which cells depend upon other cells in your worksheet. The Auditing Toolbar provides shortcuts to each of these auditing functions.

TASK 4: TO DISPLAY AND ISOLATE ERRORS USING THE AUDITING TOOLBAR

1 Click the First Quarter 1997 worksheet tab to make it the active sheet.

2 Select cell B26.

3 Choose Tools, Auditing from the menu.

4 In the cascading menu, choose Show Auditing Toolbar.

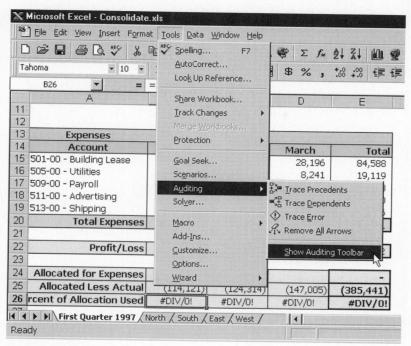

Figure 12.18

5   Click the Trace Error button 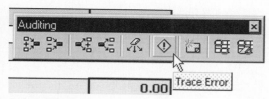 on the Auditing Toolbar.

Figure 12.19

Excel isolates the error by displaying a blue arrow, termed a ***tracer arrow***. In this case, the error results from attempting to divide the value in cell D20 by a null value in cell D24, which returns a Divide by Zero error (DIV/0!).

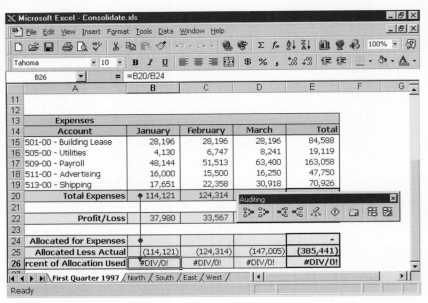

Figure 12.20

> **Tip** Although this cell currently contains a null value, you will add a projected expense value in Task 7 of this project.

6 Click the Remove All Arrows button ![icon] on the Auditing Toolbar to remove all tracer arrows from the worksheet.

As you use Excel's auditing feature, there may be times when you want to see exactly which cells are used as the source of a calculation in a formula. You can *trace precedents* to see which cells provide data to a formula. Conversely, you can *trace dependents* to see which cells depend upon a formula.

TASK 5: TO TRACE PRECEDENTS AND DEPENDENTS USING THE AUDITING TOOLBAR

1 Select cell B20 in the First Quarter 1997 worksheet.

2 Click the Trace Precedents button ![icon] on the Auditing Toolbar.

The blue tracer arrow appears as a bold line, indicating that cells B15 to B19 precede this value.

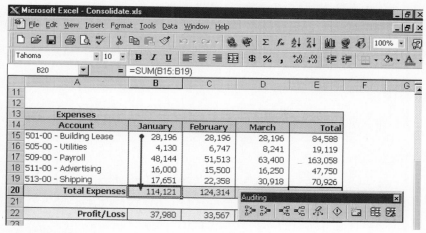

Figure 12.21

3   Click the Trace Precedents button 🔲 again. Each cell in the range is now preceded by a new symbol.
This means that the values in these cells are preceded by values in other worksheets.

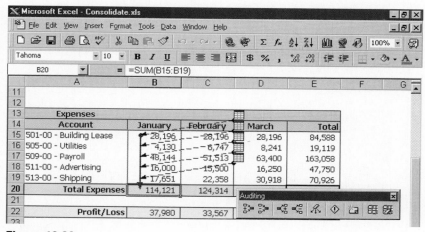

Figure 12.22

4   Double-click the Remove Precedent Arrows button 🔲 on the Auditing Toolbar to remove all precedent tracer arrows from the worksheet.

5   Select cell B15.

6   Click the Trace Dependents button 🔲 on the Auditing Toolbar to display tracer arrows indicating which formulas depend upon this cell.

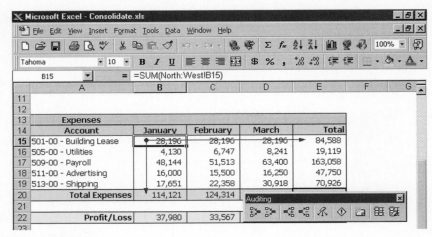

Figure 12.23

7 Double-click the Trace Dependents button 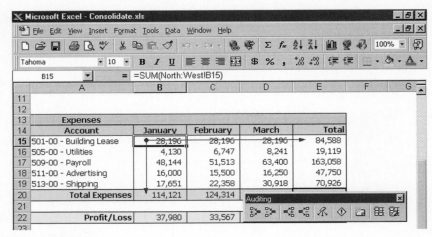 and then click the Trace Precedents button. The tracer arrows display all the cells that depend upon the value in cell B15, and the symbol extending from cell B15 indicates that this value is preceded by a value in another worksheet.

Figure 12.24

8 Click the Remove All Arrows button to remove all tracer arrows from the worksheet.

9 Close the Auditing toolbar.

Preventing Errors by Specifying Data Validation Criteria

As you develop workbooks that other may use to enter data, it is important to do what you can when constructing the workbook to prevent errors later. To help you with this, Excel supports a number of *data validation* features. These allow you to specify valid entries for a cell or range of cells and also to return a data validation message to users when they select a cell for data entry.

As you think about the structure of each regional worksheet, it should make sense that neither the revenue or expense line items will ever be less than zero. You can specify these data validation criteria and then construct a message telling users that the value entered in these cells must be greater than or equal to zero.

TASK 6: TO SPECIFY DATA VALIDATION CRITERIA AND A VALIDATION MESSAGE FOR A RANGE OF CELLS

1 Click the North worksheet tab to make it the active sheet.

2 Highlight the range B7:D9.

3 Depress the (CTRL) key and highlight the range B15:D19.

4 Choose Data, Validation from the menu.

5 Click the Settings tab in the Data Validation dialog box if it is not active.

6 Select Decimal from the Allow: list, greater than or equal to from the Data list, and type **0** in the Minimum textbox.

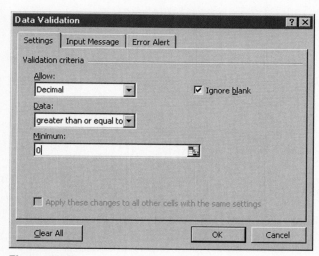

Figure 12.25

7 Click the Input Message tab in the Data Validation dialog box.

8 Click the Input Message: textbox and type **All revenue and expense values must be greater than or equal to zero!** as the message.

9 Click the OK button.

10 Select cell B7.

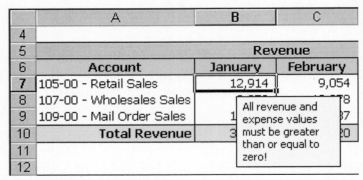

Figure 12.26

11 Type **−1** as the value for the cell and press (ENTER).

12 Click Cancel when the error message shown below appears.

Figure 12.27

13 Using the same procedures as in steps 1 through 9 above, apply the same data validation criteria and message to the remaining regional worksheets.

14 Save your workbook.

Applying Conditional Formats to Worksheet Cells

At times you may want to see at a glance the relationship between values. Although charts and graphs often represent relationships that are easily understood, Excel also supports conditional formats for the same purpose. A *conditional format* is a format such as a font color or style that Excel automatically applies to a cell if a specified condition is true.

Tip You can specify up to three conditions when applying conditional formats.

Each regional worksheet in your workbook contains a row of formulas (row 26) for displaying the percent that was actually used from the allocated budget for expenses. By applying conditional formats to these cells, you can easily see whether the actual expenses were less or more than the amount allocated for expenses.

TASK 7: TO APPLY CONDITIONAL FORMATS TO A RANGE OF CELLS

1   Click the North worksheet tab to make it the active sheet.

2   Change the width of column A to 25.00.

3   Type **25000** in cell B24, **30000** in cell C24, and **33000** in cell D24.

4   Highlight the range B26:E26.

5   Choose Format, Cells from the menu. Change the number format of the selection to Percentage, and specify two decimal places. Click OK.

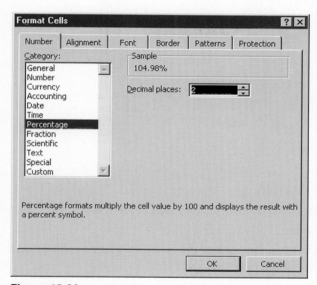

Figure 12.28

6   Choose Format, Conditional Formatting from the menu.

Troubleshooting   If the Office Assistant appears, close it.

7   Set the values for Condition 1 as shown below.

Figure 12.29

8   Click the Format button [Format...] in the Conditional Formatting dialog box.

9 In the Font tab, set the font style to italic and the color to red. Click OK.

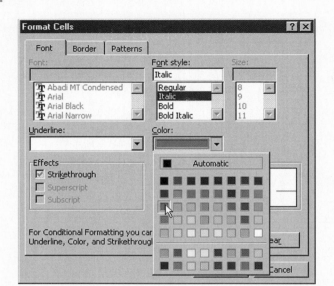

Figure 12.30

10 Click the Add button Add >> in the Conditional Formatting dialog box to add another condition.

11 Set the cell value for condition 2 to less than 1. Click the Format button Format... and set the style to italic and the color to Sea Green. Click OK.

12 Click the Add button again. Set the cell value of the third condition to equal to 1, the style to bold, and the font color to Indigo.

13 Click OK. Your settings for the three conditions should match those shown below.

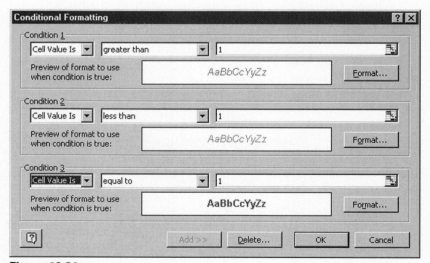

Figure 12.31

14 Click the OK button and click outside the selection to deselect it. Your worksheet will appear as shown in the following figure.

	A	B	C	D	E	F
12						
13			Expenses			
14	Account	January	February	March	Total	
15	501-00 - Building Lease	$ 9,046	$ 9,046	$ 9,046	$ 27,137	
16	505-00 - Utilities	$ 1,245	$ 1,106	$ 807	$ 3,158	
17	509-00 - Payroll	$ 11,051	$ 11,098	$ 12,554	$ 34,703	
18	511-00 - Advertising	$ 1,500	$ 1,500	$ 1,500	$ 4,500	
19	513-00 - Shipping	$ 3,403	$ 7,069	$ 8,762	$ 19,234	
20	Total Expenses	$ 26,244	$ 29,819	$ 32,669	$ 88,731	
21						
22	Profit/Loss	$ 11,749	$ 13,301	$ 15,596	$ 40,646	
23						
24	Allocated for Expenses	$ 25,000	$ 30,000	$ 33,000	$ 88,000	
25	Allocated Less Actual	$ (1,244)	$ 181	$ 331	$ (731)	
26	Percent of Allocation Used	104.98%	99.40%	99.00%	100.83%	
27						

First Quarter 1997 \ **North** / South / East / West /

Figure 12.32

You can see that the actual expenses for January exceeded the allocated expenses by 4.98%, but that the actual expenses for both February and March were less than what was allocated. The net result is that for the first quarter, the actual expenses exceeded the allocated expenses by 0.83%.

TASK 8: TO ADD CONDITIONAL FORMATTING TO THE REMAINING WORKSHEETS IN THE WORKBOOK:

1 Type the following values in cells B24:D24 of the South, East, and West worksheets, respectively:

35000	**41000**	**37000**
30000	**30000**	**40000**
22000	**25000**	**37000**

2 Click the First Quarter 1997 worksheet tab to make it the active sheet.

3 Highlight the range B7:E10, B15:E20, B22:E22, and B24:E25.

> **Troubleshooting**   Remember to depress the CTRL key to select a non-adjacent range of cells.

4 Choose Format, Cells from the menu.

5 Select Accounting as the number format. Display two decimal places.

6 Select the range B26:E26 and set the number format to Percentage, with two decimal places.

7 Select cell B24. Type **=SUM(North:West!B24)** as the formula for this cell.

8 Use the Fill Handle to copy this formula through cell E24.

9 Using the same procedures as in steps 5 through 14 of Task 7, apply conditional formatting to the range B26:E26 of the First Quarter 1997 worksheet.

10 Adjust the column widths of this worksheet as necessary to display the values in all cells.

11 Save your workbook. Rows 13 through 26 of the First Quarter 1997 workbook should appear as shown in the following figure.

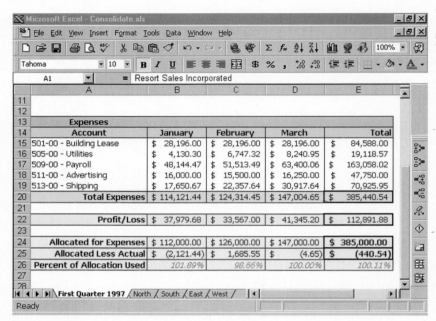

Figure 12.33

Publishing Excel Worksheets as HTML Documents for Posting on the World Wide Web or Corporate Intranet

Now that you have completed your consolidated workbook, you can publish one or more worksheets as HTML documents for posting to the World Wide Web or corporate intranet. An **_HTML document_** is a text file that includes "tags" that specify how the information will appear when displayed in a Web browser. In this way, you can share the information in your workbook with users who may not have Excel installed on their computers.

TASK 9: TO SAVE AN EXCEL WORKSHEET AN AS HTML DOCUMENT

1 Select the range A1:E26 in the First Quarter 1997 worksheet.

2 Choose File, Save As HTML from the menu as shown below.

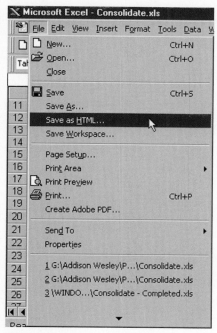

Figure 12.34

3   When the first step of the Internet Assistant WIzard appears, click Next.

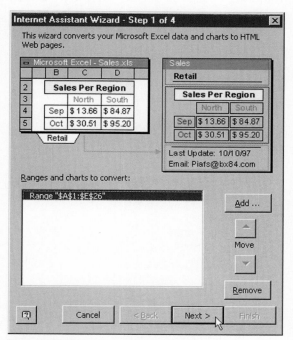

Figure 12.35

4   Accept the default option to create an independent HTML document in Step 2 of the Wizard.

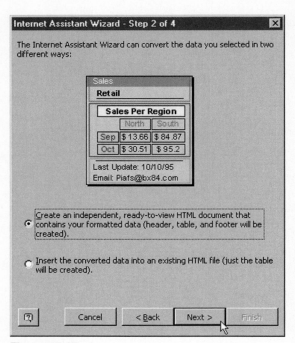

Figure 12.36

5   Click Next. In Step 3 of the Wizard, type **Resort Sales Incorporated** as the title for the document and check the option "to add a horizontal line before the converted data."

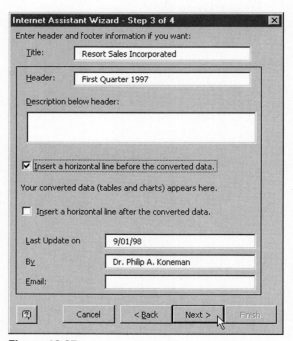

Figure 12.37

6   Click Next. In the final step of the Wizard, accept the default to save the results as an HTML document, and type **A:\Consolidate.htm** as the name for the document.

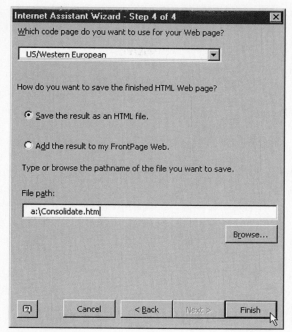

Figure 12.38

Troubleshooting Make sure you place a formatted diskette in the A: drive!

7   Click Finish. Exit Excel.

8   Open My Computer and locate the file you just created on your diskette.

9   Open the file to see how it will appear when displayed in a Web Browser.

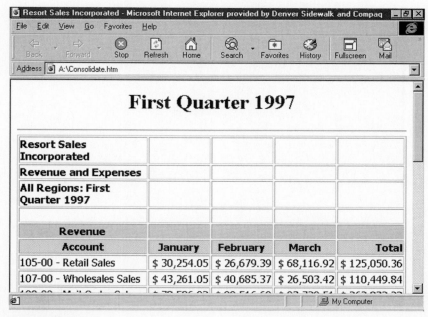

Figure 12.39

> **Tip** To view your document on the Web, you must have Internet Explorer or another web browser installed.

10 Close your Web Browser when you are finished viewing this document.

The Conclusion

You have learned how to use 3-D references to consolidate data among worksheets. The workbook you completed in this project consolidates data from multiple worksheets; it includes data validation criteria to assist users in entering data; it compares actual and allocated expenses as conditionally formatted information to allow users to see at a glance whether actual expenses were within the amount allocated; and the workbook can be posted on the Web—an ideal platform for sharing workbook information with others.

Summary and Exercises

Summary

- 3-D consolidation references allow you to share and summarize data among worksheets in a workbook.
- 3-D consolidation formulas can be copied to other worksheet cells in the same way other formulas can be copied.
- Excel includes numerous accounting formats that can be applied to currency data.
- Excel includes a variety of auditing features to locate errors in formulas, trace the cells in formulas that depend upon other cells, and determine which cells precede other cells in formulas.
- By applying conditional formats to worksheet cells, you can visually determine if a specific condition has been met.
- Excel worksheets and workbooks can be saved in HTML format for posting on a Web server, and viewed using a Web browser.

Key Terms and Operations

Key Terms
3-D references
Accounting format
Auditing Toolbar
Conditional format
Consolidate data
Data validation
Error value
HTML document

Operations
Add 3-D references to a workbook to consolidate data
Add conditional formats to worksheets
Apply accounting formats
Copy formulas that contain 3-D references
Create a data validation message
Find the source of errors
Save a worksheet as an HTML document
Specify data validation criteria
Trace dependents
Trace precedents
Tracer arrow

Study Questions

Multiple Choice

1. 3-D references that consolidate data
   a. can be entered into only one cell of a worksheet.
   b. can be entered into multiple worksheet cells.
   c. cannot contain functions.
   d. reference cells on a range of worksheets.
   e. B and D

2. To easily copy consolidation references to other worksheet cells, use
   a. copy and paste.
   b. cut and paste.
   c. the cursor to move the selection.
   d. drag and drop
   e. the Fill Handle.

3. Which of the following is a false statement concerning Accounting formats?
   a. Accounting formats can contain a dollar sign.
   b. Accounting formats can only display two places to the right of the decimal.
   c. Accounting formats can display decimal values as integers rounded to the nearest dollar.
   d. Both A and C are false
   e. Both B and C are false

4. To see what cells are used in a formula, click the _____ button on the Auditing Toolbar.
   a. Show Precedents
   b. Remove Precedent Arrows
   c. Trace Dependents
   d. Remove Dependents Arrows
   e. Remove All Arrows

5. What happens if you show precedents that appear on another worksheet?
   a. The tracer arrows will not refer to the additional worksheet.
   b. The tracer arrows will appear green in color.
   c. All tracer arrows are removed from the worksheet.
   d. An error message will appear.
   e. A symbol appears indicating that a precedent is on another worksheet.

6. If you want descriptive text to appear when a user tries to enter data into a cell, you should add which of the following to the cell?
   a. A validation message.
   b. A validation criteria.
   c. Tracer arrows.
   d. A conditional format.
   e. A 3-D reference.

7. Which statement is false?
   a. Conditional formats allow you to understand logical relationships between two values at a glance.
   b. A validation criterion is a condition that must be met before data can successfully be entered into a cell.
   c. A validation message must always accompany validation criteria.
   d. You can specify up to three conditional formats for any given worksheet cell.
   e. 3-D references always refer to multiple worksheets.

8. If you want to limit the information a user can enter into a worksheet cell, you should add which of the following to the cell?
   a. HTML tags
   b. Data validation criteria
   c. A validation message
   d. Conditional formats
   e. 3-D references

9. What is the maximum number of conditions you can specify when applying conditional formats?
   a. One
   b. Two
   c. Three
   d. Four
   e. Five

10. When you save a worksheet as an HTML document, the file is:
   a. a Word document with special formats applied.
   b. an Excel workbook formatted for display on the Web.
   c. a text file with tags indicating how the information will display in a web browser.
   d. a PowerPoint presentation formatted for delivery on the Web.
   e. none of the above

Short Answer

1. 3-D consolidation references contain which symbol immediately following a valid worksheet range?

2. How many conditions can you specify when applying conditional formats to a cell?

3. Does a 3-D consolidation reference always include a range of worksheets?

4. How do tracing dependents and tracing precedents differ?

5. Must the Accounting format display decimal values?

6. What is the difference between validation criteria and a validation message?

7. Which Toolbar contains tools for isolating errors in worksheets?

8. Which screen element is used to copy formulas to multiple cells simultaneously?

9. How do you save an Excel workbook for display on the World Wide Web?

10. Give one example of data you may want to validate as it is entered into a worksheet.

For Discussion

1. How do consolidation references differ from formulas containing lookup functions?

2. As you audit formulas in a worksheet, when should you display precedents rather than dependents?

3. What are conditional formats and why are they useful?

4. What is data validation and why is it important?

Review Exercises

1. Creating an HTML Table for a profit/loss statement

1. Create a new Excel Workbook and enter the data shown in Figure 12.39.
2. Add conditional formatting and data validation criteria to the workbook.

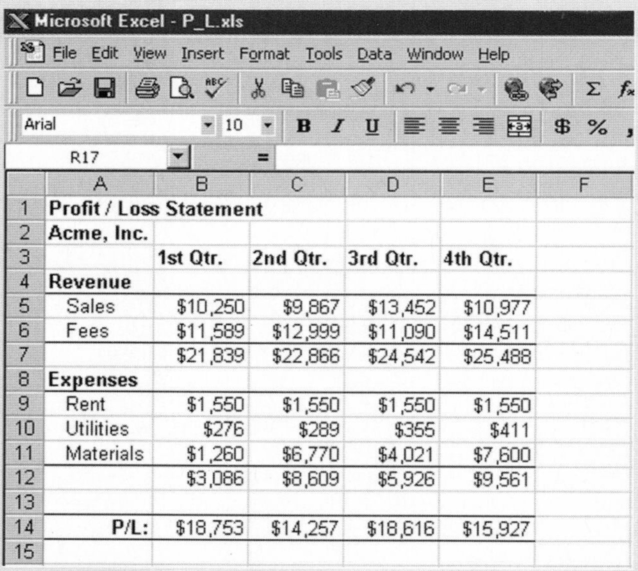

	A	B	C	D	E	F
1	Profit / Loss Statement					
2	Acme, Inc.					
3		1st Qtr.	2nd Qtr.	3rd Qtr.	4th Qtr.	
4	Revenue					
5	Sales	$10,250	$9,867	$13,452	$10,977	
6	Fees	$11,589	$12,999	$11,090	$14,511	
7		$21,839	$22,866	$24,542	$25,488	
8	Expenses					
9	Rent	$1,550	$1,550	$1,550	$1,550	
10	Utilities	$276	$289	$355	$411	
11	Materials	$1,260	$6,770	$4,021	$7,600	
12		$3,086	$8,609	$5,926	$9,561	
13						
14	P/L:	$18,753	$14,257	$18,616	$15,927	
15						

Figure 12.39

3. Save the workbook to your floppy diskette as *P_L.xls*.
4. Select Save As HTML from the File Menu.
5. View the HTML document using a web browser.

2. Using Microsoft Query to extract data from an Access database

Microsoft Office includes Microsoft Query, an application designed to retrieve data from an external database. In this exercise you will learn how to set up a link to a database and how to return data from a query into an Excel worksheet.

> **Tip** To complete this exercise, you must have Microsoft Query installed on your computer or network.

1. Copy the Access database *Resort Sales 5.mdb* from your network to a floppy diskette.
2. Launch Excel or create a blank workbook if Excel is already running.
3. Choose Data, Get External Data from the menu, and then choose Create New Query…, as shown below.

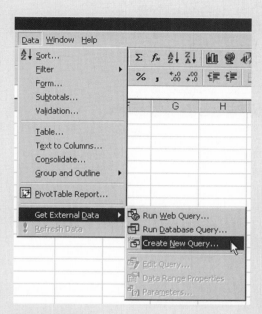

Figure 12.40

4. Highlight <New Data Source> in the Choose Data Source dialog box, if necessary.

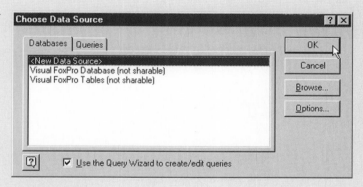

Figure 12.41

Troubleshooting   Your computer or network may display different or additional data sources.

5. Click OK. Type **Microsoft Access Database** as the name for your data source, and select the Microsoft Access driver from the list of database drivers, as shown below.

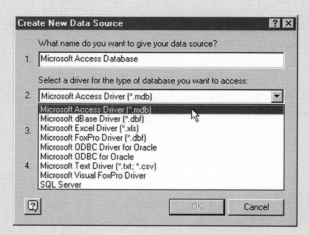

Figure 12.42

6. Click the Connect button and then click the Select button in the ODBC Microsoft Access 97 Setup dialog box.

7. Locate the *Resort Sales 5.mdb* database on your floppy diskette, as shown below.

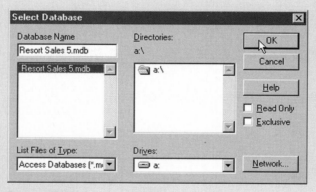

Figure 12.43

8. Click OK. The database name and path will now appear above the Select button. Click OK.

9. The Create New Data Source dialog box appears. When your settings match those shown below, click OK.

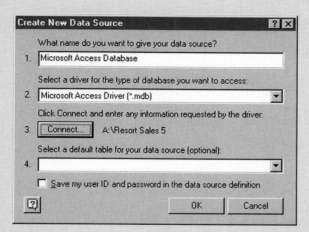

Figure 12.44

10. When the Choose Data Source dialog box returns again, click OK.

11. In the Query Wizard–Choose Columns dialog box, highlight Customer Orders in the Available Tables and Columns list. Click the > button to add all fields in the columns of your query.

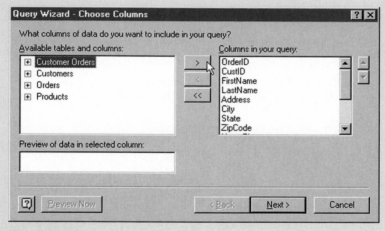

Figure 12.45

12. Click Next. When you see the Query Wizard–Filter Data dialog box to accept the default option of not filtering the data, click Next again.

13. Select Last Name in the Sort by list of the Query Wizard–Sort Order dialog box. Click Next.

14. In the Query Wizard–Finish dialog box, select the option to Return Data to Microsoft Excel if necessary. Click Finish.

> **Tip** If you want to run this query later, click Save Query. Once you save the query, it will appear in the Queries tab of the Choose Data Source dialog box whenever you run Microsoft Query from within Excel.

15. Select the option to put the data in the existing worksheet, if necessary. Click OK.

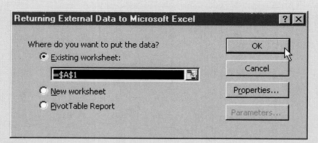

Figure 12.46

The data is returned to Microsoft Excel, as shown below. You will also notice that the External Data Toolbar is also visible on the screen. If you save your workbook, the connection between the database file and the Excel workbook will be re-established each time you open the workbook. Close your workbook when you are finished viewing the sales order data.

	A	B	C	D	E	F	G	H
1	OrderID	CustID	FirstName	LastName	Address	City	State	ZipCode
2	9	18	Fraiser	Allison	9001 Tucson Ct.	Arizona City	CA	98766-9090
3	4	25	Donald	Banes	455 S. Clover	Sunnyside	CA	78344-1000
4	20	25	Donald	Banes	455 S. Clover	Sunnyside	CA	78344-1000
5	8	4	Frank	Broadman	301 S. Mineral	Detroit	MI	45812-0000
6	2	23	James	Burns	98077 SE 44th	Madison City	CA	90655-9077
7	17	23	James	Burns	98077 SE 44th	Madison City	CA	90655-9077
8	10	15	Lawrence	Jackson	925 S. Bull Run	Amazon	MI	65122-7888
9	15	15	Lawrence	Jackson	925 S. Bull Run	Amazon	MI	65122-7888
10	19	15	Lawrence	Jackson	925 S. Bull Run	Amazon	MI	65122-7888
11	6	14	Barb	Lawson	9011 Williams Drive	Miami	OH	21190-9999
12	13	17	Warren	Lilley	P.O. Box 121	Jackson	NY	21198-2111
13	11	21	Tasha	Rogers	4 Courtside #311	Albans	NY	20233-9090
14	3	1	William	Smith	200 E. Minolta	San Diego	CA	91554-0000
15	7	27	Robert L.	Smith	677 E. Madison Grove	Dow			
16	5	26	Jane	Snider	201 S. Tulip	Gran			
17	14	26	Jane	Snider	201 S. Tulip	Gran			
18	1	3	Patricia	Snyder	4001 SE Mason	Mission	CA	92144-9243

Figure 12.47

3. Using multiple workbooks

In Projects 6 and 7 you learned how to establish links between worksheets in the same workbook. You can also use Excel to share data among workbooks by using linking formulas between the workbook files. In this exercise you will open three workbooks, and then establish links among them.

1. Open the *North.xls*, *South.xls*, and *Summary.xls* workbooks from your student diskette.

2. Resize each worksheet, to make it visible.

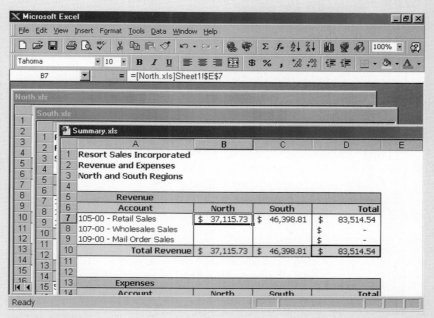

Figure 12.48

3. Click cell B7 in the *Summary.xls* worksheet. Notice that the syntax for the linking formula contains a reference to the workbook file, and the cell to display.

> **Tip** In this example each worksheet is in the same folder on your diskette. When you use linking formulas among workbooks in different folders or network drives, the path may also be included.

4. Select the range B7:C7.

5. Use the fill handle to copy the range through cell C9 of the *Summary.xls* workbook.

6. Select the range B7:C7 and select Edit, Copy.

7. Place the insertion point in cell B15 and select Edit, Paste.

8. Use the fill handle to copy the selected range through cell C19.

9. Save the *Summary.xls* workbook and close each workbook.

4. Querying from a List in Excel

Working with lists of data in Excel is often tedious. In this exercise you will learn how to create a simple form for navigating through worksheet rows, and for specifying criteria for extracting data from a list.

1. Open the *Microsoft Query.xls* workbook from your data diskette. If you do not have this file, ask your instructor how to obtain it.

2. Select the range A1:L21.

3. Choose Data, Form. The database form for the records in the Sheet1 worksheet will appear.

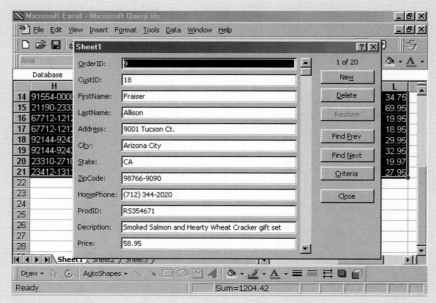

Figure 12.49

4. Click the criteria button on the form, and type **7** in the OrderID text field.

5. Click the Find Next button on the form. A record for Robert L. Smith should appear.

6. When you are finished viewing the address data, click the Close button on the form.

7. Close the workbook.

5. Adding hyperlinks to an Excel workbook

Open the *Regional Sales 3.xls* workbook that is in the Reports folder on your floppy diskette. Complete the following:

1. Select *Contents and Index* from the Help system and search for *Hyperlinks, creating*. Display the Topics Found list and select *Creating hyperlinks* to find out how to create hyperlinks.

2. Add a hyperlink in cell A2 of the North worksheet that returns to the Sales Summary worksheet.

3. Add the same link to each remaining regional worksheet.

4. Save the updated workbook in the Reports folder as *Links.xls*.

Assignments

1. Create a worksheet with a Web link

Create a new Excel workbook. Add an external link in cell A3 to Microsoft's web site (http://www.microsoft.com). Save the workbook.

2. Create an HTML Table

Create an Excel worksheet containing a list of inventory items and the quantity currently in stock. Save the Excel workbook, and then create an HTML table displaying the items and quantities. View the document using a web browser.

More Excel 97

With Microsoft Excel, you can share files with other people and work on the data collaboratively. Excel includes workgroup functions that make it easy to review other people's files and have others review your files. To distribute a workbook for review, you can send the workbook through e-mail or post the workbook to a Microsoft Exchange public folder. If you want a separate set of review comments from each person, send a separate copy of the workbook to each reviewer. To receive a cumulative set of review comments, where each person sees the comments and changes made by previous reviewers, route the workbook or post it to a public folder. When you receive the marked-up copies of the workbook, you can review and incorporate the changes in each copy, or you can merge all the changes into one copy of the workbook. With a shared workbook multiple users can open, view, and edit lists and other worksheet data. You can even add tips to individual cells to assist users in completing a copy of a shared workbook.

Creating a Shared Workbook

To set up a shared workbook, do the following:

1. On the Tools menu, click Share Workbook, and then click the Editing tab.

2. Select the Allow changes by more than one user at the same time check box, and then click OK.

3. When prompted, save the workbook.

4. On the File menu, click Save As, and then save the shared workbook on a network location where other users can gain access to it.

Tracking Changes in a Shared Workbook

To track changes in a shared workbook, do the following:

1. On the Tools menu, point to Track Changes, and then click Accept or Reject Changes.

2. If prompted to save the workbook, click OK.

3. Select the changes to review.
   - To review changes made by another user, select the Who check box, and then click the user in the Who box.
   - To review changes by all users, clear the Who check box.

- To review changes to a specific area on a worksheet, select the Where check box, and then enter a reference to the area.
- To review changes to the entire workbook, clear the Where check box.

4. Click OK, and then read the information about the first change in the Accept or Reject Changes dialog box. The information also describes any dependent changes that are affected by the action you take for this change. You may need to use the scroll arrows to see additional information.

5. To accept the change and clear its change highlighting, click Accept. To undo the change on the worksheet, click Reject.

   If prompted to select a value for a cell, click the value you want, and then click Accept.

6. Repeat steps 4 and 5 for each change, or click Accept All or Reject All to accept or reject all remaining changes. You must accept or reject a change before you can advance to the next change.

Resolving Conflicts in a Shared Workbook

Resolving Conflicts and Displaying the History of Changes in a Shared Workbook

You can resolve conflicts in a shared workbook by displaying the history of changes. When you create a shared workbook, the change history is turned on so that you can view information about previous conflicting changes. If you turn off the change history, Microsoft Excel does not preserve information about conflicting changes.

To View and resolve changes, do the following:

1. On the Tools menu, point to Track Changes, and then click Highlight Changes.

2. Select the When check box, and then click All in the When box.

3. Make sure the Who and Where check boxes are cleared.

4. Select the List changes on a new sheet check box, and then click OK.

5. When the History worksheet appears, scroll it to the right if necessary to view the Action Type and Losing Action columns.

   Conflicting changes that were kept will display "Won" in the Action Type column.

   In the Losing Action column, row numbers appear for those lines in the History worksheet that describe discarded changes.

Merging Copies of Shared Workbooks

If you plan to merge copies of a shared workbook, you must turn on the change history for the shared workbook before you make the copies for distribution to reviewers and before anyone makes any changes to the copies. You also must complete the merge within the time period you specified to maintain the change history.

To merge changes from multiple copies of the same workbook, do the following:

1. Open the copy of the shared workbook into which you want to merge changes from another workbook file on disk.

2. On the Tools menu, click Merge Workbooks.

3. If prompted, save the shared workbook.

4. In the Select Files to Merge Into Current Document dialog box, click a copy of the shared workbook that has changes to be merged, and then click OK.

5. Repeat steps 2 through 4 until all copies of the shared workbook are merged.

> **Tip**   If a cell contains a comment, the comment includes the name of the person who inserted the comment. When you merge shared workbooks and a cell has comments from more than one person, the comments appear one after another in the comment box for the cell.

To view the independent Web page you created or to see the table that was inserted in the existing Web page, you must open the HTML file in an HTML viewer. You can open the files in either Word or Internet Explorer.

Checking and Reviewing Data in Excel

When you create formulas on an Excel worksheet, you can check the data that formulas calculate. Excel can show you the cells that provide values to the formulas or the cells that depend on the formulas. Use the commands on the Auditing toolbar to locate cells that provide data to the formula in the active cell and to find the cells that depend on the value in the active cell. If your formula displays an error value such as #VALUE! or #DIV/0!, you can also use the auditing commands (Tools menu, Auditing command) to locate the cell that is causing the error.

Exporting Data to Other Applications

You can easily export data from Excel to other applications. You can export data to Access as a table, or use Copy and the Paste or Paste Special commands to embed or link data from Excel to other Office applications.

Exporting Data to Access

You can export Excel worksheet data into Access. To analyze the data from an Access table using Excel, use features in Access to import the data automatically into a new Excel workbook. If you want only a few records from an Access table, open the table and copy selected records into Excel.

Exporting Data to Other Office Applications as Linked or Embedded Data

You can use information you create in Excel in other Microsoft Office programs, and vice versa. You can share the information different ways, depending on how you want the information to appear, whether you want it to be updated if the original file changes, and with whom you want to share it.

Use the Paste Special command (Edit menu) and select the Paste link option to paste information as a linked object. Select the object type Object and Paste options to paste information as an embedded object. The Object command and most commands on the Picture submenu (Insert menu) let you insert information as either linked or embedded objects.

Linked objects and embedded objects store data differently. A Linked object in the destination file is updated automatically if the original file changes, but an embedded object is not. Use linked objects if you want the destination file to reflect any changes to the original data, or if file size is a consideration. With a linked object, the original information remains stored in the source file. The destination file displays the linked information but stores only the location of the original data. The linked information is updated automatically when the original data in the source file is changed. For example, if you select a range of cells in a Microsoft Excel workbook and then paste the cells as a linked object in a Word document, the information will be automatically updated in your Word document if you change the information in your Excel workbook.

In contrast, an embedded object becomes part of the destination file. You do not need to have access to the original data to be able to open the destination file on another computer and view the embedded object. Because an embedded object has no links to the source file, the object will not be updated automatically if you change the original data. To change an embedded object, you must have the source program (or another program capable of editing the object) installed on your computer. Double-click the object to open and edit it in the source program. Another difference between embedded objects and linked objects is that the destination file will require more disk space if you embed an object than if you link the information.

Creating Styles

You can assign a style to cells that can apply several formats in one step and ensure that cells have consistent formatting. Provided styles will format numbers as currency or percentages, and will use commas to separate thousands. You can also create your own styles to apply a particular font and font size, number formats, and cell borders and shading and to protect cells from changes.

To create a new style:

1. Select a cell that has the combination of formats you want to include in the new style.

2. Click Format, Style.

3. In the Style name box, type a name for the new style.

4. To define and apply the style to the selected cells, click OK. To define the style without applying it, click Add, and then click Close.

To apply an existing style:

1. Select the cells you want to format.

2. Click Format, Style.

3. In the Style name box, click the style you want.

Operations Reference Guide

Function	Mouse Action or Button	Menu	Keyboard Shortcut
Analysis Toolpak		Choose Data Analysis from the Tools Menu (requires the Analysis Toolpak add-in)	
Array, referencing in a formula	Type the array range in a formula and press (CTRL) (SHIFT) (ENTER) simultaneously		
AutoFormat		Select the cells and choose Format, AutoFormat	
Border, add		Select the cell(s) and choose Format, Cells, Border	
Cell, align	Select the cell(s) and click ▤, ▤, or ▤	Select the cells(s) and choose Format, Cells, Alignment	
Cell, delete		Select the cells(s) and choose Edit, Delete	
Cell, delete data in		Select the cells(s) and choose Edit, Clear	Select the cells(s) and press (DELETE)
Cell, copy	Select the cells(s) and click ▤	Select the cells(s) and choose Edit, Copy	Select the cells(s) and press (CTRL)+**C**
Cell, cut	Select the cells(s) and click ▤	Select the cells(s) and choose Edit, Cut	Select the cells(s) and press (CTRL)+**X**
Cell, format	Select the cells(s) and click appropriate formatting button (**B**, **I**, and so on)	Select the cells(s) and choose Format, Cells, and choose the desired tab	(CTRL)+1 - (one)
Cell, insert		Select the cells(s) and choose Insert, Cells	
Cell, paste	Select the cells(s) and click ▤	Select the cells(s) and choose Edit, Paste	Select the cells(s) and press (CTRL)+**V**
Cell, select	Drag mouse pointer through desired cells		Press (SHIFT)+any navigation key
Chart, create		Choose Insert, Object, Microsoft Graph 97 Chart	
Chart, move	Select the graph and drag	Select the chart, choose Format, Object, click on the Position tab	
Chart, size	Select a handle and drag	Select the chart, choose Format, Object, click on the Size tab	
Column change the width	Drag the vertical border of the column in the column indicator row	Select the column and choose Format, Column, Width	

Function	Mouse Action or Button	Menu	Keyboard Shortcut
Column, delete		Select the column(s) and choose Edit, Delete	
Column, insert		Select the column(s) and choose Insert, Columns	
Comments, add		Select the cell and choose Insert, Comment	
Data, find		Choose Edit, Find	Press CTRL+F
Data, sort	Select the cells(s) and click A↓ or Z↓	Select the cells(s) and choose Data, Sort	
Exit Excel 97	Click ✕	Choose File, Exit	Press ALT+F4
Fill, add	Select the cells(s), click the down arrow on the ▼, and select a color	Select the cells(s) and choose Format, Cells, Patterns	
Format dates		Select the cells(s) and choose Format, Cells, Number	
Format numbers		Select the cells(s) and choose Format, Cells, Number	
Header, Footer, create		Choose View, Header and Footer	
Hyperlink, add		Choose HyperLink from the Insert menu, and then specify a location	
Macro, record		Choose Macro from the Tools Menu, and New Macro	
Page break, change		Choose View, Page Break Preview, and drag the page break line	
Page break, view		Choose View, Page Break Preview	
Panes, freeze		Place the insertion below the row and to the right of the column to be frozen, choose Window Freeze Panes	
Preview	Click ◩	Choose File, Print Preview	
Print	Click 🖨	Choose File, Print	Press [ctrl]+p
Row change the height	Drag the horizontal border of the row indicator	Select the row(s) and choose Format, Row, Height	
Row, delete		Select the row(s) and choose Edit, Delete	

Function	Mouse Action or Button	Menu	Keyboard Shortcut
Row, insert		Select the number of rows you want to insert and choose Insert, Rows	
Spell check	Click 🔤	Choose Tools, Spelling	Press (F7)
Tools, Auditing, Trace Dependents	Select a cell and click 🔗 to view dependents.	Select a cell containing a formula and choose Tools, Auditing, Trace Dependents to view dependent cells.	
Tools, Auditing, Trace Error	Select a cell and click ◈ to locate errors.	Select a cell containing a formula and choose Tools, Auditing, Trace errors to determine which cell is generating the error.	
Tools, Auditing, Trace Precedents	Select a cell and click 🔗 to view precedents.	Select a cell containing a formula and choose Tools, Auditing, Trace Precedents to view precedent cells.	
Tools, Auditing, Remove All Arrows	Click 🔗 to remove all tracer arrows.	Choose Tools, Auditing, Remove All Arrows to remove all tracer arrows from the worksheet.	
Workbook close	Click ✖ in the workbook window	Choose File, Close	
Workbook, create	Click 🗋	Choose File, New	Press (CTRL)+(END)
Workbook, open	Click 📂	Choose File, Open	Press (CTRL)+**O**
Workbook, save	Click 💾	Choose File, Save	Press (CTRL)+**S**
Worksheet delete		Click the worksheet tab and choose Insert, Worksheet	
Worksheet, insert		Click the worksheet tab that should follow the new worksheet and choose Edit, Delete Sheet	
Worksheet, move	Drag the worksheet tab to new location	Select the worksheet tab and choose Edit, Move or Copy sheet	
Worksheet, name		Right-click the worksheet tab and choose Rename	
Worksheet, Save as HTML		Choose Save as HTML from the File menu	

Glossary

3-D references   Cell references appearing in formulas that refer to other worksheets in the same workbook. 3-D references allow you to share data among worksheets and workbooks.

Absolute reference   An address you use to reference a specific cell or range of cells in a worksheet; this reference, which doesn't change, is denoted with the dollar sign symbol, as in $A$1.

Accounting format   A number format that normally includes a currency symbol that is left-justified in the cell, comma separators, a decimal point, and two figures to the right of the decimal.

Active cell   The cell in which you can enter data or perform calculations. You make the cell active by clicking in the cell or by moving to the cell with keystrokes. This cell is outlined with a black border.

Alpha   The probability of making a type I error, or rejecting the null hypothesis when it is actually true,

Amortization   The process of paying a debt over time by making periodic payments.

Amortization schedule   A schedule of loan payments that includes a breakdown of the principal and interest portions of each periodic payment.

Amortization table   Another term for an amortization schedule.

Analysis of variance (ANOVA)   A statistical procedure used to test the hypothesis that means from two or more samples are equal (drawn from populations with the same mean).

Analysis ToolPak   An Excel Add-in containing many common statistical procedures.

Annuity functions   A class of financial functions in Excel that involves payments or investments at regular intervals.

ANOVA table   A table used to display the results of an ANOVA procedure.

Argument   The values an Excel function uses to perform operations or calculations.

Arithmetic operators   The operators you use to perform calculations in formulas and functions: + (addition), − (subtraction), * (multiplication), / (division), % (percent), and ^ (exponentiation).

ASCII text   A format for storing letters, numbers, and symbols according top the American Standard for Information Interchange. ASCII data can usually be shared among computers with different operating systems.

Auditing Toolbar   An Excel Toolbar for auditing formulas and finding errors.

AutoCalculate   A feature that displays a calculation in the status bar when you select a range with values.

AutoFilter   An Excel feature that allows you to find specific data within a list.

AutoFit   A feature that automatically adjusts the column or row to be just wide enough to accommodate the widest or tallest entry.

Border   A line that displays on any side of a cell or group of cells. You can use borders to draw rectangles around cells, to create dividers between columns, to create a total line under a column of numbers, and so on.

Cell   The intersection of a column and a row in a worksheet.

Chart   A visual representation of data in a worksheet.

Chart sub-type   A variation on a Chart type. For example, the column type chart has these sub-types in both 2-D and 3-D: Clustered Column, Stacked Column, and 100% Stacked Column.

Chart type   A chart that represents data in a specific format, such as columns, a pie, scatter points, etc.

Chart Wizard   An Excel feature you use to create charts. When you create a chart with the Chart Wizard, the Chart Wizard decides how the chart elements will look.

Clipboard   A memory area in which data that has been cut or copied is stored.

Coding   A method of assigning a value to a variable for use in statistical analysis. For example, by recoding nominal data for "male" and "female" as numeric data (0 and 1), this data can be used in parametric statistical procedures.

Column   A vertical block of cells in a worksheet that extends from row 1 to row 65,536.

Column indicators   The letters associated with the columns on a worksheet.

Comment   Text that you can attach to cells in a worksheet to provide additional information.

Conditional format   A format, such as cell shading or font color, that Excel automatically applies to a cell if a specified condition is true.

Consolidate data   A method of summarizing or displaying data using 3-D references among worksheets or pivot tables. Choose the Consolidate option under the Data menu.

Critical value   The value from a sampling distribution against which a computed statistic is compared to determine whether the null hypothesis is retained or rejected.

Cross-tabulation   A way of analyzing data for two variables by placing data in a row and column format.

Custom view   A method for saving the current appearance of a workbook so you don't have to change the settings every time you view or print the workbook.

Data   Facts and figures that have not been interpreted in a specific context.

Data array   A set of values appearing in a workbook that is used with certain array functions. An array is also called a table.

Data integrity   A property of computer data whereby it is consistent and accurate, and can therefore be relied upon for making decisions.

Data labels   The names you attach to different types of data in a chart. You define this setting in the Chart Options dialog box.

Data range   A block of cells used to create an element in a chart.

Data set   Data that will be analyzed by a specific statistical procedure.

Data table   A range of cells that shows how changing certain values in a formula changes the result returned by the formula. Also, a table showing the data that is used to create a chart.

Data validation   A strategy for minimizing data entry errors by limiting the values that can be entered into a cell, and optionally displaying a message about what data is valid.

Delimited   A method for separating data elements in an ASCII text file.

Delimiting character (delimiter)   The specific character, such as a comma, that separates delimited data in a text file.

Descriptive statistics   Indexes and numbers that summarize a set of data.

Dichotomous variable   A variable that takes two, and only two values.

Edit mode   The mode in which you edit the contents of a cell.

Enter mode   The mode in which you enter data in a worksheet.

Error mode   The mode Excel switches to if you make an error when entering data in a cell.

Error value   A value that is returned to a cell when an error occurs. The error value identifies the type of error.

F Distribution   A theoretical sampling distribution of F values for each combination of degrees of freedom. The F distribution is used for the ANOVA procedure.

Fill   A color or a shade of gray that you apply to the background of a cell. Also called *shading* or *patterns*.

Filter mode   The appearance of a worksheet column where a filter has been applied. In filter mode, only the data meeting specific conditions is displayed, and a filter arrow appears in the first cell of the filtered list.

Footer   Text that prints at the bottom of every page of a worksheet.

Formatting toolbar   Contains buttons and controls for formatting. To use the toolbar, click a button to perform a command or view a dialog box.

Formula   A mathematical statement that performs calculations. You create and enter formulas to perform the specific calculations needed.

Formula bar   The area at the top of the window that displays the cell address and the contents of the active cell. You can use it to enter and edit data and formulas.

Function   A mathematical statement that performs calculations. Functions are formulas that have already been created by Excel. They perform calculations that are commonly used such as calculating a sum or an average.

Gridlines   The vertical and horizontal lines in a chart that mark the values.

Header   Text that prints at the top of every page of a worksheet.

Hidden format   An Excel format specifying that row and/or column data will not be visible when the workbook is displayed on the screen.

HTML document   A document generated in Excel when you select Save As HTML from the File menu. An HTML document can be viewed on the World Wide Web or corporate intranet using a Web browser.

IF function   An Excel function containing an expression that returns one value if a condition you specify evaluates to true and another value if it evaluates to false.

Importing data   The process of converting data from a specific format so it can be used by Excel.

Information   Data that is meaningful within a specific context.

Intranet   A network within an organization that uses Internet technologies.

IPMT function   An Excel function that returns the interest payment for a given period for an investment based on periodic, constant payments and a constant interest rate.

Legend   The description of elements in a chart. You define this setting in the Chart Options dialog box.

Linking formula   An Excel formula used to share data among worksheets or workbooks. A linking formula contains a 3-D reference that includes the cell or range reference, preceded by a range of worksheet names.

Loan scenario   The principal, interest, and term values used to calculate a loan payment.

Lookup function   An Excel function that finds a specific value in a list or data array by locating one value and returning a corresponding value in the table or array.

Lookup table   An array of data that is used in conjunction with a Lookup function.

Macro   A series of commands and functions that are stored in a Visual Basic module and can be run whenever you need to perform a specific task.

Menu bar   The bar at the top of the window that contains menu options. To use the menu, click an option to display a drop-down menu, and then click an option on the drop-down menu to perform a command, view another menu, or view a dialog box.

Microsoft Map   An Excel feature that allows you to create shaded geographical maps from row or column data.

Mode indicator   A feature displayed on the far left side of the status bar. It shows a word that describes the current working condition of the program. For example, the word *Ready* means that the worksheet is ready to receive data or execute a command. Other modes include *Edit*, *Enter*, *Point*, *Error*, and *Wait*.

Multilevel sort   An Excel sort containing more than one sort criteria.

Nested IF function   An Excel formula containing more than one IF function that tests for multiple conditions.

Numeric constant   Numeric data that is entered into a cell of an electronic spreadsheet.

Office Assistant   The new Help feature that offers help on the task you're performing, often referred to as context-sensitive help.

Order of precedence   The sequence in which each operation should be performed when a formula has more than one operation. The Excel order of precedence is as follows: exponentiation, then multiplication or division (from left to right), and finally addition or subtraction (from left to right). If the formula has parentheses, the operation(s) in the parentheses are performed first.

Page break   A mark that indicates where one page ends and another one begins.

Page Break Preview   The view in which you can see where the pages will break when the worksheet prints.

Pages   Information that appears on the screen with a Web browser. HTML documents store information as pages.

Parameter   The required arguments in a worksheet function. Also, the values required by an Excel function.

Pattern   A color or a shade of gray that you apply to the background of a cell. Also called *fill* or *shading*.

PivotTable   An interactive table that summarizes and analyzes data from existing lists.

PMT function   An Excel function that calculates the payment for a loan based on constant payments and a constant interest rate.

Point mode   The mode in which you're pointing to cells to build a formula or function in a worksheet.

Posting   The process of storing Web resources on a Web server.

PPMT function   An Excel function that returns the payment on the principal for a given period for an investment based on periodic, constant payments and a constant interest rate.

Principal   The amount of money borrowed through a loan.

Print Preview mode   The mode that shows the full page view of the current page of the current worksheet. In this mode you can view additional pages of the worksheet, or you can zoom in on the page so that you can actually read the data, if necessary.

Pull technology   Displaying Web resources using a Web browser by specifically locating the resource an opening it.

Push technology   Technology for having Web resources automatically sent to one or more computers.

PV function   An Excel function that returns the present value of an investment. The present value is the total amount that a series of future payments is worth now.

Range   A block of cells selected as a group.

Rate   The periodic interest rate used to calculate a loan payment.

Ready mode   The mode in which the worksheet is ready to receive data or execute a command.

Recoded values   Nominal data converted to numeric format for use by parametric statistical procedures.

Redundant data   Data that physically is entered multiple times into worksheet cells.

Relative reference   A worksheet address that Excel automatically changes when a formula is copied to another location.

Row   A horizontal block of cells in a worksheet that extends from column A to column IV.

Row indicators   The numbers associated with the rows on a worksheet.

Run   The procedure used to play back a macro that has been recorded.

Scientific notation   A number format used for very large numbers and very small decimal numbers. For example, the scientific notation for 1,000,000,000 is 1E+09 which means 1 times 10 to the ninth power. If you enter a number that won't fit in a cell, Excel either converts the number to scientific notation or displays pound signs (#) in the cell.

Scroll bars   The bars on the side or the bottom of the window that enable you to scroll the screen vertically and horizontally.

Selection handles   The black squares that appear when a chart is selected. You use them to size the chart.

Shading   A color or a shade of gray that you apply to the background of a cell. Also called *fill* or *pattern*.

Sort criteria   The sort order specified when using Excel's sorting procedure. Up to three sort criteria can be used when sorting.

Standard toolbar   Contains buttons and controls used to perform the most common commands. To use the toolbar, click a button to perform a command or view a dialog box.

Statistical significance   A conclusion based upon a low probability that the differences returned by a statistical procedure are not due to chance.

Status bar   The bar at the bottom of the window that displays information about the current workbook.

Subtotal   A feature whereby Excel automatically adds subtotals to a list of data. When adding subtotals, the data is grouped in an outline form.

Syntax   Formula syntax is the structure or order of the elements in a formula.

Template   A workbook that contains specific content and formatting that you can use as a model for other similar workbooks.

Term   The amount of time over which a loan is repaid.

Test statistic   The value returned from a data set when using a specific statistical procedure.

Three-dimensional workbook   An Excel workbook containing more than one worksheet and linking formulas that relate data among the worksheets.

Title   The name of the chart. You define this setting in the Chart Options dialog box.

Title bar   The bar at the top of a window that displays the Minimize, Maximize/Restore, and Close buttons.

Toolbar   A bar that contains buttons for performing commands. To use the toolbar, click a button to perform a command or view a dialog box.

Transaction   A single business event, such as the sale of a product or depositing money into a bank account.

Trendline   A method based upon regression analysis to extend a trendline in a chart forward or backward beyond the actual data to show a trend.

Variable   Something that exists in more than one amount or one form.

Viewing   The process of opening HTML documents with a Web browser.

Visual Basic Editor   A special editor available in Excel for editing the commands and functions a macro stores in a Visual Basic module.

Visual Basic sub procedure   A sequence of Visual Basic statements executed as a unit.

VLOOKUP function   An Excel function that searches for a value in the leftmost column of a table, and then returns a value in the same row from a column you specify in the table.

Wait mode   The mode in effect when the worksheet is busy and cannot accept data or commands.

Web browser   A computer application that interprets the HTML tags in a Web page and formats the text and graphics for display.

Web server   A network server that stores documents and files used by Web browsers.

Web toolbar   A toolbar available in Office 97 applications for searching, browsing, and viewing Web resources. It contains buttons for Internet use. To display the Web toolbar, click the Web Toolbar button in the Standard toolbar.

To hide the Web toolbar, click the Web Toolbar button again.

Workbook A file that contains Excel worksheets. By default, a new workbook file has three worksheets.

Worksheet A page in a workbook file.

Worksheet scroll buttons The buttons you use on the scroll bar to scroll the tabs for the worksheets.

Worksheet tab A tab at the bottom of a worksheet that displays the name of the worksheet in the current workbook. Clicking a tab displays the worksheet.

World Wide Web (WWW) A system of sharing information on the Internet by posting Web resources on Web servers and accessing these resources using a Web browser.

X axis The horizontal axis in a chart. You define this setting in the Chart Options dialog box.

Y axis The vertical axis in a chart. You define this setting in the Chart Options dialog box.

Index

Notes

Notes